£10.46

182742

KW-223-897

The Bountiful Game?
Football Identities and Finances

International Football Institute

The International Football Institute (IFI) is a partnership between the University of Central Lancashire (UCLan) and The National Football Museum to advance football research and its application. The Institute was launched by Malcolm McVicar, Vice Chancellor of the University of Central Lancashire, in November 2003.

IFI has four main aims: to adopt a multi-disciplinary approach to research; to engage in football-related knowledge transfer; to disseminate its work to the widest possible audience, locally, nationally and globally; and to enhance the reputation of the University of Central Lancashire and The National Football Museum.

The Institute brings together two organizations with outstanding expertise in relation to the study of football. UCLan, the UK's fifth largest University, has a critical mass of scholars undertaking research aspects of football from a wide range of perspectives, from history and sociology, economics and business studies, to science and coaching. The National Football Museum, which explores the history of English football, has a particular international significance, as England was the birthplace of the modern game, and the Museum is also the permanent home of the FIFA Museum Collection. The Museum holds the world's finest collections of football memorabilia, totalling over 30,000 items, including the collections of the English Football Association, the English Football League and Wembley Stadium. The National Football Museum is at Deepdale Stadium, Preston, the world's oldest football league ground which is still in use today, where football has been played since 1878, and which is less than one mile from the Preston Campus of UCLan.

In September 2004 IFI held its first international academic conference, entitled 'European Football: Influence, Change and Development', which attracted over sixty delegates from around the world. The conference was led by Dr. Jonathan Magee of IFI. This volume brings together many of the papers presented at the conference. IFI is very grateful to the Editorial Board members for their contribution to the conference and to Dr. Alan Bairner and Professor Alan Tomlinson for their work as co-editors of this volume.

Kevin Moore
Director
International Football Institute
www.uclan.ac.uk/ifi

Museum Director
The National Football Museum
www.nationalfootballmuseum.com

Chelsea School Research Centre Edition
Volume 8

Jonathan Magee, Alan Bairner & Alan Tomlinson (eds.)

The Bountiful Game? Football Identities and Finances

Meyer & Meyer Sport

British Library Cataloguing in Publication Data
A catalogue record for this book is available from the British Library

The Bountiful Game? – Football Identities and Finances
Jonathan Magee/Alan Bairner/Alan Tomlinson (eds.)
Oxford: Meyer & Meyer Sport (UK) Ltd., 2005
(Chelsea School Research Centre Edition; Vol. 8)
ISBN 1-84126-178-5

All rights reserved. Except for use in a review, no part of this publication may be
reproduced, stored in a retrieval system, or transmitted, in any form or by any means now
known or hereafter invented without the prior written permission of the publisher. This
book may not be lent, resold, hired out or otherwise disposed of by way of trade in any
form, binding or cover other than that in which it is published, without the prior written
consent of the publisher.

© 2005 by Meyer & Meyer Sport (UK) Ltd.
Adelaide, Auckland, Budapest, Graz, Johannesburg, New York,
Olten (CH), Oxford, Singapore, Toronto
Member of the World
Sportpublishers' Association
Printed and bound in Germany by
Digitaldruck AixPress GmbH, Aachen
e-mail: verlag@m-m-sports.com
ISBN 1-84126-178-5

CONTENTS

UCB
182742

ACKNOWLEDGEMENTS

Thanks are due to Dr. Graham Baldwin (Chair, Strategy Group of the International Football Institute [IFI]), Kevin Moore (Director of the International Football Institute), and Emma Woodward and Gail Simpson (Conference and Event Management, University of Central Lancashire).

The contents of the book originated at the IFI Conference 2004 'European Football: Influence, Change and Development' (Preston, UK, September 2004). We are grateful to all the presenters and participants at that conference for their support and responses to versions of the chapters contained in this volume.

Thanks too to Dr Paul Downward (Loughborough University) for contributions to the review process.

And finally, we are grateful to Myrene McFee for book-making and index-compiling skills.

Jonathan Magee, Alan Bairner and Alan Tomlinson
March 2005

ABOUT THE AUTHORS

Iain Adams is Principal Lecturer in the Division of Outdoor Education at the Newton Rigg campus of the University of Central Lancashire. He has taught physical education and sport from all levels from primary school through to PhD. He became a professional football (soccer) coach in the USA after completing his PhD at The University of North Dakota in the philosophy of sport. He went on to work in teacher education in Jordan, Bahrain and Indonesia, where he was the national advisor for PE teacher education. His grandfather drove one of the first motorised ambulances on the western front where he served throughout World War I.

Alan Bairner is Reader in the Sociology of Sport at Loughborough University. He is the co-author (with John Sugden) of *Sport, Sectarianism and Society in a Divided Ireland* (Leicester University Press, 1993), co-editor (with John Sugden) of *Sport in Divided Societies* (Meyer and Meyer, 1999), author of *Sport, Nationalism and Globalization: European and North American Perspectives* (SUNY Press, 2001) and editor of *Sport and the Irish. Histories, Identities, Issues* (UCD Press, 2005). From October 2000 to October 2001 he served on a ministerial advisory panel charged with creating a soccer strategy for Northern Ireland. He is a also member of the Irish Football Association's community relations advisory group.

Simon Boyes is a Senior Lecturer at Nottingham Law School, Nottingham Trent University where he teaches sports law on the undergraduate law programme and on the Master's degree in Sports Law. He researches and publishes in the area of sports law and regulation as well as in the fields of European and public law. He is co-author of *Sports Law* (2005, 3rd Edn. London: Cavendish). Simon is currently studying towards a Ph.D pertaining to the self-regulation of sport. He is a keen supporter of Scarborough Football Club.

Babatunde Buraimo is a Lecturer at the University of Central Lancashire, Preston, England, where he teaches courses primarily in the area of sports economics and sports management. He is also a member of and researcher within the International Football Institute where he takes a keen interest in the economics of football. His research focuses on competitive balance and outcome uncertainty, the economics of broadcasting and attendance demand in football.

Garry Crawford is a Senior Lecturer in Social and Cultural Studies in Sport at Sheffield Hallam University. He has published in the areas of sport fan culture, patterns of sport related consumption and digital gaming, including the book *Consuming Sport: Fans, Sport and Culture* published by Routledge in 2004.

Paul Dietschy is Lecturer at the Université de Franche-Comté (France) and associated researcher at the Centre d'Histoire de Sciences-Po in Paris where he co-leads a seminar on sport, culture and history in Europe. He gave his PhD on football and society in Turin 1920–1960 and collaborated to the project of research on FIFA history with Tony Mason and Pierre Lanfranchi. He is a specialist of sport and football under fascism and sport and international relationships. In 2004, he published in collaboration with Patrick Clastres and Serge Laget, *La France et l'olympisme, Paris*, adpf. His bibliography can be consulted on following web-site: http://chevs.sciences-po.fr/centre/chercheurs/dietschy.html

John Doyle is a research assistant at the University of Brighton's Chelsea School. His research interests are based around sport and the media, in particular how elite European football is presented in the sports press. His doctoral study focuses on a sociological analysis of the occupational world of the football journalist.

Jack Fawbert worked as a carpenter and joiner in the construction industry for many years before returning to education, first as a mature student and later as a lecturer. After teaching for Anglia Polytechnic University and Leeds Metropolitan University, the latter as Course Leader for Sociology for six years, he recently moved to the Department of Business and Applied Social Sciences at De Montfort University, Bedford as a Senior Lecturer in

Sociology. He has previously had articles published in Sociology Review and Social Science Teacher as well as contributing chapters to two Leisure Studies Association publications. His interests are in the sociology of football, semiotics, the mass media and the contemporary study of social class and stratification.

David Hassan is a Lecturer in Sports Studies at the University of Ulster at Jordanstown. His main research interest is the relationship between sport, politics and Irish identities and he has published on this theme in various international journals. He is a former Irish League footballer with Premier Division side Cliftonville F.C.

Jessica Macbeth is a Research Fellow at the International Football Institute. She was awarded a Ph.D. in Sports Studies (University of Stirling) in 2004 for her thesis entitled 'Women's Football in Scotland: An Interpretive Analysis'. Jessica is currently developing research on partially sighted football based around fieldwork at the 2004 Partially Sighted World Championships. Particular research interests include sports subcultures, the process of socialisation into football, the meaning of football in people's lives and various issues relating to women's football and disability football.

Jonathan Magee is Chair of the Operational Group at the International Football Institute and is also a Senior Lecturer in the Division of Sport and Leisure at the University of Central Lancashire. He has published on football labour migration and football economy as well as on football identity in Northern Ireland. As a football player he was capped by Northern Ireland at every level to Under 21, represented Northern Ireland, Ireland and Britain in international university tournaments, participated in the 1991, 1993 and 1995 World Student Games, won a variety of medals in the Irish League and the English non-league and also played in the European Cup Winners' Cup in 1993 and 1994.

Stephen Morrow is Senior Lecturer in the Department of Sports Studies at the University of Stirling. He is a Chartered Accountant and his research concentrates on financial aspects of the football industry. He is the author of *The People's Game? Football, finance and society* (Palgrave, 2003) and numerous academic papers in this area. In 2001 Stephen received one of the first FIFA Havelange Research Scholarships for his project 'The Ownership and Governance of European Football Clubs'. His most recent work is a project on 'Image management in football club annual reports' funded by the Institute of Chartered Accountants of Scotland (ICAS).

Antoine Mourat is preparing a PhD in contemporary history at the Université de Franche-Comté. The topic of his thesis is 'Birth and development of football professionalism in Franche-Comté'.

Trevor Petney was born in 1952 in Adelaide, Australia. he took his undergraduate degree at the University of Adelaide and his PhD at Flinders University of South Australia in zoology and ecology, respectively. He worked at Yarmouk University in Jordan from 1982 to 1985, and at Rhodes University and the Veterinary Research Institute at Onderstepoort in South Africa from 1985 to 1989. Thereafter he has lived and worked near Heidelberg in Germany, returning to work in Australia during the European winter. Dr Petney has published over 60 papers primarily on ecological topics. He is married with two children. Two of his uncles fought in World war I with the Australian contingent, one of whom won the MM in 1918.

Raffaele Poli studied geography at the University of Neuchâtel, in Switzerland, where he works both at the local Geography Institute and at the International Centre for Sports Studies (CIES). He is currently preparing a PhD on African players' mobility in European professional football clubs co-tutored by the Geography Institute of the University of Neuchâtel and the Centre of Study and Research on Sport and Olympism of the University of Franche-Comté, in France. He has written two books in French published by the CIES editions: *Football in the Ivory Coast* (2002) and *The International Migration of Footballers* (2004).

Alan Tomlinson is Professor of Leisure Studies at the University of Brighton, where he leads the Sport and Leisure Cultures group in the Chelsea School. He is also head of research in the Chelsea School Research Centre, and deputy chair of the university's Research Degrees Committee. Professor Tomlinson studied humanities and sociology at the University of Kent, and took master's and doctoral degrees in sociological studies at the University of Sussex. His research interests are in the application of a critical sociology of consumption to the analysis of sport and leisure.

Stephen Wagg is Reader in Sport and Society at Roehampton University in London. He is the author of *The Football World* (Harvester Press, 1984) and editor of *Giving the Game Away* (Leicester University Press, 1995) and *British Football and Social Exclusion* (Routledge, 2004). With John Williams, he also edited *British Football and Social Change* (Leicester University Press, 1991). He also writes on the politics of cricket, of comedy and of childhood. His latest book is *Cricket and National Identity in the Postcolonial Age* (Routledge, 2005).

John K. Walton is Professor of Social History in the Department of Humanities, University of Central Lancashire, Preston, UK. He has published extensively on the social and cultural history of tourism, resorts, sport and regional identities, especially in Britain (above all Blackpool and Lancashire) and Spain (San Sebastián and the Basque Country). His most recent books are *The British Seaside: Holidays and Resorts in the Twentieth Century* (Manchester University Press, 2000), and (with Gary Cross), *The Playful Crowd* (New York: Columbia University Press, forthcoming 2005).

INTRODUCTION

IDENTITIES AND FINANCES IN FOOTBALL CULTURE

Alan Bairner, Loughborough University
Jonathan Magee, University of Central Lancashire
Alan Tomlinson, University of Brighton

The widely quoted description of (association) football as 'the beautiful game' is attributed to the legendary Brazilian footballer Pelé. As with any such phrase, it can be made to mean whatever the user chooses: it can refer to football as an object of adulation, an aesthetic activity, a public drama, a physical spectacle, a psychological addiction. Something in football has this essential yet elusive core that has drawn in millions of players from almost every country of the world over the last century and a half, and many more millions of spectators eager to share in the public enthusiasm for the game. This book makes no attempt to explain the worldwide appeal of the sport in all of these dimensions. Rather, it offers another interpretive label for exploring the central features of the game, mostly in its professional forms, but also in terms of wider forms of participating and playing. The beautiful game may have captivated crowds generation after generation, but behind the scenes at the stadia and the television companies and the governing bodies it has been somewhat uglier, generating economic battles, financial scandals and status struggles at all levels, from the local community to the trans-national world of international sports diplomacy. The beauty of football has been regularly soiled by the beast at the heart of the football culture. So this book turns from the beauty of football to consider, instead, something of the history, character and currency of football, 'the bountiful game': in the first section, instances of the power of the game to confer, sustain and evoke identity;

3

and, in the second, the financial rewards seemingly on offer which, though promised, may not always be delivered.

Still, the bountiful game can offer much that is valuable, 'good' and rewarding to players, owners and fans. But where it offers power, fame and riches, such bounty can also attract reward-seekers and opportunists, hungry for returns of both status and money. The history of the game is a mosaic of the interrelationship of these dimensions, and crises in and transformations of the cultural and economic dimensions of the game have been recurrent in football's unfolding narrative.

Adjectival labels have hardly been in short supply in studies and commentaries on English football. Social historian James Walvin's classic study branded professional football the 'people's game' (Walvin, 1975). His commentary a quarter of a century on, in mock celebration of the tenth anniversary of the FA's Premier League, recognised football's tenacious grip on popular consciousness even throughout periods of dramatic transformation: "It is the same game then and now; the same game the world over; the only game" (Walvin, 2001: p. 282). Critic and commentator Hunter Davies (1972) took the rallying chant of the Tottenham Hotspur club as a source for his portrait of the professional game in *The Glory Game*. David Conn, investigative journalist and reporter on the business side of the modern game (Conn, 1999), lent an air of irony to the romanticised description in his work on the seamier side of the game's finances (Conn, 2004). *Daily Mail* investigative reporter Tom Bower (2003) reassembled cases and stories of greed and vanity to expose the endemic nature of corruption across financial aspects of the game's administration. Such themes are addressed in this collection by Babatunde Buraimo and Jessica Macbeth, David Hassan, and Stephen Morrow in chapters dealing with football crises in England, Northern Ireland and Scotland respectively.

The English game has exhibited these various cultural and economic dimensions in shifting balances. At its culturally most rooted, football was a strong economic force within a traditional class-based culture. What Walvin (2001: p. 93) calls a "communal fizz" characterised English football in the period just after World War II. The first season after the war yielded 35.5 million spectators for England's professional Football League. Two seasons on, the League attracted a record aggregate attendance of 41.25 million. In 1949, an Amateur Cup final staged at Wembley, London, attracted 90,000 spectators. But football was not alone in its popularity. As Walvin notes: "Football and cricket grounds, cinemas and seaside resorts, all brimmed with people desperate for a return to life's familiar pleasures" (2001: p. 92). In 1946 1,635 million tickets were sold for movies at British cinemas. This was a revival of the established leisure patterns of the inter-war years. Football was part of a calendar of leisure limited by financial constraints, lack of personal mobility, and restricted consumer choice, but held close to the heart by a loving and predominantly male working-class public. A decade or so on, within a society moving in directions away from forms of traditional manufacturing work and offering a myriad of alternatives for leisure and consumption, football could not possibly sustain its prominence in the sporting culture of the nation, regions and communities.

The well-documented reforms to the base of the professional game — abolition of the maximum wage in January 1961, and the legal condemnation of the retain-and-transfer system as "an unjustifiable restraint of trade" in July 1963 (Wagg, 1984: pp. 101–20) — ushered in a new phase in the evolution of the game. Television coverage acted as a magnet for sponsors and the professional game was catapulted into the heart of the emergent consumer culture, creating celebrities and stars from George Best to Paul Gascoigne and David Beckham and onwards to Wayne Rooney (no coincidence that three of these should have been based at different stages of their careers at glamour club Manchester United). Such stars would be irresistible to an expanding popular media hungry for headlines, and the case of Gascoigne (Whannel, 2002) demonstrated the prescience of Chas Critcher (1979) in identifying the dislocated superstar in his typology of the professional player. Critcher showed that the world of traditional football was undergoing tumultuous cultural change.

There is much valuable scholarship telling the story of these developments and changes, and looking at the challenges for the future (Garland *et al.*, 2001). Such challenges have intensified in the period from the 1960s onwards, from threats emanating from the hooligan fan culture, through to the tragedies of Bradford, Heysel and Hillsborough, and the economic transformation of the game with the creation of the Premier League in 1992. At the Heysel Stadium in Brussels in 1985, 39 (mostly Juventus) fans were killed in a stadium disaster at the European Cup final against Liverpool. Just weeks before, 56 fans were killed at Bradford City's ground when a fire swept through the old wooden stand — a tragic symbol of the vulnerability of the old football culture to the new forces of legislative, cultural and economic reform. Just under four years later, in April 1989, 96 Liverpool fans died in the Hillsborough disaster at Sheffield Wednesday's ground. Three years later the Premier League was in place, all-seated stadia were the order of the day at the top level of the English game, and Rupert Murdoch's Sky TV operation and rival forces began to change the rhythms of the everyday football culture in irreversible ways. In the early 1980s some traditionalists might have wondered how the commercial influences had won the day in allowing shirt sponsorship; twenty years later you would need a personal organizer to keep pace with the television and sponsor-led match schedule, and you could catch a live transmission every day of the week, wondering how the proud logo on the player's chest had given way to the sponsor's name.

This book offers a contribution to the understanding of how, throughout cultural and economic changes on a seismic scale, football could maintain a strong fan base and continue to offer a valuable source of meanings for its followers. In fact, reforms at the upper levels of the game and revivals at the lower levels have in some real and desirable ways expanded the fan base. All-seated stadia allow small people to see, infirm people to sit, women to feel unthreatened by roving male predators. As Burnley fought out a rugged goalless draw in a derby encounter with Blackburn Rovers in the FA Cup in February 2005, in one of the heartlands of the history of the English professional game, a capacity crowd could generate an atmosphere equal to any recalled from the post-war boom years. In one part of the stadium, people took up their seats but then stood for the duration of the match, with children actually standing on their seats — reminiscent of those who took orange boxes to stand on into the packed terraces of the grounds of the 1940s and 1950s. The previous afternoon, five or six miles away, Accrington Stanley played the leaders of the Nationwide Conference top tier, the north London club Barnet. Defeated only four times so far that season, the Londoners were outrun and outfought by the Accrington side, losing 4–1 and wondering what — besides the icy winds howling into the ground from the East Lancashire Pennine moors — had hit hem. Almost 2,000 spectators, including coach-loads of Barnet fans, enjoyed the match. Hardcore Stanley fans stood ecstatically by their banner 'Accrington Stanley — the club that wouldn't die', fuelling the hope that one day the club might be restored to the very top tier, as it was — along with Blackburn and Burnley — when it was one of the twelve founding clubs of the Football League in 1888. Accrington had tumbled out of the League, bankrupt and humiliated, in 1962, not to be reformed until 1968. No stranger to controversy, the club was without a mascot for its victory against Barnet. Stan the Monkey — aka Alan Smith, a 50 year-old local man — was helping the local constabulary with its inquiries into allegations of child abuse. The club acted quickly, informing the Accrington Observer that, until further notice, matches would take place without the club mascot. Undeterred on the publicity front, some Accrington enthusiasts ensured a Stanley presence during the major football occasion of the area's weekend. During Burnley's game with Blackburn, the following day, a plane flew over the ground Turf Moor, trailing a banner 'Accrington Stanley — Pride of Lancs'. All of this must be set within a context in which the industrialist Jack Walker had bankrolled Blackburn Rovers to the Premiership title in 1994-5, just half a decade or so after Burnley had avoided dropping out of the Football League by winning its last match of the season.

The sense of history, cultural affiliation and identity that continues to sustain examples of local rivalry comparable to those in the East Lancashire case has the potential to outlast the financial fluctuations of the game's economy. It is not only Liverpool, Manchester, or Glasgow where such cultural values are publicly, passionately, often wittily and sometimes dangerously, expressed. Fans might know that the financial books of the club are a bit dodgy; that, in the words of former Tottenham Hotspur and England manager Terry Venables, referring to his dealings with the then manger of Nottingham Forest Brian Clough: 'Cloughie likes a bung' (Bower, 2003: p. 62). But at the match between Derby and Nottingham Forest at the end of 2004, in the old Second Division of pre-Premier League days, or first division of post-Premier League days [now the (Coca-Cola) Championship], the sell-out crowd revelling in the memory of the recently deceased Brian Clough was not the least concerned about the bungs. He had won undreamt-of honours for what were, at the time he took over, clubs in decline. Fans at both clubs were less interested in economic scruples than glory on the pitch. Whether at the men's World Cup where FIFA finances (ticket prices apart) are of no concern to the average fan, or the Olympics where the luxurious lifestyle of Olympic freeloaders or the corrupt shenanigans of its apologists are of no widespread concern to the crowds, it is as if the start of the sporting action suspends an everyday morality. Fans and sponsors, identities and profits — this tempestuous mix of meaning and money has long explained the draw of sport and, in particular, football in modern culture.

The local and community base of football provides countless moments in which this mix can be explored. It is in underpinning, sometimes jeopardising, and often revitalising such moments and encounters of wider cultural and economic import that football has had such an enduring history. Football has had many cultural and economic crises and challenges, and yet despite moral panics about crowd safety, concern about the morality of the football culture and recurring financial difficulties, it has remained the most resilient of cultural forms (Tomlinson, 1983). Grasping the nature of identities as expressed in and around the game, and the nature of financial forces making and reshaping it, are tasks central to the understanding of such a history and to the educated debate that should inform the game's future.

In the remaining sections of this chapter we reflect more upon the contribution of the idea of identities to that debate, and provide a picture of the financial patterns characterising the professional game in England and beyond.

Although sport in general and football in particular are commonly praised for their role in the maintenance of distinctive regional and national identities in the face of global trends towards cultural homogeneity, literature also points to the extent to which football's close relationship to the construction and reproduction of collective identities can have harmful as well as beneficial consequences (Bairner, 2001). It is undeniable that many of the world's great club rivalries — Celtic versus Rangers, Arsenal versus Manchester United, Barcelona versus Real Madrid and so on — appear graphically symbolic of an unchanging modern world. The colours, the sounds, the passions are resonant of a century or more of political and cultural difference as well as of intense competitiveness on the field of play — as John Walton demonstrates in this volume with his examination of the place of football in the hearts and minds of the Basque people. Those who bemoan what they perceive as a gradual but inevitable transition towards global cultural uniformity should be partially reassured as events unfold at Celtic Park, Old Trafford or the Camp Nou as raw atavistic tensions take over, if only for the duration of a football match (Andrews, 2004; Burns, 1999; Murray, 2000). Yet many of globalisation's fiercest critics are almost certain to feel uneasy about football's displays of local, regional and national rivalries. There are times where the sanitised world of global consumer capitalism seems like an altogether more comfortable place to be than in the streets surrounding major football stadia on match days when the particularisms involved in supporting a club or a country assume sinister and threatening forms. The point is forcefully brought out in this collection by Jonathan Magee. The fact is that, because football, perhaps more than any other sport, plays a crucial role in the reproduction of identities that might otherwise be closer to extinction, it also contributes to the persistence of animosities that are fundamental to socio-political and ethnic division. Furthermore, although evidence exists that football can act as a bastion in the face of global pressures leading to uniformity, it is equally apparent that the game itself has not been impervious to those selfsame pressures.

It is ironic when association football is the subject of debate to note that globalisation is often equated with Americanisation. In virtually no other field of human endeavour, one might think, has the United States played a less significant role in the shaping of global culture than in 'soccer' (Markovits and Hellerman, 2001). Despite or perhaps because of the international success of the country's women's international players, football remains marginalized in the USA's sporting culture — further evidence, one might argue, of the absence of cultural homogeneity on a world scale. In numerous ways, however, the American (or to be more precise the consumer capitalist) approach to organising, packaging and buying into sport has impacted on a game that the country itself has largely ignored, at least as a form of mass entertainment. Penalty shoot-outs, squad numbers, electronic scoreboards, watching games on television in bars are all features of 'the bountiful game' in many European countries and all were introduced to an American sporting public long before they crossed the Atlantic. So too are all-seated stadia with almost identical catering facilities and only minor architectural differences. Gone, or going at least at the highest levels of football, are the days when drawn cup ties would be replayed ad nauseam until a winner emerged, when team jerseys were numbered from one to eleven, when half-time scoreboards consisted of a series of letters beside which eager volunteers would append results once they had been heard on the radio and when televised football was restricted to a handful of games each season. Fast disappearing too are the terraces on which, for generations, fans stood huddled together, sometimes with tragic consequences (Walker, 2004; Scraton, 2004).

Another development that serves to weaken the close ties that once existed between football clubs and their local communities is the movement of players. This issue is addressed directly in this collection by Raffaele Poli and more obliquely by Stephen Wagg. It must be recognised of course that this particular phenomenon has been part of the professional game since the late nineteenth century when players from Scotland, Wales and Ireland began to move to English clubs in their quest for fame and fortune. Yet, as recently as 1967 it was still possible for Celtic to win the European Cup with a team comprised in its entirety of players born in Glasgow and its surrounding areas. Today, however, throughout the football world, the idea of a local hero has assumed an altogether different meaning. The player in question may well be a hero in the eyes of fans from a specific locality but it is increasingly unlikely that he himself will be 'local'. Furthermore, there is a growing likelihood that many of the fans themselves will not be 'local' either. As with playing, fandom has always been characterised by a degree of mobility. Indeed the emergence of so-called super clubs, although clearly facilitated by economic and social change in relatively recent times, owes much to the fact that even in the first half of the twentieth century, fans felt no obligation to support their local teams, with some preferring instead, for a variety of reasons, to opt for major city clubs. With the advent of cheap flights, satellite television, the creation of iconic media stars and the aggressive marketing of club merchandise, the choice of supporting a team based in another part of the country or in a different part of the world has become much easier to make. Indeed, as Garry Crawford reveals in his chapter in this book, as a consequence of technological developments fans are now in a position to choose between the virtual world of football or the 'real' one.

None of this is intended to deny that local identities are still well served by football clubs. It is important though to look a little more carefully at what that claim actually means. For example, if one takes the example of three leading clubs in the English east midlands — Derby County, Leicester City and Nottingham Forest — it is immediately apparent that the vast majority of the fans of each team comes from the cities of Derby, Leicester and Nottingham respectively, or else from towns and villages in the vicinity of these three cities. On that basis, one might argue that the clubs, for good or ill, help to maintain the existence of local identities and rivalries which would otherwise be threatened by the lure of Arsenal, Chelsea, Manchester United or Liverpool or even of Barcelona, Bayern Munich, Juventus and Real Madrid. On the other hand, this assumption fails to take into account the fact that the demography of the cities involved has changed dramatically since the end of the Second World War. Each now possesses a significant black and/or Asian population. Yet the overwhelming majority of fans at Pride Park Stadium, the Walkers Stadium and the City Ground are white (although no longer almost exclusively male) with the local ethnic minorities being disproportionately represented only amongst the staff of the catering outlets and in the ranks of the match day stewards. To that extent therefore, and without going into all of the reasons for this situation, many of which have been rehearsed elsewhere (Back *et al.*, 2001; Carrington and McDonald, 2001), suffice to say that although the clubs in question are indeed closely linked to the defence of local identities, these identities themselves are connected to communities that no longer exist, at least in their original forms. Another example of this phenomenon, whereby the football club becomes the symbol of an imagined or remembered local community, is explored in this collection by Jack Fawbert. The West Ham fans discussed by Fawbert no longer live in the east end of London. Yet their attachment to their club is deeply interwoven with feelings about community and place. In real terms, however, the local population — many of them of Bangladeshi origin — are scarcely represented by their 'local' football club.

There is no doubt that football clubs are major signifiers of the types of identity that many feel are threatened by globalisation. This in itself is evidence of the bounty that is bestowed by the game. The consequences of this, however, should not be regarded as uniformly positive. Nor should we be led into the trap of believing that the relationship between football clubs and local identities is relatively straightforward. As in so many other ways, what 'the bountiful game' giveth it is more than capable of taking away. An identity that is capable of resisting the trend towards global homogeneity is not intrinsically good. What really matter are the meanings that lie behind that identity (and are communicated to others) and the types of behaviour that the identity in question inspires.

In terms of financial matters, football's status is equally ambiguous. The game has possessed the ability to generate money almost constantly since its codification in England in 1863. With the increasing popularity of the game as a spectator event, attendance fees were charged which in turn created financial conditions for players to be rewarded for their participation (Holt, 1990; Russell, 1997; Walvin, 1994). Income generation and player remuneration thus became an inherent aspect of the development and global growth of the game throughout the twentieth century.

The emergence of football as a professional entity appealed not only to paying spectators but also to newspaper owners and editors, radio broadcasters and subsequently television companies, most notably the British Broadcasting Corporation which first screened highlights of the English league's Division One matches on Match of the Day in August 1964. As John Doyle's chapter in this book shows, the written word and football remain intimately connected. It is television, however, that has exerted a more profound influence on football in the contemporary era. Yet, after a number of years of sustained coverage by the BBC, relations between the broadcasting companies and the football authorities reached a low point in the 1980s with the result that highlights of English league football were 'blacked out' for a couple of seasons.

Given that this blackout occurred only twenty years ago, English football has experienced remarkable financial growth in the intervening period, particularly since the early 1990s, and it is no exaggeration to say that the sport is now a multi-billion pound entertainment industry in its own right. In order to appreciate the scale of football's financial operation, one needs to dwell on the significance of the year 1992 for the modernisation of the game, and subsequently for its economic development and, as Simon Boyes shows in his chapter in this collection, its legal regulation, not only in England but also in Europe. That year two new leagues were created: the FA Premier League and the UEFA Champions League. The former was established by the Football Association in England as a breakaway league above Division One of the Football League and secured a £304 million five year broadcasting contract from British Sky Broadcasting. The UEFA Champions League on the other hand was a remodelling of the European Champions' Cup. Rather than being a new league in its own right, this competition replaced the traditional knock-out style cup with a mini-league format which filtered through to a final match. This overhaul was designed to create extra games which brought associated revenue such as ticket sales and broadcasting rights but also ensured that Europe's top clubs had regular exposure in a prolonged European competition. In effect, UEFA had created a tournament for the elite clubs in Europe.

Fundamentally these two competitions were at the forefront of a process of monumental change in both England and Europe, but to understand in greater detail the scale of the finances involved in this new economic market, the findings of Deloitte's 'Football Money League' (2005) are worth considering. The report provides an overview of the financial revenue of European football's top 20 clubs based on income generation for 2003/4. By way of placing the report in context the report the editor notes that:

> Revenues have continued to grow since our last edition, continuing a long term trend. In the first edition, back in 1996/6, the 20 clubs' combined income was 1.2 billion euros — this year's top five clubs earned almost as much as that between them and the top 20 clubs collectively generate almost 3 billion euros, a compound growth of 14% per year. (Jones, 2005: p. 4)

Central to the revenue-generating power of such clubs is money accrued from broadcasting rights, but the report suggests that "clubs are not purely reliant on broadcasting revenue — and many have moved to successfully develop their other primary revenue streams. UK clubs, in particular, have developed their stadia into a key source of income, with revenues from stadium operations on matchday and non-matchday rising accordingly" (Jones, 2005: p. 4). It is anticipated that the revenue of 2 billion euros will be exceeded in 2004/5.

The centrality of the English Premiership as one of world's core leagues is reinforced by the appearance on the list of Manchester United (1st), Chelsea (4th), Arsenal (6th), Liverpool (10th), Newcastle United (11th), Tottenham Hotspur (14th), Manchester City (16th) and Aston Villa (20th). It is remarkable that English football, given its 1980s era of television blackouts, serious spectator disorder and a ban from European club football, is now the dominant league in terms of generating income from match days, broadcasting and commercial activities.

Associated with the rapid commercial boom of the 1990s was the Bosman case, a landmark employment ruling that provided occupational mobility for professional footballers across the European Union. Without the need for a transfer fee at the end of a player's contract this 'Bosman-type' player was vital to a fluid and increasingly rich football labour market. Freed from contract shackles that bound so many of their predecessors, the footballers of the mid-1990s were able to secure increased salaries from clubs scared of losing their top stars on a 'Bosman' (Magee, 2002). However the rapid change in employment conditions, combined with the increases in revenue flowing from the game, has allowed the player representative (or agent as he or she is popularly known) to rapidly secure a central position in the football marketplace.

Initially the player representative negotiated contract terms on behalf of a client for a percentage cut of the deal but it quickly became evident that player trading, with under-contract as well as Bosman-type players, was a lucrative and fruitful business. Not only did player salaries increase in this period: so too did the number of transfers as a network of representatives emerged across the world and player mobility intensified. Whilst player representation is an under-researched academic area, it is apparent that it is in Europe that the key deals take place as the leagues of England, France, Germany, Italy and Spain play host to 44% of the total number of agents licensed by Fédération International de Football Association (FIFA).

This is not surprising, as it is in these leagues that the most lucrative contracts are offered. Nevertheless, the emergence of player representatives in such high numbers has made transfer activities in the football economy extremely difficult to manage and police, with tales of dodgy deals and corrupt transfers becoming regular occurrences. Clearly the football business at the core European level is awash with cash but, as has been pointed out earlier in this chapter with regard to English football, the game continues to experience serious crises. At a time when 'the bountiful game' is at its most popular and financially lucrative, poor management practices threaten rather than secure its future, proving that football operates like no other business in the industrial sector.

David Conn (2004) sub-titles his latest book 'searching for the soul of football'. His search takes him from the heights of Arsenal and the lows of Sheffield Wednesday's recent history to the community roots of the game at smaller clubs such as Crewe Alexandra, Bury, and non-league Glossop North End. He notes the 'oddly passionless' atmosphere at an Arsenal-Chelsea match (p. 10), and his investigative journey celebrates the commitment and passion of fans of the smaller clubs, surviving and reviving without any significant support from football's new riches in the post-Premier League era. A central theme in his analysis of the contradictions of 'the beautiful game' is the betrayal of the game's wider interests by a Football Association increasingly dominated by the narrow and self-serving interests of Premier League chairmen. Conn captures in evocative fashion the persisting cultural vibrancy of football, but also condemns the motives of the money-seekers who have moved into controlling positions in the game since the formation of the Premiership. Conn's search is an idealistic, romantic one, championing the minnows of the football world. His analysis of a truly rounded, balanced football club and culture takes him outside the cocooned ranks of the Premiership elite. It is to Crewe that he turns to evoke the soul of the game. Dario Gradi has been the manager at Crewe Alexandra Football Club since 1983, and his Christian chairman John Bowler believes that "football has a special place in society. It unites people around a common cause, and we have a responsibility to use that to benefit the community" (p. 263). Gradi has presided over well in excess of a thousand games. The club makes a profit. Young players are nurtured through the ranks and in some cases move on to success at the very top. The fans respect and support the club and its community programme, and companies clamour to sponsor the club:

And with all that, they are arguably competing way above their natural level, lasting five seasons in the First Division before going down then bouncing straight back again. Crisis in football: what crisis? (Conn, 2004: p. 263)

Conn's study warns that the new riches at the top level of the game have inflated the cost for fans so that new generations scarcely feature at the matches: "In 2003, just 7 per cent of season ticket holders [in the Premiership] were aged 16–24" (Conn, 2004: p. 63). The increasingly expensive glossy product of the Premier League has a real problem in that, despite superficial financial prosperity, it may be offering a cultural product with a diminishing core following, susceptible to the whims of a media-savvy generation of consumers with little in the way of deep-rooted commitment to the game and its traditions and legacies.

There is no denying the extent to which association football has inserted itself into the psyche of millions of people worldwide — most notably men although, as Jessica Macbeth indicates in this volume, the game also has a significant and growing role to play in the lives of many women. A magnificent mythology surrounds the game. Whether true or false, the story of football's transcendent appeal, even amidst the horrors of trench warfare, which is recounted and reassessed in this book by Iain Adams and Trevor Petney, is a classic example. More mundane perhaps but arguably even more revealing is Paul Dietschy and Antoine Mourat's chapter which focuses on the relationship between sport and industrial development.

Arthur Hopcraft's 'football man' of the 1960s was a cultural figure soaked in tradition and sentimentality (Hopcraft, 1968), but Hopcraft noted the emerging features of a game on the eve of transformation: increasing primacy of youth; the way in which the game was being "played at sprinter's pace" (p. 227), and more explosively; contempt for referees; and pressure whereby "managers grow more tense and anxious by the month" (p. 227). His comments were prescient, and Steve Redhead has taken the English Premier League as an ideal illustration of "the speeding-up of sport in modernity" (2004: p. 4), an example in popular culture of the theorist Paul Virilio's concept of "accelerated culture in the instant present" (p. 5).

Yet despite such extensive changes, football remains recognisable in the landscape of contemporary culture. Any appraisal of football's balance sheet to date would almost certainly arrive at the conclusion that 'the bountiful game' has operated in credit more than in debt. Without ignoring its negative aspects, it is still possible to celebrate the game's overall contribution to modern society. The challenge, however, is to ensure that it can remain both morally and financially sound and continue to bestow its manifest bounty upon future generations of admirers.

References

Andrews, D. L. (ed) (2004) *Manchester United: A thematic study*. London: Routledge.

Back, L., Crabbe, T. and Solomos, J. (2001) *The changing face of football. Racism, identity and multiculture in the English game*. London: Berg.

Bairner, A. (2001) *Sport, nationalism, and globalization: European and North American perspectives*. Albany, NY: State University of New York Press.

Bower, T. (2003) *Broken dreams — vanity, greed and the souring of British football*. London: Simon & Schuster/Pocket Books.

Burns, J. (1999) *Barça. A people's passion*. London: Bloomsbury Publishing.

Carrington, B. and McDonald, I. (eds) (2001) *'Race', sport and British society*. London: Routledge.

Conn, D. (1997) *The football business: Fair game in the '90s?*. Edinburgh: Mainstream.

—— (2004) *The beautiful game? Searching for the soul of football*. London: Yellow Jersey Press.

Critcher, C. (1979) 'Football since the war', pp. 161–184 in J. Clarke, C. Critcher and R. Johnson (eds) *Working-class culture: Studies in history and theory*. London: Hutchinson.

Davies, H. (1972) *The glory game*. London: Weidenfeld and Nicolson.

Deloitte's Football Money League: The climbers and the sliders (2005). London: Deloitte and Touche (Sport Business Group).

Garland, J., Malcolm, D. and Rowe, M. (eds) (2000) *The future of football — challenges for the twenty-first century*. London: Frank Cass.

Holt, R. (1990) *Sport and the British — a modern history*. Oxford: Clarendon Press.

Hopcraft, A. (1968) *The football man — people and passions in soccer*. London: Collins.

Jones, D. (2005) 'Introduction' in *Deloitte's Football Money League: The climbers and the sliders*. London: Deloitte and Touche (Sport Business Group): p. 4.

Magee, J. (2002) 'Shifting balances of power in the new football economy', pp. 216–239 in J. Sugden and A. Tomlinson (eds) *Power games: A critical sociology of sport*. Routledge: London.

Markovits, A. S. and Hellerman, S. L. (2001) *Offside: Soccer and American exceptionalism*. Princeton, NJ: Princeton University Press.

Murray, B. (2000) *The Old Firm. Sectarianism, sport and society in Scotland*. Edinburgh: John Donald.

Redhead, S. (2004) *Paul Virilio — theorist for an accelerated culture*. Edinburgh: Edinburgh University Press.

Russell, D. (1997) *Football and the English*. Preston: Carnegie Publishing.

Scraton, P. (2004) 'Death on the terraces: The contexts and injustices of the 1989 Hillsborough Disaster', *Soccer and Society* Vol. 5, No. 2: pp. 183–200.

Tomlinson, A. (ed) (1983) *Explorations in football culture* (LSA Publication No. 21). Eastbourne: Leisure Studies Association.

Wagg, S. (1984) *The football world — a contemporary social history*. Brighton: The Harvester Press.

Walker, G. (2004) 'The Ibrox Stadium disaster of 1971', *Soccer and Society* Vol. 5, No. 2: pp. 169–182.

Walvin, J. (1975) *The people's game*. London: Allen Lane.

────── (1994) *The people's game. The history of football revisited*. Edinburgh: Mainstream Publishing.

────── (2001) *The only game: Football in our times*. London: Longman.

Whannel, G. (2002) *Media sport stars — masculinities and moralities*. London: Routledge.

PART ONE

IDENTITIES

GERMANY 3 – SCOTLAND 2, NO MAN'S LAND, 25th DECEMBER, 1914: FACT OR FICTION?

Iain Adams, University of Central Lancashire
Trevor Petney, University of South Australia

Introduction

The story of football being played between British and German troops at Christmas in 1914 has become an established part of World War I legend. The truce of Christmas 1914 in France and Belgium has been the subject of debate from the moment of its occurrence. Many old soldiers refused to believe that any sort of truce had occurred, let alone one in which games of football were played by the opposing armies. Whitehouse, a veteran of the 1914–1918 war, stated "I have always doubted this particular legend, and my disbelief is continually heightened by every magazine illustration that accompanies the story of this Christmas fraternisation." He supported his view by stating that:

> The author was not in France at this time, but in conversations with men who were in the British lines that Christmas, not one encountered any evidence of the incident. In fact, most of them stated that they had not heard of it until some time later, after being wounded or returned to England for leave or rest. (Whitehouse, 1964: p. 38)

Since that time, television programmes such as the BBC documentaries *Christmas Day Passed Quietly* (1968) and *Peace in No Man's Land* (1981) and books such as Brown and Seaton's (1984) *Christmas Truce*, Weintraub's (2002) *Silent Night* and Jürgs' (2003) *Der Kleine Frieden im Grossen*

Krieg have proved that the truce did occur. However, individual soldiers' stories that the troops from Germany and Britain played football together have not proved possible to corroborate.

Perhaps the best known and most detailed account of football between British and German troops is by Oberstleutnant Johannes Niemann of the 133rd Royal Saxon Regiment:

> We came up to take over the trenches on the front between Freling-hien and Houplines, where our Regiment and the Scottish Seaforth Highlanders were face to face. It was a cold, starry night and the Scots were a hundred or so metres in front of us in their trenches where, as we discovered, like us they were up to their knees in mud. My company commander and I, savouring the unaccustomed calm, sat with our orderlies round a Christmas tree we had put up in our dugout.
>
> Suddenly, for no apparent reason, our enemies began to fire on our lines. Our soldiers had hung little Christmas trees covered with candles above the trenches and our enemies, seeing the lights, thought we were about to launch a surprise attack. But, by midnight it was calm once more. Next morning the mist was slow to clear and suddenly my orderly threw himself into my dugout to say that both the German and Scottish soldiers had come out of their trenches and were fraternising along the front. I grabbed my binoculars and looking cautiously over the parapet saw the incred-ible sight of our soldiers exchanging cigarettes, schnapps and chocolate with the enemy. Later a Scottish soldier appeared with a football which seemed to come from nowhere and a few minutes later a real football match got underway. The Scots marked their goal mouth with their strange hats and we did the same with ours. It was far from easy to play on the frozen ground, but we continued, keeping rigorously to the rules, despite the fact that it only lasted an hour and we had no referee. A great many of the passes went wide, but all the amateur footballers, although they must have been very tired, played with great enthusiasm. Us Germans really roared when a gust of wind revealed that the Scots wore no draws under their kilts — and hooted and whistled every time they caught an

impudent glimpse of one posterior belonging to one of 'yesterday's enemies'. But after an hour's play, when our Commanding Officer heard about it, he sent an order that we must put a stop to it. A little later we drifted back to our trenches and the fraternisation ended.

The game finished with a score of three goals to two in favour of Fritz against Tommy. (MacDonald, 1988: p. 46–47)

However, Niemann was not sure of the identity of the unit opposite. In a letter to the BBC, Niemann (1968a) asked if the producers of *Christmas Day Passed Quietly*, then in production, could identify the Scots regiment. Later, in a letter to Reverend Vernon Sproxton, producer of the programme, Niemann (1968b) expressed the thought that it may have been the Scots Guards because a description of the truce written by 'Sir Hamilton' of the Scots Guards was very similar to his own experience. A further letter (1968c) concludes that it must have been either the Seaforth Highlanders or the Scots Guards. In *Das 9. Königlich Sächsischee Infanterie-Regiment Nr. 133 im Weltkrieg 1914–18* (1969), a war history of the 133ʳᵈ, a description of the Christmas Truce by Niemann states that the 133ʳᵈ were in the trenches between Armentières and Frelinghien and only identifies the troops opposing them as Scottish, *Schotten* (1969: p. 32). The consistent feature in the description of the opponents is that they are kilted, a highland regiment.

The Seaforth Highlanders

Niemann's narrative in MacDonald (1988) and in his letter to Sproxton (Niemann, 1968c) names the Seaforth Highlanders as possible opponents. The 1ˢᵗ Battalion of the Seaforth Highlanders (1/Seaforth Highlanders) were part of the 19ᵗʰ Indian (Dehra Dun) Brigade of the 7ᵗʰ (Meerut) Division that had arrived in France in October 1914. They held part of the line in the neighbourhood of Richebourg–St. Vaast and Neuve Chapelle throughout the winter 1914–1915 (Sym, 1962). The battalion was in the trenches at Festubert from the 16ᵗʰ to the 23ʳᵈ December and were in billets on Christmas Day (War Diary, 1/Seaforth Highlanders). Numbers 3 and 4 Companies of the 1/Black Watch (Royal Highlanders) reinforced the battalion from the 21ˢᵗ to the 23ʳᵈ December.

The 4/Seaforth Highlanders (Ross Highland) were also part of the 19th Indian (Dehra Dun) Brigade of the 7th (Meerut) Division. They were one of the first Territorial Battalions of the British army to be assigned active overseas service, arriving in France on the 6th November, 1914. On the 18th December, it was assigned to the 7th Division and joined it on the 20th December near Neuve Chapelle (Sym, 1962). The battalion went into the reserve trenches on Rue des Chavattes between the Richebourg–St.Vaast-Hulloch Road and the River Loisne (Westlake, 1997). These trenches were about 400 yards behind the firing line of the 6th Gurkhas. The unit left the trenches on the 23rd December and on Christmas Day marched to Robecq, 10 miles west of Vielle Chapelle (War Diary, 4/Seaforth Highlanders). A private from the 4/Seaforth mentions beating the 4th Saxon Regiment 6–2, however another private, in a letter published in *The Football Times* (1915), supports the War Diary; "On Christmas Day we hoped to have a rest, but no luck. We have marched about ten miles away from the lines."

The 2/Seaforth Highlanders were part of the 10th Brigade of the 4th Division. This division was assigned the St Yves/Ploegsteert Wood area with its left flank parallel to, and south of, the River La Douve. The battalion was in the trenches just to the north of Ploegsteert Wood over the Christmas period, having relieved the 1/Royal Irish Fusiliers. They left the line on the 27th December at 18:00 returning to billets at La Crèche. They have been placed as opposite the 28th Bavarian regiment by both Brown and Seaton (1984) and Weintraub (2002), using evidence from Corporal John Ferguson. In *The Saturday Review*, he described the truce: "It was like being in a different world. There we were, Xmas Day and able to walk about with our heads up — some of our men even left the trench to play football" (Ferguson, 1915: p. 605–606). *The Scotsman* (1915) also published a letter from a Seaforth Highlander in which he said "in fact, some of our fellows were playing football along the firing line — rather a curious affair after such revengeful attacks on each other".

Francis Gale, of the Royal Garrison Artillery, remembered that football matches between British and German troops had been seen from their observation post situated in the Château de la Hutte behind Hill 63 (Rossignol Hill) on the north-western fringe of Ploegsteert Wood. In *The Daily Chronicle* (1926) he stated that they were instructed not to send over the planned 'Christmas Greeting' as instructed by HQ because:

> A telephone message was received that our boys and the Jerries were fraternising and even playing football at the time. This could plainly be seen from our o.p., a big chateau. The infantry were the Royal Irish Fusiliers, the Warwicks, Gordon Highlanders and I think the Royal Dublin Fusiliers, belonging to the 4th Division.

However, the Gordons were in the 3rd Division whereas the 2/Seaforths were in the 4th Division. Additionally, the Royal Irish Fusiliers had just been replaced in the line by the 2/Seaforth. Lt Kurt Zehmisch of the 11th Company of the 134th Saxon Regiment noted in his diary that they were in the trenches alongside Ploegsteert Woods, south of Ypres. He went into No Man's Land with a burial party after a truce had been negotiated and met an English party; both sides engaged in conversation and assisted burying the other's dead. After the dead were buried:

> A few Englishmen brought a football from their trench and a vigorous game began. All of this was so strange and wonderful, and so it appeared to the English officers as well. In this way the Christmas Festival, the Festival of Love, brought together the hated enemies as friends. This Christmas Festival will always remain unforgettable in my memory. I told them that we did not want to shoot on the second Festival Day (Boxing Day), they agreed to that. That evening, their officers asked if we could have a big football competition between the two sides next day. We could not say definitely as we were getting a new commanding officer the next day. We parted towards evening with a warm handshake and returned to our trenches, but around 7:00pm we were relieved by the 1st Company. (Zehmisch, 1914)

The 2/Seaforth were too far north to have fraternised or played football with the 133rd Royal Saxon Regiment, but they were probably part of the group that Gale saw playing football and they possibly played against the 134th Saxons. The 1/Seaforth and the 4/Seaforth were out of the lines on Christmas Day. The other regiment specifically mentioned by Niemann (1968b and c) was the Scots Guards.

The Scots Guards

The 1/Scots Guards were part of the 1st (Guards) Brigade, 1st Division assigned to the area north of Givenchy, east of Bethune. Half of the battalion was in billets on Christmas Day but three of its companies were in the trenches near Cuinchy (Westlake, 1997).

The 2/Scots Guards were part of the 7th Division, 20th Brigade which was assigned to the area of the Sailly-sur-la-Lys to Fromelles road. The battalion was in the line near Rouges Bancs, about 2.75 kilometres north-east of Aubers. Lt. Sir Edward Hulse provided a description of the frater-nisation between his troops and the Germans that is well known. The Germans opposite were mainly from the 158th Regiment and the 11th Jäger Battalion of the 25th Westphalian Brigade (Brown and Seaton, 1984). Some dispute over the identity of the German troops has occurred; Major Thomas in a 1934 article claimed that the German unit involved was the 2nd battalion of the 15th Regiment of which he was adjutant (Brown and Seaton, 1984). Jürgs (2003) stated that the 2/Scots Guards were opposite the 55th Infantry Regiment and that Hulse had asked a couple of Saxons if their officers had a specific wish over Christmas, such as to discover where the British machine guns were hidden; there was no right moment to get away from the fighting. Hulse mentioned that on his return to the front line, after reporting the truce to battalion headquarters, his trenches were empty, contrary to orders. There were over 150 troops fraternising in front of his trenches and similar groups all the way down the battalion's lines and extending to the 8th division on his right. Hulse did not mention football being played, although Lt. Colonel Fisher-Rowe of the Grenadier Guards wrote on the 27th December that "They [the Germans] wanted to play the Kiddies [2/Scots Guards] at football yesterday but the Kiddies couldn't supply the ball" (Brown and Seaton, 1984: p. 144). Gunner Ben Bloye of the Royal Garrison Artillery remembered being in a forward observation post and that "a football match was fixed up in No Man's Land, but fell through for the lack of a ball, although at Ypres, my Scots Guard friend did play football with the Germans, using rolled up coats as goal posts" (Bloye, 1979: p. 8). However, neither Scots Guards battalions was at Ypres and, therefore, could not have played in Bloye's friend's game. They could not have fraternised or played football with the 133rd

Royal Saxon Regiment either, as both battalions were too far south. Also, The Scots Guards are not a kilted regiment. Niemann's description of the 133rd Royal Saxons playing football with a kilted regiment limits the British units that could have been involved.

The other kilted regiments in theatre

The 1/Gordon Highlanders were a part of the 8th Brigade of the 3rd Division assigned to the northern area of the British front in the Kemmel area. They were relieved by the 1/Royal Scots Fusiliers from the trenches east of Kemmel on the 21st January and went into billets in Westoutre (Westlake, 1997).

The 2/Gordon Highlanders and the 6/Gordon Highlanders were both in the 20th Brigade of the 7th Division near the Sailly-sur-la-Lys to Fromelles Road. Westlake (1997) reported that the 2/Gordons spent Christmas in flooded trenches and no shot was fired by either side. The 6/Gordons were a territorial unit that had arrived in France on the 5th December and were on the edge of the road about 60 yards from the German trenches. They were adjacent to Hulse's Scots Guards and shared the fraternisation with them. The Gordon's chaplain, the Reverend J. Esslemont Adams conducting the joint burial service in No Man's Land (Brown and Seaton, 1984). They were too far south to have fraternised and played football with Niemann's 133rd.

The 1/Queen's Own Cameron Highlanders had taken part in the attack on Givenchy on the 21st December and were relieved from the front line on the 22nd December and went into bivouacs west of Cuinchy. They moved back into the front line on Christmas Day, along with the 1/Coldstream Guards, replacing the 1/Black Watch in the trenches to the north of Givenchy (Westlake, 1997). The 2/Black Watch had been relieved from the trenches in the Festubert sector on the 13th December. They moved back into the reserve trenches at Rue de l' Epinette on the 21st. The battalion moved to Le Touret on the 24th, Paradis on the 25th, Ecquedecques on the 26th, and Amettes on the 27th. The 5/Black Watch, a territorial unit had arrived in France on 13th November, 1914 and attached to the 24th Brigade of the 8th Division. Some companies were in billets on the 25th and the others were in reserve. The 2/Queen's Own Cameron Highlanders arrived in France at Havre on the 20th December and were in reserve digging trenches north-east of Aire-sur-la-Lys until the end of the year (Westlake, 1997). The 1/Queen's Own Cameron High-landers and 5/Black Watch were too far south to be Niemann's footballers and the 2/Queen's Own Cameron Highlanders, the 1/Black Watch and the 2/Black Watch were not in the trenches.

Two territorial units based in England were kilted: the 14/ (County of London) Battalion (London Scottish) and the 10/ (Scottish) Battalion (Territorial Force), otherwise known as the Liverpool Scottish. The London Scottish had arrived in September and had been in continuous action throughout October and November, mainly around Ypres. On the 21st December they moved to Cuinchy and then into the line in the Givenchy area on the 22nd. The Liverpool Scottish had arrived in November and begun front line duties in the Kemmel sector. Therefore, the London Scot-tish was too far south and the Liverpool Scottish too far north to have fraternised with the 133rd (Westlake, 1997).

The 1/Argyll and Sutherland Highlanders had been in Dinapora, India, at the outbreak of war and only arrived in France on the 20th December, 1914. They went into billets at La Poudriere on 21st January before commencing trench induction with the 2/Duke of Wellington's Regiment on the 30th January in the Messines sector (Westlake, 1997).

The 2/Argyll and Sutherland Highlanders had been in billets in the Lunatic Asylum just to the south-east of Armentières since the 11th December and on the 19th December received orders to relieve the 1/Middlesex Regiment in the Houplines sector on the 20th December. Lt. Hutchinson (1936: p. 225) of 'B' Company noted that the battalion "paraded for trenches 4 p.m." on the 20th December and commenced the take-over at 17:00 completing it that evening (War Diary, 2/Argyll and Sutherland Highlanders). This would place their trench position within an hour's march of their billets. The first part of this march would probably have been over the main road from Armentières to Houplines through Nouvel Houplines, then south-east on the road towards Pont Ballot before heading north-east on a dog-leg road towards L'Aventure. However, the last section would have been cross-country and single file along a sap (communication trench). The inclement weather conditions of the previous month and the need for quiet to avoid enemy artillery attention would have made taking over the "worst trenches on earth ... poured with rain ... slimy and damnable" a slow process (Hutchinson, 1936: p. 225). It is doubtful that the trench positions could have been much more than four kilometres from the billets. Robinson (1968), the farmer from Les Cigalons Farm near Frelinghien, described to Sproxton how Niemann regularly revisited the site of his war service. Niemann had searched for, and found, the remains of La Moularderie Farm which had been "obliterated" in the 1914–1918 war and never rebuilt. La Moularderie had been in the proximity of where Niemann had frequently served. A trench map from 1915 (Bridger, nd) shows La Moularderie 3.1 kilometres from the Lunatic Asylum and about 300 metres north-west of the dog-leg on the Houplines-L'Aventure road.

Hutchinson (1932: p. 47) noted that he could hear German transport travelling along the Radinghem-en-Weppes road "bringing up the German rations, in the same way as they must have heard the wheels of our wagons rumbling through the streets of Houplines and down the dog-leg road". The battalion War Diary notes that on the 23ʳᵈ December German transport could be heard moving west to east. This would, possibly, place the transport on the Radinghem-en-Weppes to Quesnoy-sur-Deule road. The British supply wagons from Battalion headquarters in Houplines were probably following the route the soldiers would have taken. This would place the Argylls about 1 kilometre north-east of Houplines and about 1.5 kilometres south of Frelinghien. This is firmly in the area of Niemann: "on Christmas Eve we had to relieve at the front by Armentières-Frelinghiem" (*Das 9. Königlich Sächsischee Infanterie-Regiment Nr. 133 im Weltkrieg 1914–18*, 1969: p. 32).

The 2/Argylls certainly fraternised with the German unit opposite them. Hutchinson (1936: p. 226) noted that there was a German band in the trenches on the 24ᵗʰ December and "we sang in turns — Germans and ourselves. Sergeant M. exchanged badges with a German officer. Much shouting. On the *qui vive* all night." Candles and Christmas trees had appeared on the German parapets and shouted invitations had ended in an agreement that two representatives of each side could meet in No Man's Land. One of the two Germans had worked as a waiter in Glasgow and spoke good English. Lt. Ian Stewart of 'A' Company was one of the Argylls' representatives and was given a photograph of the 133ʳᵈ Royal Saxon Regiment's pre-war football team and a cigar in exchange for a tin of bully beef (Brown and Seaton, 1984). Hutchinson (1932: p. 62) noted "to our immediate front were the 133ʳᵈ and 134ᵗʰ Regiments of the XIX Saxon

Corps." This partially supports one of his earlier statements (writing under his middle name of Seton, 1931: p. 138) that said the Argylls had chatted with some Germans on the 25th December and "they gave us cigars and cap badges. They were men of the 133rd and 139th Regiments of the XIX Saxon Corps." In his autobiography *Warrior*, Hutchinson (1936: p. 226–227) wrote of Christmas Day:

> In the afternoon war ceased and we advanced across out trenches and chatted with the Germans. Most amusing. Can this be war? Some had played football against Glasgow Celtic. All were certain of a victory in about six months, for Germany, and the end of the War. They gave us cigars and cap badges. They were men of the 113th and 139th Regiments of the XIX Saxon Corps.

However, in *Warrior*, Hutchinson, possibly for narrative effect, has brought together the events of several short truces during December 1914 and January 1915 in the Houplines-Bois Grenier sector. These truces had been initiated when one of tributaries of the River Lys broke its embankment and flooded the trenches on both sides, leaving all the soldiers exposed to fire from the other side. Hutchinson (1932: p. 58) described the troops as being "watchkeepers of the waterworks. For the holding of the allied line before Armentières at this season had degenerated to little else." He described how the opponents' trenches, like his, had flooded in the night forcing both sides to build replacement breastworks above ground. The Argylls and their counter-parts were in plain sight as dawn broke; Hutchinson waved, "someone waved back and hulloaed...thus commenced an unwritten armistice covering a front of some miles" (Hutchinson, 1932: p. 61).

The confusion of German regiment numbers, 113th, 133rd, 134th, and 139th, across Hutchinson's writing and the War Diary may be the result of the Argyll's being where German Regiments were juxtaposed or because German units relieved each other over the extended 'live and let live' period (Ashworth, 1980) of flooding and Christmas. The 134th Saxon Regiment were in the same brigade, the 89th, of the 40th Division as the 133rd (Cron, 2002) but on Christmas Day were in the trenches at La Basseville, near Warneton, opposite the British at St. Yves (Weintraub, 2002) and possibly playing football with the 2/Seaforth. Also

Hutchinson's narrative of the truce includes episodes involving Ration Farm, the battalion headquarters in late December when the 2/Argylls had moved to the front line slightly further south in the Bois Grenier sector (War Diary, 2/Argyll and Sutherland Highlanders). Furthermore, it is possible that the opposing troops were less than candid with each other and supplied false information, such as unit identity, during the fraternisation.

It appears highly probable that it was the 2/Argyll and Sutherland Highlanders who were the kilted soldiers opposite the 133rd Royal Saxon Regiment on Christmas Day. However, neither the War Diary nor Hutchinson (1932, 1936; Seton, 1929, 1931) mention actually playing football against the Germans. There was certainly a football culture prevalent in the 2/Argyll and Sutherland Highlanders and this was apparent during the fraternisation period:

> No battalion can be recruited in the City of Glasgow without its strong quota of football enthusiasts. The rival claims of the Clyde-bank and Partick clubs were always subject for vigorous debate. We had with us representatives of both teams, while on the other side were men who had played for the Leipzig team visiting Glasgow during the previous season. The occasion of cessation from active war was an invitation to a football match to be played in No Man's Land. The plan was eagerly fostered. (Hutchinson, 1932: p. 62)

Unfortunately the high command heard about the truce and ordered that "warlike measures against the enemy must be adopted forthwith", resulting in Hutchinson writing a letter to the Germans telling them "war will be declared at 10 a.m. to-morrow morning" and destroying any hopes of a football match. A German Feldwebel took the letter "presumably to the officer commanding the 134th Saxon Regiment" (Hutchinson, 1932: p. 63). Hutchinson was himself a keen footballer and recollects playing for the company on the 27th December on "awfully sloppy ground" (Hutchinson, 1936: p. 227). Private Collier, Number 2 platoon of A Company of the 2/Argylls, observed that some of the battalion did play football on the 25th December; "some of the men in the Platoon on our left had made a 'ball' from paper, rags and string and they went their 'dinger' for about twenty minutes, until the 'ball' fell to pieces and that was that" (1965: p. 6).

An anonymous Sergeant of the 5th Scottish Rifles wrote a letter home that was published in *The Glasgow News* on the 2nd January, 1915, in which he said that he had been on guard on the road to the trenches:

> Some of our boys (the Argyll and Sutherland Highlanders) visited the Germans in their trenches, wished them a Merry Christmas, and agreed to have a truce for 24 hours. They also had a football match between the two lines of trenches and exchanged gifts of cigars and chocolates.

Captain James Lochhead Jack, who had served with Argyll and Sutherland Highlanders in the South African War, was in the trenches next to the 2/Argyll's with the 1/Cameronians (Scottish Rifles) and remarked:

> It seems that on Christmas Day the 2/Argyll and Sutherland (in trenches next to ours) actually arranged to play a football match versus the Saxons — whom we consider to be more human than other Teutons — in No Man's Land that afternoon. Indeed someone in my trench told me of the proposal at the time, but I scouted so wild an idea. In any case, shelling prevented the fixture. (Terraine, 2000: p. 94)

The more war-like nature of the Prussians or of Jack's troops was confirmed by the 2/Argylls: "on our right where the Cameronians are opposed by Prussians, neither side left their trenches, and firing began there almost before our people had separated" (War Diary, 2/Argyll and Sutherland Highlanders). Brown and Seaton (1984 p.110) cited an entry from Jack's diary that "there was no truce on the front of my battalion", but he did record a truce on either side of his unit.

Thus chronologically and geographically, the 2/Argylls were the most likely kilted regiment to have played football with the 133rd Royal Saxon Regiment.

The pitch

Many veterans stoutly denied any football occurred claiming that the state of the ground made any game impossible. Private Alexander Runcie of the 6/Gordon Highlanders near the Sailly-sur-la-Lys to Fromelles Road observed that:

Some chroniclers of the truce incident have claimed that a football match was played in no man's land; this is not the case as the shell-holes, ditch, barbed wire and churned-up condition of this part of the ground rendered it impossible to do so. (Brown and Seaton, 1984: p. 145)

Jürgs (2003) stated that there was too much barbed wire, ammunition, and cracks from freezing to make games possible in places. However, it had been a comparatively mobile war for the first five months and it was only in early December 1914, after the 1ˢᵗ Battle of Ypres, that the armies dug in and the classic trench warfare of World War I began. In many areas there were relatively few shell holes and rabbits and hares foraged in the abandoned fields of cabbages and turnips in No Man's Land. Bairnsfather (1937: p. 120) remarked that, on Christmas Day, he had "hung around a ploughed field the better part of a day, talking to, and being photographed with, a group of German soldiers in what was then the middle of No Man's Land". Ploegsteert through to Rue de Bois were known as 'cushy sectors' as they had yet to suffer much shelling and fighting. Tree lines and hedges still existed as heavy shelling had not generally appeared (artillery was to grow more powerful, sophisticated and effective as the war progressed) and the typical barren terrain of the later years of the war had yet to be created.

The winter of 1914 was very wet, creating thick mud in the low-lying lands around the River Lys. December rainfall was 1.99 inches above average (Brown and Seaton, 1984). Clark (1991) found only 18 dry days between the 25ᵗʰ October, 1914 and 10ᵗʰ March, 1915 and the temperature was below freezing on 11 of these days. Trenches had flooded along the front and soldiers on both sides had been forced to create breastworks above ground level. Hutchinson described the conditions of a trip to Battalion headquarters along a communication trench waist-high with water:

I took off my boots and hose, securing the former with their laces round my neck, then draped the kilt as a cloak over my shoulders; holding my shirt high, I waded through thick slime to hear the wisdom of those who presided over the destinies of the battalion. (Hutchinson, 1932: p. 58)

However, the temperature fell towards Christmas and Hutchinson (Seton, 1931) stated that it was snowing on the 22nd and 23rd of December. The weather turned cold and clear on the 24th, "a glorious afternoon" according to a Field Artillery officer writing to *The Times* (Weintraub, 2002: p. 21). It turned bitterly cold during the evening of the 24th causing the mud to harden, pools to freeze, and forming hard rime frost that covered the trees, ruined buildings, and the corpses of men and sheep; "a Christmas-card Christmas Eve" according to Albert Moren (Brown and Seaton, 1984: p. 60). The low temperatures hardened the ground and made playing football more feasible on Christmas Day than in less severe weather.

The lack of corroboration

Most of the evidence for football during the Christmas Truce has come from second hand reports, soldiers who saw others or heard of others playing. One soldier of the Hampshire regiment reported seeing a football match on his left involving the 10th Division; "one of their number having found in the opposing unit a fellow member of his local Liverpool football club" (Terraine, 1979: p. 785). However, the 10th Division was not in France at that time and the soldier may have meant the 10th Brigade. If so, then this supports the observation of Francis Gale from the Château de la Hutte. Where there are first-hand reports such as Niemann's, there is little or no corroboration from the other side. However, Niemann's story is supported by Hugo Klemm and, somewhat, by Collier. Klemm, also of the 133rd Royal Saxon Regiment, recalled that "Everywhere you looked the occupants from the trenches stood about talking to each other and even playing football" (Weintraub, 2002; p. 119). Klemm and Niemann were in different companies of the 133rd, Klemm's company was billeted in Pont Rouge (Brown and Seaton, 1984) whereas Niemann's was billeted in "the vegetable farm village of Frelinghien" (*Das 9. Königlich Sächsischee Infanterie-Regiment Nr. 133 im Weltkrieg 1914–18.*, 1969: p. 32). Klemm mentions his company officer, Lieutenant Grosse, meeting an English officer and agreeing on procedures to bury the dead (Brown and Seaton, 1984). Was this Stewart of the Argylls?

Many photographs of the Christmas Truce have appeared (Brown and Seaton, 1984; Weintraub, 2002) as affordable cameras were generally available and had been packed into soldiers' kitbags. This was against regulations because the War Office and Admiralty had initially banned soldiers taking photographs at the front and had restricted visits of war correspondents which also limited official photographs (Lytton, 1921). Brown and Seaton (1984) point out that there was a general crackdown on cameras after the Christmas Truce but papers, such as the *Daily Mail,* were still offering payment for front line photographs throughout most of 1915. According to both Jürgs (2003) and Niemann (*Das 9. Königlich Sächsischee Infanterie-Regiment Nr. 133 im Weltkrieg 1914–18.* 1969), British officers had cameras and photographed a war game. Niemann's story of the truce in the regimental war history also describes a German soldier taking photographs.

> Then a Scotsman dragged out a football and a proper game of football developed with our caps laid down as goal-posts on the frozen meadow, which was quite a thing. One of us had a camera and the two teams got themselves into a group with the football in the middle; the game ended in a 3–2 victory for Fritz. (*Das 9. Königlich Sächsischee Infanterie-Regiment Nr. 133 im Weltkrieg 1914–18,* 1969; p. 32)

However, no photographs of British and German troops playing football against each other have surfaced. It is possible that such evidence may have been destroyed in the heavy bombing of World War II. The Saxon home cities of Leipzig and Dresden were particularly affected.

There are other secondary sources that may allude to the 133rd Royal Saxon Regiment's game. A Royal Army Medical Corps major wrote in *The Times* of 1st January 1915 that "The —— Regiment actually had a football match with the Saxons, who beat them 3–2!!!" Weintraub (2002) found evidence that the 104 and 106 French regiments reported kilted Scots playing football with the Germans.

Hutchinson's story of discussing, planning and arranging a football match with the 133rd/134th Saxons that was prevented is supported by a letter from a highland officer in *The Glasgow News* as well as by Captain James Lochhead Jack:

> One great big sergeant had toured Britain with the Leipsic (sic) team, and beat Glasgow Celtic 1–0 ... we arranged, however, to

have a two hours interval on Boxing Day, from 2pm to 4pm, for a football match. This, however, was prevented by our superiors at headquarters. (*The Glasgow News*, 2nd January 1915)

Research by Christian (1994) failed to find evidence of a football match between a team from Leipzig and Celtic. Hutchinson was a prolific writer and it is possible that the highland officer who wrote to *The Glasgow News* was Hutchinson himself. It is perplexing that Hutchinson, a football player, did not mention the football match but did write about trying to organise a game. This may throw doubt on Niemann's story because it seems certain that the 133rd were opposite the 2/Argyll's. However, Hutchinson was a career officer and may have been circumspect about truce activities that were not used for useful work such as strengthening defences. He does not mention Stewart obtaining a football photograph. It is possible that if Niemann's match did occur, it was out of sight of Hutchinson and was a relatively small event. Hutchinson stated that three companies of the Argyll's were in the line on Christmas Day holding about 1,200 yards; each company responsible for about 400 yards (Seton, 1931). Collier (1965) was in 'A' Company and mentioned football to his left. Only three companies would have been in the line with one in reserve. Therefore if it was not Hutchinson's 'B' Company that played it would have been 'C' or 'D' and Hutchinson would have been on the right of Collier, next to Jack's Cameronians. This would place Collier's football at a minimum of 400 yards from Hutchinson and a maximum of 1,000 yards. With trees and hedgerows as well as the breastworks over head-high, it is possible that Hutchinson would not have seen a small kick-about half a mile away. Also, Hutchinson may have been trying to organise a 'proper' game and natural football scrimmages amongst young men were not worth mentioning in his eyes.

There are a number of possible reasons for the general lack of corroboration of the football stories of the truce. One is that observers told the subjective truth, what they felt and imagined, rather than the objective truth, what actually happened. Also, soldiers often live on a diet of rumour and partly explained facts and these rumours coalesce as fact. Soldiers on both sides were often unaware of the accurate details of the event in which they were participating; they were in the 'fog of war'.

Soldiers were often not aware of what was going on even in fairly close proximity to each other. It was very early in the trench war; trees and hedges were still common across the land and would have limited visibility in some places. Lt. Zehmisch (1914) of the 134th Saxons wrote that he found out about the developing truce by field telephone from 'A' Company of his regiment. Information tended to spread back and forwards from the trenches rather than along the trenches due to the administration structure of armies at war, the difficulties of traversing along flooded trenches and the danger of moving out of trenches.

Soldiers who had heard stories may have embellished them to make them more authentic, making distinguishing fact from fiction more difficult over time. A Hampshire soldier may have seen a football match up the line on his left and may have been told that the 10th Division had arrived at the front. By adding the two together, he tells a more believable story to his family and friends. Stories may have also been enhanced through 'kidology' to develop a picture of normality at the front, so lowering the anxiety levels of family on the home front.

As the war progressed, it is probable that some British soldiers felt guilt at having participated in the Truce and did not write about it or removed it from their diaries. The Royal Welch Fusiliers found themselves being spat upon by French women as they left the trenches after fraternisation became public knowledge (Brown and Seaton, 1984). Shortly after Christmas, many soldiers would have found out about the 16th December German naval bombardment of West Hartlepool, Scarborough and Whitby that resulted in the deaths of civilians (*The Illustrated London News*, 1914).

Similarly, many soldiers would have believed the Germans stepped across the boundaries of 'civilised' war with the use of flame throwers and gas in 1915 and concluded that the fraternisation over Christmas 1914 had been a mistake. This would have been reinforced by the mass casualties of 1915–1916 signalling that the amateur 'sportsmanship' ethic of the war was truly over.

Also, it is possible that many reports of the fraternisation were stopped or altered through censorship. Letters home were censored, often with a soldier's name and unit being removed on published letters. The truce was not approved by the High Command on either side. Jürgs (2003) notes that very little was written about the period of the 24th to 27th December in the *Regimentstagebuchern* (regimental records). Similarly British Battalion Diaries are very terse over fraternisation; these diaries were probably being written by career officers, usually Lieutenant-Colonels, who could possibly have been thinking of their careers as they wrote up the daily events. In true military style, the 2/Argyll and Sutherland Highlanders' War Diary laconically recorded the events of the 25th and 26th of December:

> 25th Very quiet day. Germans came out of their trenches unarmed in afternoon, and were seen to belong to the 133rd and 134th Regiment.

> The position was reconnoitred by Lieut Anderson. The Germans asked for leave to bury 10 dead. This was granted.

> 26th relieved by Sherwoods. (War Diary, 2/Argyll and Sutherland Highlanders)

Conclusion

Niemann's account of the 133rd versus a Scottish regiment at football has become a classic war story. The veracity of the story appears to be supported by the use of it in the regimental history, *Das 9. Königlich Sächsischee Infanterie-Regiment Nr. 133 im Weltkrieg 1914–18*. However, Dominiek Dendooven (2004) of the Documentary Centre of the In Flanders Field Museum feels that the regimental history was produced by Niemann. Niemann became aware of Hulse's letters, along with others, through a book of British soldiers' letters from World War I published in Hamburg (*Das 9. Königlich Sächsischee Infanterie-Regiment Nr. 133 im Weltkrieg 1914–18*, 1969).

It is generally accepted that British and German troops fraternised during the Christmas 1914 period over about two-thirds of the British lines (about 20 miles). Thousands of soldiers were involved and most would not have spoken the other side's language. In many cases, though, officers would have been able to converse: Lt Zehmisch, 134th Saxon Regiment, noted "We were soon joined by two or three English officers and we conversed in French, English and German" (Zehmisch, 1914). Football had become an established part of British culture by 1914 and was developing into a popular mass sport in Germany, especially amongst the young age group who were being recruited into the army (Hesse-Lichtenberger, 2003). British troops reported several instances of Germans asking how specific British professional teams were doing. Lieutenant Brockbank's [(1914), 6/Cheshires] diary entry of football being played between British and German troops makes it appear to be the natural thing to occur: "Someone produced a little rubber ball so of course a football match started". Football could be described as the *lingua franca* of the truce. It was one of the things that the British and German soldiers had in common along with their vulnerability, fear, and their mutual enemies of cold, wet, rats, lice, hunger and the high command. For a brief period of time football offered an escape from their fear and anxiety. It may have provided a confirmation of the community of man and given a sense of normality to the surreal world of the trenches. They could be themselves, free from the commands of their military superiors, playing something they could control and own, re-establishing, albeit very briefly, a measure of autonomy.

It is improbable that a 'proper' football match occurred in the chaotic world of the front line of Christmas 1914; Jürgs (2003) comments that reports of proper matches with referees and timekeepers are a legend. However, it would seem to be highly likely that football was played in a true playful manner in many places. Jürgs (2003: p. 176) remarked that as the soldiers used an empty tin to play football they were running around like children: *"Wie die Kinder rennen sie hinter ihren seltsaamen Fussballen her"*. Jürgs reported that the players were cheered by those in the 'stands' which were the parapets of the trenches. If anybody did keep the scores, one of the ad hoc games was possibly 133ʳᵈ Royal Saxon Regiment 3, Argyll and Sutherland Highlanders 2.

References

Ashworth, T. (1980) *Trench warfare 1914–1918: The live and let live system*. London: Macmillan.

Bairnsfather, B. (1937) 'Memories II — Bruce Bairnsfather looks back', in E.D. Swinton (ed) *Twenty years after: The Battlefields of 1914–1918: Then and now*. London: George Newnes Limited, pp. 117–122.

Bloye, B. (1979) 'That extraordinary Christmas 1914', *Gunner Magazine*, December: p. 8.

Bridger, G. (nd) *The Imperial War Museum Trench Map Archive on CD-Rom*. Uckfield: The Naval and Military Press.

Brockbank, C. B. (1916) *Diary of a lucky man in the War 1914–1916*. Cheshire Military Museum.

Brown, M. and Seaton, S. (1984) *Christmas Truce*. London: Leo Cooper Ltd.

Christian, E. (1994) 'The Christmas Truce', *Gunfire*, 28.

Clark, A. (1991) *The donkeys*. London: Pimlico.

Collier, F. C. (1965) 'No 'ell in Houplines: Christmas Day, 1914', *The thin red line*, January: pp. 6–7.

Cron, H. (2002) *Imperial German Army 1914–18: Organisation, structure and Orders-of-Battle*. Solihull: Helion and Co.

Das 9. Königlich Sächsischee Infanterie-Regiment Nr. 133 im Weltkrieg 1914–18. (Hamburg: Private Publication, 1969).

Dendooven, D. (2004) Documentary Centre of In Flanders Field Museum. Conversation with the author, 27th October.

Ferguson, J. (1915) *The Saturday Review*, (25th December, 1915).

The Football Times (9th January, 1915), letter from a private, The 4/Seaforth Highlanders.

Gale, F. J. (1926) *The Daily Chronicle*, (24th November, 1926).

The Glasgow News (2nd January, 1915), letter from a sergeant of the 5th Scottish Rifles and a letter from an officer of a Highland Regiment.

Hesse-Lichtenberger, U. (2003) *Tor! The story of German football*. London: WSC Books Ltd.

Hutchinson, G. S. (1932) *Warrior*. London: Hutchinson & Co.

———— (1936) *Pilgrimage*. London: Rich & Cowan.

The Illustrated London News, (26th December, 1914).

Jürgs, M. (2003) *Der Kleine Frieden im Grossen Krieg*. München: C. Bertelsmann.

Lytton, N. (1921) *The press and the General Staff*. London: W. Collins and Son.

MacDonald, L. (1988) *1914–1918: Voices and images of the Great War*. London: Michael Joseph.

Niemann, J. (1968a) Letter to the BBC. BBC Written Archive Centre, Caversham Park. T24/32/1 18th October 1968.

———— (1968b) Letter to the Reverend Vernon Sproxton. BBC Written Archive Centre, Caversham Park. T24/32/1, 20th October 1968.

———— (1968c) Letter to the Reverend Vernon Sproxton. BBC Written Archive Centre, Caversham Park. T24/32/1, 8th December 1968.

Robinson, V. (1968) Letter to the Reverend Vernon Sproxton. BBC Written Archive Centre, Caversham Park. T24/32/2, 4th November 1968.

The Scotsman (7th January, 1915), letter from a Seaforth Highlander.

Seton, G. (1929) *Biography of a batman*. Hampton: IMCC Ltd. (reprinted from *The English Review*, August, 1929).

——— (1931) *Footslogger: An autobiography*. London: Hutchinson & Co.

Sym, J. (1962) *Seaforth Highlanders*. Aldershot: Gale & Polden Ltd.

Terraine, J. (1979) 'Christmas 1914, and after'. *History Today*, December: pp. 781–789.

Terraine, J. (ed) (2000) *General Jacks diary 1914–18*. London: Cassell Military Paperbacks.

The Times (1st January, 1915), letter from an RAMC major.

War Diary, 2nd Argyll and Sutherland Highlanders, The Regimental Museum, Stirling Castle.

——— 1st Seaforth Highlanders, The Highlanders Museum, Fort George, Inverness.

——— 2nd Seaforth Highlanders, The Highlanders Museum, Fort George, Inverness

——— 4th Seaforth Highlanders, The Highlanders Museum, Fort George, Inverness.

Weintraub, S. (2002) *Silent night*. London: Pocket Books.

Westlake, R. (1997) *British battalions in France and Belgium 1914*. London: Leo Cooper.

Whitehouse, A. (1964) *Epics and legends of the First World War*. London: Frederick Muller Ltd.

Zehmisch, K. (1914). Diary (photocopy at Documentation Centre), Flanders Fields Museum, Ypres.

THE MOTOR CAR AND FOOTBALL INDUSTRIES FROM THE EARLY 1920S TO THE LATE 1940S: THE CASES OF FC SOCHAUX AND JUVENTUS

Paul Dietschy & Antoine Mourat
Université de Franche-Comté
Centre d'Histoire Contemporaine & UFR STAPS Besançon

Introduction

Even though introducing football at the end of the nineteenth century was a sign of modernity for the pioneers of Italian and French sport (Lanfranchi, 1994), it took a certain time for the 'Latin cousins' to acquire a quality of play and organisation comparable to that of the teams affiliated to the (English) Football Association. Indeed, just after the end of World War I, the sportsmen and journalists from both sides of the Alps who watched the FA Cup final did so with admiration and envy. Many would have liked to play to more than a hundred thousand spectators and be able to choose professionalism without being condemned for it in countries where the level of the game and the infrastructure trailed behind.

Nevertheless, in less than thirty years the face of football changed dramatically in both France and Italy as both countries took the path of professionalisation and modernisation. This transformation was more evident in the home country of Giuseppe Meazza where the *squadra azzurra*, with only professional players, won two World Championships in 1934 and 1938. In France the results of the national team on the eve of World War II were not as striking, but football had become the most popular sport and was played in large and modern stadiums like Colombes in the Paris suburbs or the Stade Vélodrome in Marseilles.

Even though one can find the same development in other countries in mainland Europe, France and Italy are the most interesting to consider because modernisation there had its roots in two cities entirely devoted to the motorcar industry: Turin in the Piedmont in the North-West of Italy; and Sochaux, a small city bordering Montbéliard in the East of France. The owners of FIAT and Peugeot, Edoardo Agnelli and Jean-Pierre Peugeot respectively, played a crucial role in promoting professionalism and in the modernisation of the game: in other words, in the rationalisation of this new economic activity and the transformation of the football match into a show for the crowds. It is the role of these two actors and these two clubs, Juventus of Turin and FC Sochaux, that will be analysed in this chapter.

Firstly their role in the passage from 'shamateurism' to open and official professionalism will be discussed. This means going back to the models that inspired them and the resistance they encountered. Subsequently, the means used to bring down the last bastions of amateurism will be examined.

The ties between football and manufacturing industries in those days will also be explored. For instance, did the promoters of professionalism introduce the spirit of industrial management into the world of sport? What were the effects of private investment in the football field? Was football an instrument in the paternalistic policy of the two companies with the purpose of maintaining social order through sport? Did the teams and the stars become sports icons to be used for the promotion of the two makers' brands and products?

Finally, by analysing the diverging trajectories of the two clubs after World War II it will be revealed that two models were created regarding the relationship between football and industry. These were, namely, a policy of stardom that prevented the total absorption of the Turinese upper-middle class club into the biggest Italian industrial conglomerate, and a policy of training young players within a professional sports association as an integral part of the second-biggest French car manufacturer.

The introduction of professionalism at Juventus and FC Sochaux: 1923–1932

Two reference models: England and Central Europe

During the first quarter of the twentieth century English football was still admired, not to say venerated, by the French and Italian sportsmen. This attitude appears clearly in the pages of *Hurrà*, the newsletter Juventus created for its members in May 1915 at the time when Italy entered the Great War. Four years later the same newspaper dedicated pages of its coverage to English football, notably its professional status and the FA Cup. For the majority of the club's members, the British model then appeared to be the direction Juventus in particular and Italian football in general should follow. That is why it was decided to build a new football stadium just like the English ones. After collecting capital of one million lire they built and inaugurated the *Campo Juventus* in Corso Marsiglia in 1922, and with the rather lax security rules of the day the stadium held between twenty and forty thousand spectators. Thus football could then become one of the crowd's favourite recreations in a city that already had 400,000 inhabitants.

However, leaders and members of the club had reached their financial limits in building the stadium. To fully follow the English model it was necessary to buy and pay quality Italian and even foreign players, and only a patron of a certain calibre could provide the necessary funds to ensure such recruitment. Those were the conditions when Edoardo Agnelli, the son of FIAT's founder, was elected president of Juventus on 24 July 1923. Through FIAT or with their own fortune, the Agnelli family had acquired (in addition to competing or complementary companies in the mechanical industry) chain stores like La Rinascente and insurance companies. Football could thus be considered another investment choice, though certainly not very profitable, for some of the enormous profits the Agnelli made during World War I through the sale of arms and munitions (Castronovo, 1977).

Be that as it may, rather than importing English players and trainers at astronomical prices, Agnelli and Juventus, after setting their heart on the most promising Italian players like Virginio Rosetta, chose to recruit in Central Europe and Hungary in particular. From Hungary they hired an excellent trainer, Jeno Karoly, the midfielder Viola and the club's first star, the forward Ferenc Hirzer. Thus thanks to an expensive recruitment drive early in the season and the competence of the trainer Karoly, Juventus won its first Italian Championship in 1926.

There is no evidence that Jean-Pierre Peugeot, president and owner of the Peugeot motorcar, had any direct contacts with Edoardo Agnelli or indeed used the latter's experience and methods to develop his own club. On the other hand, he was certainly aware of the interest of some big European and French companies in promoting sports, and in particular football, among the working classes after the end of the World War I (Fridenson, 1989). For example, the Bayer Group established Bayer Leverkusen in Germany in 1904 as the first works sports club, whilst PSV Eindhoven in Holland was founded by employees of Phillips in 1913. Thus in 1929 Peugeot set up FC Sochaux as a professional team and, as in the cases of Bayer Leverkusen and PSV Eindhoven, the club was financially dependent on the parent company. Even though none of these clubs had already taken the step to professionalism, these examples seem to have partially influenced the type of professionalism that was developed at Sochaux. Later, in 1937, Jean-Pierre Peugeot organised a trip to England so that his players could watch the British professional players and thus improve their knowledge of top-level football. The Sochalians left for London on 6 November 1937 to watch the First Division match between Chelsea and Sunderland.

Nevertheless, in the same way as Agnelli, Jean-Pierre Peugeot preferred to buy the services of players less expensive than British ones. Central to this decision was that the technical ability of the Central European players gave them a reputation for efficiency and an artistic aura (Lanfranchi and Taylor, 2001) and several foreign players and trainers were recruited from Switzerland and the countries of the old Austro–Hungarian Empire.

The break from amateurism

Even if it was easy for 'captains of industry' like Peugeot or Agnelli to recruit players, changing the existing rules regarding amateurism turned out to be a difficult matter, and Juventus and Sochaux immediately met with strong resistance to their crusade for professional football. Initially the managements of the federations and the opposing teams refused to change the players' status and abandon amateurism, despite the fact that the subject had been hotly debated since the early twenties and that the national federations as well as the sports press repeatedly castigated the 'shamateurism' (Wahl, 1989; Papa and Panico, 1993).

At the beginning of the 1923–4 season, Pro Vercelli took their former player Rosetta to a sport court, and the Football League of northern Italy cancelled the results of four matches Rosetta had played in for Juventus, removing all chance of the club winning the championship that season. Rosetta was accused of having been given a fictitious job in order to be recruited into the ranks of Juventus (Ghirelli, 1990). Even though the new president of the Italian Federation, the fascist Leandro Arpinati, eventually accepted professionalism in 1926 by issuing the Viareggio charter that distinguished between amateurs and 'non-amateurs', he remained mistrustful of captains of industry like the Agnelli who invested in football. The fact that a Juventus player was convicted of corruption during a match with local rival Torino in 1927 did not help to improve the mood against professionalism (Dietschy, 1997).

At Sochaux, Jean-Pierre Peugeot also encountered difficulties in getting the professionalism of his players accepted, even though questions of a political nature interfered very little in the debate on professionalism in France. When he initially employed players to play at gala-matches, he infringed the federal rules that prohibited the open use of remunerated players and attracted the animosity of some less fortunate competitors. Worried that other better-known clubs would take advantage of this breach of amateurism, the *Fédération Française de Football* refused to authorise the Sochalian team to play in the first division championship. To reach the elite level with (officially at least) amateur players, the club had to negotiate every level of the sport's hierarchy starting with the regional championships — which Jean-Pierre Peugeot had refused to do. The club's first major achievements provided a certain notoriety as they defeated Olympique de Marseille, the current French champions, on 26 January 1930 and then the Belgian national team a fortnight later (Dorier, 2001).

That same year, Jean-Pierre Peugeot put the game's authorities on the spot again by setting up his own competition — the 'Sochaux Cup' — in which the best French clubs, like FC Sète or Racing Club de Paris, were invited to participate. This trophy allowed the club to establish its popularity and also to gain a new legitimacy by measuring itself against the best French teams of the day. The parallel competition was a success — FC Sochaux won the inaugural trophy — and to some extent the competition replaced the official championship. After only two years, the Sochaux Cup was replaced in 1932 by a professional French Championship, among the creators of which were Sochalian leaders like

Robert Dargein and Samuel Wyler. Thus the strategy of skirting around the rules, matched with the superiority of industrial capital, won over the associations in this case.

A policy of stardom

On mainland Europe at this time the *années folles* had already consecrated the cult of big sports stars like the French boxer Georges Carpentier, the 'divine' tennis woman Suzanne Lenglen and the star of the 1924 Olympic Games in Paris, swimmer Johnny Weissmuller. Sport was not only seen as a means to educate youth morally and physically but it was also a show with artists and celebrities. Even though Agnelli and Peugeot insisted on the virtues of work and humility in their respective companies it was quite a different matter in their football clubs during the first years of their presidencies. Thus they clearly chose to distinguish themselves from the competition through a 'star' policy.

The first Juventus star was Raimundo Orsi who played for Argentina at the Olympic Tournament of 1928. Even though Argentina was beaten by Uruguay in the final, Orsi's talent did not go unnoticed by European experts and led to his recruitment by Juventus in 1929. Very soon his 'royal' remuneration of 8,000 lire a month — approximately seven times the salary of a university professor or a magistrate — and a powerful FIAT 509 to drive around Turin caused a stir (Ghirelli, 1990). However, within the context of Juventus's ultra defensive game, Orsi and his compatriot Cesarini possessed superior technical skill and Orsi was key to the five championship titles won by Juventus from 1931 to 1935. Furthermore Orsi was rather good-looking and played the violin with virtuosity: he quickly became the ladies' favourite in the Italian sports arena of the 1930s.

When Jean-Pierre Peugeot decided to establish a high quality team at FC Sochaux in 1929, he wanted it to be a leading club not only to enhance the name of his motorcars but also to create a new distraction in the industrial *Pays de Montbéliard* (Goux, 1986). In order to start a team that had fighting spirit but which was also attractive to the crowds, Peugeot needed to recruit football players with recognised talent. Thus the first appearances of the team gave the Franc-Comtois spectators the opportunity to get to know a certain number of internationally known players, both French and foreign (Baudouin, 1984). Some Sochalian players played in the first World Cup in 1930 and French centre-forward Lucien Laurent scored the first goal ever in World Cup's history. Even though the salaries of the Sochalian stars were nowhere near those at Juventus, they were often three to four times higher than those of Peugeot's best workers and clearly distinguished them from the industrial proletariat in the Montbéliard area.

Once professionalism had been accepted by the French Federation in 1932, FC Sochaux continued to distinguish itself through the 1930s by an expensive recruitment policy to reinforce a team that during that decade won the *Coupe Sochaux* once, the *Coupe de France* once and the French Championship twice.

Juventus and FC Sochaux: two versions of industrial modernity

Professional management

Between the two wars Juventus did not officially maintain any direct ties with FIAT. The main administrators, with the exception of Edoardo Agnelli, were owners of small enterprises or members of civil society like the vice-president Sandro Zambelli or the solicitor Enrico Craveri (Dietschy, 1997). Even though it took full advantage of the fortune and generosity of the number one Italian car maker, it wished to maintain that the traditions of the club — based on the upper middle-class values of the Turinese society such as a good education, temperance and seriousness — were respected. This bourgeois ethic was evidently shared by Edoardo Agnelli, whose motto was said to have been: "something well done could always have been done better" (Pennacchia, 1985). The absence of first-hand information about the actions of the FIAT heir, because of his refusal to give interviews and also because the family archives are practically inaccessible, make it difficult to be exact about the way the football club was managed.

However, press coverage, and in particular *La Stampa* of which Agnelli was the president, reflects that players were managed in a way that represented the workforce and would spread the same FIAT message of the value of effort and discipline. As goalkeeper Giampiero Combi says in a *La Stampa* interview (6 May 1934), the style of the team can be characterised in two words: *lavorare e tacere*, that is, "work and shut up!". From the early

1930s the players were asked to attend the *circolo Juventus* in the centre of the city the afternoon after a training session to play music or cards in family surroundings. Thus the club leaders and members could keep check on the players' company and make sure they did not succumb to the temptations of alcohol or amorous wanderings (Dietschy, 1997). It is clear that, having invested heavily to recruit high quality players in the 1920s, Juventus sought to carefully manage such players which permitted the club to be more careful in the 1930s in order that excessive transfer costs did not accrue. This behaviour was in contrast with that of clubs in southern Italy which spent recklessly on players who were already on the decline.

In the case of Sochaux an industrial logic was applied even more directly to the sports arena. The professionalisation of the Sochalian club applied not only to the players but also to its management and trainers: the reins of the team were held by specialists from industry paid by the club (such as Robert Dargein, commercial manager of the Peugeot factories in Bordeaux and also an amateur footballer) or by specialists from the world of sport like Victor Gibson, the English trainer with the best reputation in France in the 1930s (Lanfranchi and Wahl, 1995). Their status as salaried employees took away any right of the players to interfere in the decision-making of the club and reduced them to mere conduits for the orders given by the managers, with the trainer becoming a kind of foreman (Wahl, 1989).

This subordination of the players was reinforced by the fact that the management structure of FC Sochaux was practically identical to that of the Peugeot Group and all the key positions in the club were held by members of the firm's board. It is quite clear that the club's leaders wished to apply rational management and a separation of responsibilities, and that these were the great principles of economic rationalisation that were in fashion in the motor industry in those days (Cohen, 2001). Thus FC Sochaux served as a bridge for transferring industrial standards to the world of sport and for applying the scientific organisation of the workplace to the world of football.

Football: the image of a modern and healthy life

Juventus and FC Sochaux had something else in common during the 1930s — they both attracted more spectators when they were not playing at home. In Turin the workers preferred the rival Torino AC while the spectators at Juventus's Sunday matches represented approximately two and a half per cent of the Piedmontese city's inhabitants. In Sochaux, a modest town, the number of spectators was the lowest for any French Championship team. The real Juventus supporters were found in the *Mezzogiorno* whilst most FC Sochaux supporters were located in Paris and the major provincial cities.

The admiration for the two teams was less due to their repeated successes than to selecting players that embodied certain admired aspects of modern life at the time, like youth, dynamism and speed. For the inhabitants of the poor areas in the south of Italy, Juventus players personified the 'Italian Detroit': that is, a city that had been a location for modernity in Italy that was not only the cradle of the motorcar but also that of the cinema (Rondolino, 1993). With pictures in magazines such as *Il Calcio Illustrato* showing players climbing aboard a 1st class carriage, driving a big car or on holidays on the Mediterranean coast, the *juventini* footballers represented a dream of prosperity, but also the power of the north — specifically of Piedmont — that helped to forge a second reunification of the Peninsula based on sport.

At Sochaux the symbols were more down-to-earth and the owners invested in an infrastructure that was quite new for those days. A brand-new stadium with roofed grandstands, La Forge, was opened in November 1931 (Baudouin, 1984) which permitted the players to take advantage of optimal playing conditions. As the club's captain remarked in 1937: "At FC Sochaux we are particularly favoured. Thus our infirmary has much equipment that you don't find in other clubs" (quoted in Baudouin, 1989: p. 51).

Nevertheless this both hedonistic and hygienic representation of modern life stops where the eulogy on morality and sports values begins. The good footballer was also a good father and husband who preferred going to bed early rather than going dancing or meeting undesirable people. He was an apostle of a sound life whose aim was to make sure his dependents were looked-after in the future. In the 1930s articles or books about players like Virginio Rosetta at Juventus or Etienne Mattler at FC Sochaux highlighted the fact that they worked seriously and with self-sacrifice whilst also investing their savings carefully. On the occasion of his 42nd selection for the national team (which was a record at that time), and as a compensation for his exemplary behaviour as a professional player, Mattler was given a bank book containing 11,000 Francs in his daughter Nelly's name. It was the result of a vast subscription among the inhabitants of the *Pays de Montbéliard* and corresponded to the annual salary of a Peugeot worker.

From paternalism to advertising

If prudent managers like the Agnelli or Peugeot enter the sphere of football it is evidently not just for sporting reasons. Initially, football could appear to be a prolongation of the paternalism practised in the industrial enterprises, operated by the likes of Agnelli and Peugeot. For example in October 1923, three months after Agnelli's election as president of Juventus, FIAT's workers were invited to see free of charge the matches played by the first team. This measure does not appear to have produced the hoped for results with the Turinese workers, who preferred to support Juventus's rivals, Torino AC.

From the middle of the 1920s the colourful and noisy *tifo* of the *Toro* fans is ascribed to its working-class character and, as the novelist Mario Soldati observed (Soldati, 1964), the rivalry between the two clubs reflected a sporting metaphor for the opposition between the two 'cities': the bourgeois centre represented by Juventus and the proletarian sur-roundings by Torino. The sports paternalism of Agnelli thus did not produce immediate results at Juventus. Rather, the *Gruppo Sportivo* FIAT played that role in the 1920s by offering the opportunity for its workers and employees to play football or other sports at a low price. The president of *Gruppo Sportivo*, the lawyer Benignetti, suggested that it was a question of a "huge program of physical training, harmony and fraternisation between all the FIAT workers' families" (quoted in *Il Paese Sportivo*, 11 June 1925). Implicit in this was the intention to maintain social order and peace among employees through sporting activity and engagement.

A similar objective was found at Peugeot where every effort was made to associate the club and its players with the 'wider Peugeot family'. Thus home games were preceded by a procession through the streets of Montbéliard, led by the Peugeot band, and various attractions in the vicinity of the stadium were offered free of charge by the Sochalian factory management. The football provided a playful touch to the paternalistic social system established by the firm which included the Peugeot band and social measures from the distribution of food to the extension of the opening of the infirmary beyond normal working hours (Goux, 1986).

Apart from its social role within the company, the football team also served to promote Peugeot products. More directly at Peugeot than at FIAT, football was a way of maintaining a sporting image that had been gained in the early part of the century through motor car races. The national influence and the achievements of FC Sochaux promoted publicity for the 'Lion Brand' and the company's dealers were asked to contribute when the team travelled to away matches. The *réclames* that were subsequently published in the sports papers linked the quality of the FC Sochaux team with that of the Peugeot motor car.

In the case of Juventus, FIAT's quasi-monopolistic situation in the Italian market and Edoardo Agnelli's personal commitment made this advertising form less apparent or necessary. Nevertheless, the players were regularly shown in the sports magazines, photographed with their cars, and the connection between the image of power and excellence of FIAT and the five consecutive titles won by the club from 1931 to 1935 was evident to most *tifosi* throughout Italy.

Diverging trajectories

The shock of World War II

During World War II the cities of Turin and Sochaux were both partially destroyed by RAF bombing (Castronovo, 1987 and Martin, 1994). The bombing raids, and more generally the political and economic upheavals caused by the war, had profound effects on football, particularly in the east of France. The Vichy government's sports policy — established by the former tennis champion Jean Borotra, Commissioner of Education and Sports until April 1942 — created great difficulties for the organisation of professional football as advocated by Peugeot. Seeking to reinvigorate French youth both morally and physically, while in secret preparing for potential revenge attacks against Nazi Germany, Jean Borotra tried to progressively eradicate professionalism, particularly in cycling, boxing and football (Gay-Lescot, 1991).

From 1942 when Colonel Joseph Pascot replaced Borotra at the head of the Commission, the French Club Championship disappeared to be replaced by a Championship of Provinces to which Franche-Comté, the region that FC Sochaux represented, was not invited. The Sochalian players were instead asked to play for the Nancy-Lorraine team. Even though this transfer was successful in the sense that the new team won the French Cup in 1943, it also undermined the club's sports structure at a time when the Peugeot factories were weakened, first by the bombings and then by the liberation struggle. Consequently in the autumn of 1945, lacking financial support from the company, the club had to abstain from participating in the new first division championship (Baudouin, 1984).

In Turin the situation was rather different. For ten years the club had had to make do without the direct support of Agnelli. Then during the summer of 1935 Edoardo Agnelli was killed in an airplane accident and was replaced by Emilio de La Forest, a 'gentleman' fascist without any significant financial resources but with many ideas. In 1940 he was thus the first president of an Italian club to offer an annual subscription for all the season's matches, which temporarily increased the number of spectators who came to support Juventus (Dietschy, 1997). In 1943 Juventus was placed under the control of Piero Dusio, the owner of the sports car company Cisitalia. Employed as workers in Cisitalia, the players thus avoided being drafted into the Salò Republic's troops or sent to work in Germany. Finally the Agnelli family returned to Juventus in September 1947 when Gianni Agnelli, the son of Edoardo and grandson of FIAT's original founder, became the president of the club at the ripe old age of 26.

In Turin as at Sochaux the war had thus been a period of turbulence which had created a serious break in the history of the clubs. The leaders at each club had to reconsider their respective sports strategies and from then on their policies diverged to give rise to two distinctive models of professional football management.

FC Sochaux — the forced choice of training

Unlike a Louis Renault or a Marius Berliet, both of whose enterprises were nationalized in 1945, Jean-Pierre Peugeot did not collaborate with the

Germans during the occupation of France. For that reason he is considered by historians as a *patron résistant* who tried to avoid aiding the Nazi war-effort (Marcot, 1999). As a result his company came out of the conflict on its knees, and it took time for Peugeot to recover its pre-war productive capacity (Loubet, 1990).

At the end of the war there were therefore other priorities than football at Peugeot. At one time it was a matter of completely stopping football activity, which was considered too expensive. One of the directors of the Sochaux factory, Gaston Turin, managed to convince the owners to finance a new professional team within a strict management policy that did not recruit foreign stars or international French players at extravagant prices in order to assure the survival of the club. Promoted to the position of President of the club, Gaston Turin established a new strategy based on the location and training of young players that the club has adhered to and respected ever since. In 1949 this strategy led to the creation of the *Ecole des Lionceaux* (Lion cubs' school), a genuine training centre aided by Peugeot dealers who found promising young football players and provided part-time jobs in the factory in Sochaux. Subsequently recruited players would be allowed to play in the second-team as well as the inter-factory Cup with the aim of integrating the more talented players into the first team at some future point. The success of this youth policy later allowed the club to open the third national training center, after Nantes and Saint-Étienne, in France in 1974 (Lanfranchi and Wahl, 1995). Since then several big names in French football such as Bernard Genghini, Yannick Stopyra, Franck Sauzée and more recently Benoît Pedretti and El-Hadji Diouf have started their careers in Sochalian colours.

Juventus, FIAT and Gianni Agnelli

The elevation of Gianni Agnelli to the leadership of Juventus at 26 years of age came out of respect for his father's memory, but was also because he was considered too young to take over the management of the FIAT empire that had been led by the engineer Vittorio Valletta since 1943. Moreover, Valetta did not appear in any hurry to give up his position in favour of the young Agnelli (Castronovo, 1999), so Gianni Agnelli was encouraged to find hobbies to fill his life as a bachelor and a rich heir. Football, in the form of Juventus, thus became one of Agnelli's occupations.

Agnelli however did not revolutionise football management at the end
of the 1940s or in the early 1950s but rather modernisation was due to
their rival club Torino A.C. (Dietschy, 2004). Gianni Agnelli broke with
the discreet habits of his father Edoardo and regularly gave interviews, as
well as becoming close to the players. In the mid 1950s he invested in
foreign players: Scandinavian followed by British and then South
Americans. The most notable 'captures' were the Welsh international John
Charles and Argentinean Omar Sivori. John Charles was attracted to
Juventus by a significantly higher remuneration at a time when salary
levels in Britain were capped by the maximum wage. Indeed Charles (1962:
p. 45) observed that "there is no maximum wage in Italy. In fact there is
no maximum to anything".

Match bonuses were set according to the desires of the flamboyant
Gianni Agnelli, a sign that Agnelli did not appear to have followed a rational
management model during his early years at the head of the club. Instead
he sought to use his generosity to promote the interests of Juventus, and
by using the FIAT commercial network he was able to secure some of the
best players from rival clubs. John Hansen, a Danish player, had been
recruited after the 1948 Olympic Games and was paid more than
1,500,000 lire a month, the equivalent at the time of £900 (Dietschy, 1997).

Though these extravagant expenses contributed to building the legend
of the heir of the most powerful family in Italy, they also had repercussions
for the development of football in Italy. Agnelli's financial largesse — like
that of other Italians such as the Neapolitan ship owner Achille Lauro,
president of *Napoli* — transformed the Italian Championship into one of
the most attractive and most cosmopolitan in Europe, but also paved the
way for the financial crisis that shook the game in the 1950s (Papa and
Panico, 2000). Personal largesse also created a situation of dependence
between the clubs and their rich sponsors which, on the one hand, created
a management without economic rationality and, on the other, made the
clubs extremely vulnerable in the event of the benefactor removing or even
losing his fortune.

Conclusion

Though other examples, Italian or French, could have been chosen to identify the spearheads of modernisation in European football between the 1920s and the 1950s, the cases of Juventus and FC Sochaux nevertheless remain fundamental for starting such an analysis. It was Edoardo Agnelli and Jean-Pierre Peugeot who delivered the first blows against amateurism that led to professionalism in Italy in 1926 and in France in 1932. They were also the leaders of two clubs that put in place professional management structures which strengthened the position of football as a modern sport. In different contexts, despite the common tie through the automobile industry, the two clubs can be identified as representing two models of the bond between football and industry. Up to the middle of the 1950s, Juventus was transformed into a free-spender supported by the generosity of the richest and most powerful industrial family in Italy. Its sphere of influence was more national than local and its sporting success and the aura of its stars contributed to a mirage in a country that was still poor and trailed behind centres of modernity in north-west Europe.

The case of Sochaux totally integrates the football club into a company strategy aimed at both the modernising of traditional paternalism and reinforcing the sports image of Peugeot. The route followed by FC Sochaux was thus narrow and became narrower during World War II as the aim was to maintain a professional team consisting initially of stars while preaching, through sport, the virtues of hard work, clean living and seriousness among its workers. This was gradually replaced by a more careful approach to economic management, leading to the production of young players for the world of high-level sports through the company and through FC Sochaux.

In 2005 — and despite the changes in the management of Peugeot and the choice of presidents from outside the founding family, the recent death of Gianni Agnelli and his brother Umberto — the ties uniting the two clubs and the car manufacturing industry from where they came were still not severed. It is true that other partners such as media companies, commercial sponsors or local communities largely financed the club's existence; and, moreover, the relationship between the clubs and their parent enterprises had long been institutionalised. Juventus was still regarded as a daughter company to the FIAT parent company and thus had to make a profit. The political and union context that led to a weakening of anti-capitalistic tendencies altered the *raisons d'être* of these clubs: they no longer serve as a social 'sedative', and they have to adapt to the new rules of modern marketing. Yet, paradoxically, while adapting to these new standards of professional sports modernity, Juventus and FC Sochaux continue, into 2005, to remain true to themselves and their inter-related origins.

References

Baudouin, G. (1984) *Histoire du FC Sochaux-Montbéliard*. Roanne: Horvath.
——— (1989) *Mattler*. Belfort: France Régions.
Castronovo, V. (1977) *Giovanni Agnelli. La Fiat dal 1899 al 1945*.Turin: Einaudi.
——— (1999) *FIAT 1899-1999. Un secolo di storia italiana*. Milan: Rizzoli.
Charles, J. (1962) *The gentle giant*. London: The Soccer Book Club.
Cohen, Y. (2001) *Organiser à l'aube du taylorisme. La pratique d'Ernest Mattern chez Peugeot*. Besançon: PUFC.
Dietschy, P. (1997) *Football et société à Turin 1920-1960*. Unpublished PhD Thesis, Lyon: université Lyon-II.
——— (2004) 'The Superga Disaster and the Death of the 'Great Torino'', *Soccer and Society* Vol. 5, No. 2: pp. 298-310.
Dorier, F. (2001) *FC Sochaux-Montbéliard*. Joué-lès-Tours: Alan Sutton.
Fridenson, P. (1989) 'Les ouvriers de l'automobile et le sport', *Actes de la Recherche en Sciences Sociales* No. 79: pp. 50-62.
Gay-Lescot, J. L. (1991) *Sport et éducation sous Vichy 1940-1944*. Lyon: Presses Universitaires de Lyon.
Ghirelli, A. (1990). *Storia del calcio in Italia*. Turin: Einaudi.
Goux, J. P. (1986) *Mémoires de l'Enclave*. Paris: Mazarine.
Il Paese Sportivo, 11 June 1924.
La Stampa, 6 May 1934.
Lanfranchi, P. (1994) 'Exporting football: Notes on the development of football in Europe' in Giulianotti, R. and Williams, J. (eds), *Game without frontiers. Football, identity and modernity*. Arena: Aldershot: pp. 23-45.
Lanfranchi, P. and Taylor, M. (2001) *Moving with the ball. The migration of professional footballers*. Oxford, New York: Berg.

Lanfranchi, P. and Wahl, A. (1995) *Les footballeurs professionnels des années trente à nos jours*. Paris: Hachette.

Loubet, J.L. (1990) *Automobiles Peugeot, une réussite industrielle 1945–1974*. Paris: Economica.

Marcot, F. (1999) 'La direction de Peugeot sous l'occupation: pétainisme, réticence, opposition et résistance', *Le Mouvement Social* No. 189: pp. 27–46.

Martin, C. (ed) (1994) *Sochaux d'hier à aujourd'hui*. Sochaux: MJC.

Papa, A. and Panico, G. (1993) *Storia sociale del calcio Dai club dei pionieri alla nazione sportiva (1887–1945)*. Bologna: Il Mulino.

———— (2000) *Storia sociale del calci. Dai campionati del dopoguerra alla Champions League (1945–2000)*. Bologna: Il Mulino.

Pennacchia, M. (1985) *Gli Agnelli e la Juventus*. Milan: Rizzoli.

Rondolino, G. (1993) 'Una grande tradizione di cinema' in Castronovo, V. (ed), *Storia illustrata di Torino, Torino nell'età giolittiana*. Turin: Elio Sellino, pp. 1661–1680.

Soldati, M. (1964) *Le due città*. Milan: Garzanti.

Wahl, A. (1989) *Les archives du football. Sport et société en France 1880–1980*. Paris: Gallimard/Julliard.

NORTHERN IRISH SOCIETY AND FOOTBALL IN THE IMMEDIATE POST-WORLD WAR II ERA: JIMMY JONES AND SECTARIANISM

Jonathan Magee
International Football Institute
University of Central Lancashire

Introduction

In divided societies such as Northern Ireland, it is no surprise that the majority of socio-political research into sport has focused on ethno-sectarian issues and religious divisions. In particular, research into football has demonstrated that "sport in Northern Ireland has been shown to consolidate the division between the unionist and nationalist communities ... As a consequence, Irish League football has been portrayed as a consistently divisive arena. The charge is not unwarranted" (Bairner and Walker, 2001: p. 81).

Arguably the worst incident of sectarian violence in Irish League football occurred on 27 December, 1948 when Belfast Celtic player Jimmy Jones was seriously injured by supporters of Linfield at the end of a match between the two clubs. Belfast Celtic and Linfield were rivals from neighbouring Belfast districts drawing their supporter bases from opposite communities; whilst sectarian disturbances were common at matches between the two clubs, Boxing Day 1948 was especially grave. The date became permanently embedded in the game's historiography when officials of Belfast Celtic withdrew the club from the Irish League in May 1949, with the spectre of sectarian violence a key, though not sole, factor.

The demise of Belfast Celtic, including the events of Boxing Day 1948, has been well covered in the literature (c.g. Coyle, 1999; Kennedy, 1989; Sugden and Bairner, 1993; Tuohy, 1978) and it is accepted that whilst

Jones was of the same (Protestant) religion as his attackers the attack was nonetheless motivated by sectarianism. The focus of this study however is to place Jimmy Jones at the centre of events and use his own testimony to explore the *Protestant-on-Protestant* nature of the attack and, in particular, the intra-community relationship between Jones and Linfield FC.

This approach duly extends knowledge of Boxing Day 1948 beyond ethno-sectarian factors and redresses "the tendency to focus on the Boxing Day [1948] incident with little reference to what was happening at the time, not only in the wider community but also within Linfield Football Club itself" (Bairner and Walker, 2001: p. 86). It also adds to a growing body of work in both sports history and in the sociology of sport devoted to the cultural meaning of individual athletes. Whilst Andrews and Jackson (2001), Cashmore (2002) and Whannel (2002), amongst others, have made a significant contribution in this regard by examining the social significance of star performers, this chapter, like the previous study by Bairner and Walker (2001), demonstrates that lives more ordinary can also offer important insights into extraordinary social developments.

Further, this contribution responds to, albeit with a historical example, Bairner's (2002: p. 193) comment that "there is a real need for more research into the relationship between sport and intra-community rivalry within both the Ulster unionist and Irish nationalist traditions, not least in order to reveal that the contestation for positions of power is in no way confined to disputes between the two traditions".

Context

The late 1940s was politically sensitive for Northern Ireland and the Unionist majority. With Unionist votes lost to the Northern Ireland Labour Party (NILP) and pressures from the Anti-Partition League (APL) to end the constitutional existence of Northern Ireland, the success of Independent Unionist candidates over those of the Ulster Unionist Party (UUP) revived the UUP's "deep-rooted fear of Unionist fragmentation leading to weakness regarding the defence of the constitutional position of Northern Ireland" (Walker, 2004: p. 89). In addition, the Irish Free State declared itself a Republic in 1948 and withdrew from the British Commonwealth, increasing Unionist fears of a pending all-Ireland state.

It is against this highly charged political backdrop that the Linfield–Belfast Celtic game was played out. Therefore "the riot at the match has to be placed in the broader political context of heightened tensions over the constitutional position of Northern Ireland. Although it had always been the dominant political issue, the security of the state appeared to Unionists to be facing its gravest threat since its foundation" (Bairner and Walker, 2001: p. 90).

Nowhere was the dominance of Protestantism within Irish league football more visible than in the form of Linfield FC. Founded in 1886 by employees of the Ulster Spinning Company in a Protestant district of south Belfast, Linfield's early successes established them as the premier club. As Linfield grew in stature the unmistakable sense of Protestantism set the club apart from Irish League clubs in other Protestant districts and they soon gained "a reputation for ethnic exclusivity ... for having appeared to have adopted a policy at various stage ... of not signing Catholic players or, indeed, employing Catholics in any capacity" (Bairner and Walker, 2001: p. 83). This reputation permitted Linfield to draw upon supporters from outside their locality (Bairner, 1997; Bairner, 2001; Bairner and Shirlow, 1998; Magee, 2005) and, whilst Protestant exclusivity has always been denied by the club (Brodie, 1985), Linfield has been accurately described as "the Protestant symbol" (Sugden and Bairner, 1993: p. 131), "the representatives of Ulster loyalist identity" (Bairner, 2001: p. 33), "a Protestant club for Protestant people" (Bairner and Walker, 2001: p. 84) and a "club which is traditionally and, for the most part, accurately identified with the Protestant and Unionist tradition" (ibid: pp. 81–2).

Whilst Linfield had acquired an overwhelming Protestant image, the impression of Belfast Celtic as an Irish nationalist club was established on rather more tenuous grounds. Critically, however:

> ... in the eyes of Protestants, Belfast Celtic were already guilty by association; it was a nationalist side for nationalist players and supporters ... In a society where myth is more often potent than fact, however, the popular image of Celtic was kept alive by friend and foe alike. (Sugden and Bairner, 1993: p. 81).

The idea of Belfast Celtic as a nationalist club has since been disputed (Coyle, 1999; Kennedy, 1989; Sugden and Bairner, 1993; Tuohy, 1978) but the perception was nonetheless real in the Protestant community of the late 1800s.

Belfast Celtic's first Irish League game against Glentoran, a mainly Protestant club from Belfast's shipyard arena, resulted in sectarian violence between rival supporters and further violence transpired when the clubs met again later that season. According to Sugden and Bairner (1993: p. 81):

> From then onwards, games featuring the club [Celtic] and rivals Linfield and Glentoran, both supported for the most part by Protest-ants, were frequently marred by crowd disturbances ... It was clear from the outset that these incidents had sinister political overtones. Thus, it was scarcely surprising that as political tensions heightened, crowd trouble at matches between Celtic and their Belfast rivals worsened.

Although ethno-sectarian tension in football at this time was not restricted to intra-Belfast rivalries, particularly when Dublin clubs visited Belfast, it was the Belfast Celtic–Linfield/Glentoran axis that resulted in the most serious sectarian disturbances.

The rivalry between Belfast Celtic and Linfield increased as Celtic successfully challenged Linfield's early supremacy and it was further accentuated following Linfield's move to their Windsor Park ground in 1905 which brought the clubs into close proximity to one another. Sectarian violence at matches between the two clubs became a regular feature and in the 1912–3 season one match was abandoned while the return game was marked by sporadic gunfire from Linfield supporters. Gunfire, this time from Belfast Celtic supporters, also featured at a match in 1920.

The Government of Ireland Act (1920) resolved the situation for southern clubs who withdrew from the Irish League to enter the newly created League of Ireland in the Irish Free State. From this point on:

> ... association football was to be organized separately in the different states of Ireland, with the Irish League and the Irish Football Association continuing to preside over the game's affairs in the

northern side of the border, and the League of Ireland and the Football Association of Ireland (F.A.I.) assuming control in the south … [and] the impact of political and cultural division was now more overt than had been the case before partition. (Sugden and Bairner: pp. 73–4)

Whilst the complexities of organising football in the two Irish states caused confusion in the international arena, the reorganization of the Irish League to contain only northern clubs isolated Belfast Celtic as the sole Catholic-supported club.

Commenting on a later period of Irish league history and the cases of Derry City and Cliftonville, Bairner and Walker (2001: p. 83) note that these clubs were "the most visible outsiders in a league in which most clubs attract mainly Protestant fans and where the dominant ethos at most grounds is one that is supportive of unionist hegemony". The same comment can be applied to Belfast Celtic and in an attempt to stem sectarian disorder the Irish Football League (IFL) barred Belfast Celtic from competing during the 1924–5 season.

In this context it is remarkable that Belfast Celtic not only survived such difficulties but did so with distinction. Indeed the inter-war period saw Belfast Celtic become the dominant force as they won 11 Irish League championships, eclipsing both Linfield (six championships) and Glentoran (three championships). The sporadic pattern of football during the 1940s because of World War II further extended Celtic's dominance and, when football resumed its normal course in 1946–7, Belfast Celtic were at the pinnacle of Irish league football.

Therefore the ascendancy of the nationalist-perceived Belfast Celtic over Linfield in the immediate period following World War II had significant political value when considered alongside the Unionist view that the constitutional position of Northern Ireland was in danger. Linfield supporters, and indeed Protestant supporters of other clubs, could conceivably have regarded Belfast Celtic's continued supremacy as symbolic of the threat posed by the 'other' to the Northern Irish state. Hence the political uncertainty at this time intensified the ethno-sectarian rivalry between Belfast Celtic and Linfield, a rivalry of which Jimmy Jones became an intrinsic part.

The early career of Jimmy Jones

James Jones was born on 25 July 1928 in Keady, County Armagh, but moved to Lurgan in the same county in his early years. The family had an impressive football pedigree with Jimmy being the cousin of Jack Jones, Linfield captain in their Irish Cup victories of 1930 and 1931, who had featured in the same Irish team in 1933 alongside his brother Sam and brother-in-law Billy Mitchell. The Joneses' football fraternity extended to the Burnison family, also of Lurgan, which had provided four Irish international players in the early 1900s.

Regarding the Burnison-Jones football dynasty, football historian Malcolm Brodie (1980: p. 43) observed that "there could be few families who have contributed so much to the game in Ireland as the Joneses and the Burnisons". Continuing the family tradition in football, Jimmy Jones first came to prominence as a fifteen year old with Lurgan club Sunnyside of the Amateur League during the 1943/4 season and the next season moved to fellow Lurgan club Shankill Young Men (YM), also of the Amateur League.

At the time, Jack Jones was scouting for Linfield and influenced his young cousin to sign for the club in July 1945 ahead of approaches from other Irish League clubs. Jimmy Jones was a notable capture for Linfield at a time when the club was struggling to compete with Belfast Celtic. Despite having recognized a promising opportunity at Linfield, Jones recounted[1] that things did not go well:

> I signed for Linfield because of Jack [Jones] and went to train at Windsor Park with Walter Sloan and the first night nobody ever said anything to us ... Walter got a [pre-season] match but I didn't get anything ... I went to play for the Swifts [Linfield's reserve team] but was twelfth man away at Lurgan Rangers. There were no subs then and I just got fed up with that and went back to Shankill Young Men. Nobody at Linfield said, 'Jones, where did you go?' and I have often wondered why [I was allowed to leave].

Jones, angered by Linfield's treatment, returned to Shankill YM but remained registered with the club for the remainder of the 1945/6 season.

Linfield's apathy towards and subsequent negative judgment of Jones was brought into question after he scored a double hat-trick (six goals) in Shankill YM's Clarence Cup match with Hilden Recreation of Lisburn not long after his aborted spell with Linfield, a feat that impressed a particular spectator:

> At the end of the match I was tackled by this fella. I did not know who he was. He grabbed me by the arm and said 'would you sign a form for [Belfast] Celtic?' and I says 'I already signed for Linfield at the start of the season'. Just like lightening he says 'I'll see you on the 20th of May'. That was when your amateur contract expired. The man disappeared as quick as he came … It was Elisha Scott, the manager of [Belfast] Celtic … and sure enough he turned up at our house on 20th May [1946].

Jones's goal-scoring feats had not only alerted Belfast Celtic: Distillery and Glentoran also tried to sign the player without realizing that Jones was a current Linfield player.

Despite Jones's performances and the interest shown in him by other Irish League clubs, Linfield never invited Jones back even though he was still their player. This further angered Jones who by then "had made up my mind I wasn't signing for another senior [Irish League] club. I'd had enough of them. I went back to Shankill [YM] as it was handy and I enjoyed it. I had no intention of playing in the Irish League".

Jones reaches 'paradise'

Despite Jones's strong views on Irish League clubs Elisha Scott eventually persuaded him to train with Belfast Celtic midway through the 1946/7 season. Jones recalled how he "was pressurized that much by him [Scott] I gave in. It was the only way to stop him coming to the house". Initially Jones was unwilling to commit to Celtic because of his Linfield experience but a key moment changed his mind:

> Scott got me in the room and threw this wad of notes, big white fivers, on the table and he says 'There you are, count that'. It was two hundred pounds and he says 'It's yours. All you have to do is sign that [professional] form' and I couldn't refuse. I never had any

regrets about it. They [Celtic] were some outfit ... They were the top-notchers ... Linfield were fighting a losing battle ... The green and white kit I thought was great. Wherever you went you were never allowed to think you were going to get beat. Scott had it drummed into you that if you don't win you'll not be here.

Having signed, Jones was unable to break into the Celtic team that won the Irish Cup, City Cup and Gold Cup that season (1946–7) and spent a formative period in the reserves.

The next season, 1947–8, saw the 19 year-old Jones make his debut and establish himself in a Celtic team that went on to win the Irish League Championship, the Gold Cup and the City Cup. During the season the club also went on a 31 match unbeaten sequence with Jones contributing a debut season tally of 63 goals, reward not only for Scott's persistence but also for his judgment of Jones's talent. Jones's immediate impact with Belfast Celtic also drew attention to Linfield's error of the season before not least because not only had Jones proven his ability at Irish league level but he had done so with Linfield's main rivals.

In an attempt to rectify the situation, Linfield secretary Joe Mackey made an illegal approach to Jones during his debut season with Celtic. Jones explained "that Linfield were trying their damnest to sign me, offering me more money to leave Celtic but I wasn't interested. I was telling Joe Mackey I was staying at Celtic but he was having none of it. I got sick of him and he didn't like me for it". A further surreptitious approach by Mackey lead to a change of tact in his next (illegal) meeting with Jones during which he sought to capitalise on Jones's clear Protestant heritage, including membership of the Orange Order:

He [Mackey] then says to me that I shouldn't be up there [at Celtic Park] and should be with them and that my rightful place belonged there with them. I didn't like that and I told him I'd already been at Windsor Park and they got rid of me and not to give me any of that. He kept making approaches to me about this but I wasn't interested, I wanted to play for Celtic and he didn't like it. I don't think he forgave me for it and I didn't like him for that, pressurizing me that way. He wasn't a very nice man.

It is difficult to distinguish whether Mackey's attempt to influence Jones on religious grounds was a personal decision or a club one but nonetheless it failed.

Not only was Jones encouraged to stay at Celtic Park for football reasons, but Linfield and/or Mackey had been mistaken in thinking that Jones's personal heritage would be a problem at Celtic Park:

> The supporter base was very much Nationalist from the Falls and Andersonstown. Belfast Celtic had nothing republican about them. Their support was mostly Catholic although there were a lot of Protestant supporters of Celtic. The greater majority of their supporters were Catholic but nothing was emphasized, unlike Linfield. Their supporters sang *The Sash* but Celtic, there was never any sectarianism ... The support was greatly Catholic but it was different with the players. A great many were Protestant and that was that. We were winning and no one cared ... That 1947–8 team had at least five Protestants in it and there was no problem with that ... There were also players from the Republic of Ireland who travelled to play but we were all great mates ... It didn't matter who you were. There were no [sectarian] remarks passed ... Everyone was the best of mates.

Jones reckoned that the inclusive atmosphere at Celtic Park was maintained by Elisha Scott's management style that nullified comments of a religious or political kind even though:

> Scott himself was a Protestant who made no bones about it ... anywhere at all he went he [made it known he] was a Protestant alright... There was no mistaking that but it [sectarianism] never came into the dressing room. He made sure of that. If he heard anything being bantered like that he would say 'That's enough. We'll have none of that in here [dressing room]' and it would stop just like that.

Jones did however recall how players would joke about the subject behind Scott's back and recalled a tale of how fellow player Charlie Tully would refer, without seriousness or cynicism, to the number of Protestants in the team before then ribbing those players who travelled from the Republic of Ireland to play. This account gains further credibility as a result of Brodie's (1980: p. 58) description of Tully as "Ireland's leading soccer extrovert.

Known as the Clown Prince of Football, a virtuoso in a jersey, he was an irrepressible, jovial character whose wisecracks and stories will be forever told".

Therefore the insights into Belfast Celtic, as revealed by Jones, contrasted with the popular image of the club. The inclusive attitude of Belfast Celtic at the time permitted space for 'Protestant heroes' like Scott and Jones, signifying a willingness on the part of Celtic's mainly nationalist supporter base to endorse inclusion in what were volatile political times. Had Jones played for a different manager or indeed been less successful as a player his spell at Celtic Park may have been different but as it was "my membership of the Orange [Order] was never mentioned to me at all in my time at Celtic. No one was bothered about it".

Despite poor relations with Linfield officials, and in particular Joe Mackey, Jones believed that in his debut season with Belfast Celtic he had established:

> ... a good relationship with Linfield supporters because of Jack [Jones], and there was never any bother between them and me really ... Because of the Jack factor Linfield supporters knew who I was, knew of me and knew of Jack, my cousin, and of where I came from.

Jones knew however that fellow Celtic players were treated differently by Linfield supporters with Catholic players subjected to sectarian abuse while Protestant players were derided for playing for the 'other'. As is now known, Jones was mistakenly idealistic about his relations with Linfield supporters and unaware of the impact of his contributions to the successes of Linfield's 'other'.

The 1948/9 season

The first trophy of the 1948/9 season was the City Cup, played in league format between the twelve Irish League clubs with each team playing each other once. Going into the tenth and penultimate game, Belfast Celtic and Linfield were joint top and scheduled to play each other at Celtic Park on 30 October, 1948.

Played in front of 20,000 spectators, Belfast Celtic won a dramatic match 2–1. For most of the second half Linfield played with ten players as a clash between Celtic's goalkeeper, Kevin McAlinden, and Linfield's Billy Simpson forced the injured Linfield player to leave the pitch. According to Jones, "Kevin hit Simpson hard and the [Linfield] crowd didn't like it. They gave him some awful stick [verbal abuse] for the rest of the game". As well as being barracked during the game, McAlinden received death threats, purporting to be from Linfield supporters, following the game.

The final matches in the City Cup took place the following Saturday and Celtic won theirs to secure the trophy narrowly ahead of Linfield. The structure of the season meant that the Irish League championship began the next weekend and Celtic and Linfield set the early pace. The fixture list scheduled the two clubs to play each other on Boxing Day at Windsor Park and only one point separated them at the top of the table. The match also brought the resumption of the McAlinden–Simpson battle and Jones recalled that there were pre-match concerns regarding the safety of Celtic goalkeeper McAlinden.

Jones himself was in good form by the time of the match, having already scored 33 goals, and recalled "a huge crowd that day, they were packed in, hanging from the rafters, nobody could move. There was easy 35 or 40 thousand there and the atmosphere was electric". Typical of important matches, the opening was tense but a critical incident involving Jones and Bob Bryson, Linfield's centre-half, toward the end of the first half intensified the atmosphere:

> Bob hit me [in a challenge for the ball]. It wasn't an awful foul to be honest with you. Whatever happened I was lying on the ground after being knocked down. The referee gave me a free kick but I can honestly say it wasn't a bad foul and Bob didn't think so either. I was lying on the ground and Bob went to kick the ball at me. Whenever he turned round he saw the referee had give me a free kick and went to kick the ball at me. I just stuck my foot up like that [motions by lifting his foot and showing the sole of his shoe] against the ball to block it and he kicked the ball. It was like in a block tackle and as he kicked the ball which was against my foot you heard the crack of his leg, just like a rifle shot. You see, I never touched Bob Bryson in that incident.

Bryson was carried off and shortly afterward Linfield were reduced to nine players when Jackie Russell received a severe blow from the ball to the chest and was carried off. The match ended scoreless at half-time but Celtic was clearly in the ascendancy given their two player advantage.

During the half-time interval it became known that Bryson had broken his leg and although Linfield secretary Joe Mackey announced the unfortunate news on the public address system, Jones confirmed that the Celtic camp was not informed:

> ·   We were in the dressing room and I didn't know Bob Bryson had broken his leg ... Joe Mackey announced it over the tannoy system ... I didn't know any of this when I took the field for the second half but I knew the atmosphere had got worse. I did not know why. I just thought it was because it was a big game ... Looking back, someone should have told us about Bob but I think that was done on purpose. Mackey knew what he was doing and that I was playing away at the far end in the second half and he saw his chance what with the things that went on between us.

Thus the second half started without the Celtic players either knowing about Bryson or why the atmosphere had further degenerated.

In the second half Linfield played toward their supporters in the Spion Kop — the terracing at the end of the ground adjacent to the players entrance — with Celtic attacking their own supporters in the Railway Stand at the opposite end. Linfield supporters were also in the South Stand and its Enclosure while more Celtic fans were opposite in the Gallaher Blues Stand. Not long into the second half Linfield's Simpson exacted revenge on Celtic goalkeeper McAlinden with a hefty challenge and tempers were further frayed in the 72nd minute when Linfield's Albert Currie and Celtic's Paddy Bonnar were dismissed for fighting. Thus the remainder of the game was played out between ten Celtic and eight Linfield players.

Just as it seemed that the match would end scoreless, Celtic was awarded a penalty in the 80th minute which Harry Walker scored. According to Jones, "Linfield then piled forward and had us penned back even though we had two extra players" and subsequently equalised in the 86th minute. The goal resulted in around 300 Linfield supporters encroaching onto the playing area in celebration, causing the re-start to be delayed. The match ended 1–1 in semi-darkness, a fair result in Jones's view, but events were to quickly worsen:

> At the end I chased a ball away out on the left wing [in front of the Gallaher Blues Stand]. We were playing into the goals at the Railway End ... and I was away in that far left corner when the referee blew the whistle. I didn't think there was any problem and shook hands with Alfie McMichael [Linfield right back] and went to walk off as usual. The whole crowd came over the walls [at the South Stand Enclosure and Spion Kop] and I thought 'what the hell is going on here?'.

Jones focused his attention on Kevin McAlinden, assuming that the Celtic goalkeeper was in danger following his clashes with Linfield player Simpson, but "he [McAlinden] was playing up at the Spion Kop goals and was away like a rocket up the players' tunnel". However McAlinden, along with Celtic right back Robin Lawlor, was manhandled though not seriously injured by Linfield supporters before reaching safety.

By now Jones was stranded near the centre circle as one of the few, if not the only, Celtic player left on the pitch and was trying to make his way diagonally across the pitch to the players' tunnel by weaving in and out of Linfield supporters:

> I couldn't get up to the players' exit in the corner at Windsor [Park] as the crowd came all around from the Spion Kop and the South Stand. I ran over to the side [South Stand] as there was police all around there during the match but when I got there, there were no police as they had all moved up to help the players off. I tried to run up the track and somebody pushed me over the wall onto the terracing [into the Enclosure in front of the South Stand]. I got up to run down the terracing to the [players'] tunnel but somebody else tripped me and then somebody else jumped off the wall onto my leg. The impact shattered my shin bone in five places. My right leg is an inch shorter now.

Lying on the ground with a shattered leg, Jones was at the mercy of the crowd:

> One fella threw himself down on top of me and I thought he was attacking me too! The police arrived on the scene. They had the batons drawn and they were just pushing them [Linfield

supporters] back. Fellas were kicking at me. They [police] could
have hit them across the head with the blooming things [batons]
and got the right ones. The police, I thought, weren't very
effective that day and if it wasn't for the fella on top of me I don't
know what else would have happened. He helped me more than the
police did.

It transpired that Jones's saviour was Sean McCann, a Ballymena United
player, who left his seat in the South Stand to help Jones.

The police presence brought eventual, if delayed, calm and the badly
injured Jones was taken to the dressing room but encountered a further
problem as an argument between Linfield and Celtic officials developed
over his treatment. Celtic officials, and in particular Elisha Scott, believed
that the severity of Jones's injury merited immediate hospital treatment
whilst Linfield preferred that their club doctor treat Jones at the ground.
One can only assume that Linfield officials relented as an ambulance took
Jones, accompanied by Scott — who Jones described as having "tears
rolling down his cheeks. He was livid at what had happened" — to hospital.
That night in the Musgrave Park Clinic Hospital Jones was operated on
by Mr. Withers, a top surgeon of the time.

Jones's rehabilitation involved a four-month stay in hospital, a further
three operations to re-set his leg and a long spell in plaster. At this point
Jones was pessimistic as to any future involvement in football:

I never thought I'd be able to play football again. I didn't have much
intention to play again … I couldn't see it myself. After all, I was in
plaster for eight and a half months and walked with a limp after
that.

Indeed it took Jones until the end of 1949, a year after the attack, to walk
without the aid of a walking stick by which time he had won £4,361 in
compensation from Belfast Corporation, the licensing municipal authority, for malicious injury, loss of earnings and his share of a pending transfer
to English professional football that had never materialised. Despite a
lengthy court case which involved many witnesses, including Jones, the
referee, Belfast Celtic and Linfield officials no one was ever charged with
attacking Jones.

As for Belfast Celtic, the 1948/9 season brought victory in the City Cup and a second-place finish behind Linfield in the Irish League championship. In May 1949, club officials sent a resignation letter to the IFL's Management Committee and whilst Boxing Day 1948 was not the only factor in the club's demise, it was an influential one. That month the club embarked on what turned out to be a farewell excursion to the United States and even defeated the Scottish national team in New York. Alhough he did not go on the trip, Jones was still listed in the official tour programme.

Conclusion

Despite injuries sustained on Boxing Day 1948, Jones resumed his Irish League career in 1950/1 with Glenavon of Lurgan and played until 1964[2]. His scoring record of 332 goals in 285 matches placed him 22nd in the 1997 FIFA list of the world's national top division goalscorers of all time with a ratio of 1.16 goals per league game. However it is perhaps Boxing Day 1948 for which Jones is best remembered.

Central to the events of Boxing Day 1948 is the complex relationship between Jones and Linfield FC. The relationship was soured by Linfield's rejection of Jones who subsequently became successful with Linfield's chief rivals and duly rebuffed Linfield's various approaches to return. Had Jones re-emerged with an Irish League club other than Belfast Celtic — hence one with a mainly Protestant outlook — his career might have assumed less significance in the eyes of men such as Joe Mackey, who had played the Orange card and lost.

During the interview with Jones, it became clear that he had a somewhat naïve understanding of the ethno-sectarian climate surrounding the Belfast Celtic–Linfield rivalry, the symbolic status afforded to Celtic's prolonged dominance over Linfield, and how he was a key player for Linfield's 'other'. Jones was in a curious position as a former Linfield player with family connections to the club and an overtly Protestant heritage who, nevertheless, became instrumental in exacerbating Linfield's problems at the hands of their chief rivals. To this day, Jones appears to have missed the significance of his impact in the political context at this time, and that — like it or not — he was more than just a football player.

The success of Belfast Celtic at the expense of Linfield inevitably had serious implications in ethno-sectarian terms in the immediate post-World War II period when Unionists increasingly feared the threat of an all-Ireland state. The anomaly is that Belfast Celtic's successes were greatly assisted by Protestants like Elisha Scott, Harry Walker and Jimmy Jones who found comfort in and helped to create an inclusive atmosphere which refutes the view of Belfast Celtic as a nationalist club. However, as this chapter has shown, contrary perceptions of Belfast Celtic, particularly from those connected to Linfield like Joe Mackey, remained strong.

Jones made reference to the sectarianised nature of Linfield and Mackey's notion that Windsor Park was "the rightful place" for Protestant players. Conversely, Belfast Celtic supporters deserve credit for widely accepting players with Protestant heritages, like Jones, which no doubt greatly assisted in nullifying the impact of external political and religious factors as insisted upon by Scott. This can be considered a sign of just how inaccurate the labelling of Belfast Celtic as a 'nationalist' club was.

Whilst Jones offered strong testimony that he regarded himself the victim of a revenge attack stage-managed by Joe Mackey on Boxing Day 1948, consideration needs to be attributed to broader factors. Whilst there is no doubt that Jones suffered horrific injuries, he acknowledged that he was not the original target for rampaging Linfield supporters — Kevin McAlinden was — and thus was something of a secondary target. When McAlinden reached safety it is likely that Linfield supporters then turned their attention to the remaining Celtic players on the pitch, of whom Jones would have been among the last. At this point it is likely that Jones was then attacked by Linfield supporters fuelled, and almost certainly blinded, by sectarianism because he was playing for Linfield's 'other', as opposed to being prioritized by the strained relations Jones had with Linfield.

Some Linfield supporters may have been further influenced to attack Jones because of his disloyalty to the Protestant cause, but Jones fails to realise that his contributions to Belfast Celtic's success would have resulted in him being re-imagined by Linfield supporters as a 'Fenian-lover' at a nationalist club. In broader terms, Jones would thus have been considered either part of the "disloyal elements" (Patterson, 1996: p. 3), like Unionist voters disaffecting to the NILP, or seen as an "enemy within" (Dixon, 2001: p. 50) like the APL. These would have been reasonable perceptions in what were politically insecure times for Protestants who perceived a genuine threat to the constitutional security of Northern Ireland. Critically, Jones fails to appreciate the political currency afforded to football at this time and in particular the Belfast Celtic–Linfield rivalry of which he was a part.

In examining the relationship between Jones and Linfield it has become apparent to the author that further research is required to achieve greater clarity regarding Boxing Day 1948. This chapter has demonstrated that there are factors beyond ethno-sectarian ones that need to be considered to fully understand the single most damaging football event in Northern Ireland's history. For instance, it is worth considering whether the depth and intensity of the *football* rivalry, as opposed to the ethno-sectarian rivalry, between Belfast Celtic and Linfield affected the events that day. As part of this it would be interesting to know if any other personal duels, like that between McAlinden and Simpson, existed as undercurrents to the match, and also whether incidents from previous matches had a bearing.

As for the Jones–Linfield relationship, there is also room for further research as the discord between the two did not end with the court case of 1949. Not only did Jones resume his playing career with Glenavon but he was a significant player in their 1950s and early 1960s successes as Linfield's chief challengers. In fact, Jones was captain of the Glenavon side that defeated Linfield 5–1 in the 1961 Irish Cup Final, a match which Jones describes as his "personal revenge against Linfield".

As a final point, the example of Protestant Jimmy Jones who acquired 'hero status' at Belfast Celtic offers a contrasting example to Catholic player and trainer Gerry Morgan's 'hero status' at Linfield, as identified by Bairner and Walker (2001). Thus this chapter reaffirms Bairner and Walker's (2001: p. 86) claim that "there are subtle nuances which do not conform to the general pattern [of sectarianism] and which, as a result, shed interesting light on the role of football in the history of Northern Ireland".

Notes

[1] An interview with Jimmy Jones was conducted by the author on 22 July 2003 in Lurgan, County Armagh; all quotations of Jimmy Jones that are reported in this chapter are from this interview.

[2] In 18 seasons in the Irish League with Belfast Celtic, Glenavon, Portadown and Bangor Jones won 15 trophies, represented (Northern) Ireland three times and

scored 1 goal, made 6 appearances in European club tournaments and scored 2 goals, and scored 11 goals for the Irish League Select XI. Jones's career goal tally across all competitions was difficult to accumulate but he did score a total of 96 goals for Belfast Celtic (1947/8 — 1948/9) and 614 for Glenavon (1951/2 — 1961/2). The tribute headline in *Ireland's Saturday Night* (15 February, 1997), "Jimmy knew where the net was...", succinctly summed up Jones's remarkable career.

References

Andrews, D. L. and Jackson, S. (eds) (2001) *Sport Stars. The cultural politics of sporting celebrity*. London: Routledge.

Bairner, A. (1997) '"Up to their knees"? Football, sectarianism, masculinity and Protestant working-class identity', in P. Shirlow and M. McGovern (eds) *Who are 'The People'? Unionism, Protestantism and Loyalism in Northern Ireland*. London: Pluto Press, pp. 95–113.

—— (2001) *Sport, nationalism and globalization: European and North American perspectives*. New York: State University of New York Press.

—— (2002) 'Sport, sectarianism and society in a divided Ireland revisited', in J. Sugden and A. Tomlinson (eds) *Power games: A critical sociology of sport*. London: Routledge, pp. 181–195.

Bairner, A. and Shirlow, P. (1998) 'Loyalism, Linfield and the territorial politics of soccer fandom in Northern Ireland', *Space and Polity* Vol. 2, No. 2: pp. 163–77.

Bairner, A. and Walker, G. (2001) 'Football and society in Northern Ireland: Linfield Football Club and the case of Gerry Morgan', *Soccer and Society* Vol.2: No. 1: pp. 81–98.

Brodie, M. (1980) *100 Years of Irish Football*. Belfast: Blackstaff Press.

—— (1985) *Linfield 100 Years*, Belfast: The Universities Press (Belfast) Ltd.

Cashmore, E. (2002) *Beckham*. Cambridge: Polity Press.

Coyle, P. (1999) *Paradise lost and found. The story of Belfast Celtic*. Edinburgh: Mainstream.

Dixon, P. (2001) *Northern Ireland: The politics of war and peace*. Hampshire: Palgrave.

Ireland's Saturday Night, 30th October 1948; 15th February 1997.

Kennedy, J. (1989) *Belfast Celtic*. Belfast: Pretani.

Magee, J. (2005) 'Football supporters, rivalry and Protestant fragmentation', in A. Bairner (ed) *Sport and the Irish*. Dublin: University College Dublin Press, pp. 172–188.

Patterson, H. (1996) 'Unionism in power', in A. Aughey and D. Morrow (eds) *Northern Ireland politics*. Longman: London, pp. 3–10.

Sugden, J. and Bairner, A. (1993) *Sport, sectarianism and sport in a divided Ireland*. Leicester: Leicester University Press.

Tuohy, M. (1978) *Belfast Celtic*, Belfast: Blackstaff Press.

Walker, G. (2004) *A history of the Ulster Unionist Party: Protest, pragmatism and pessimism*. Manchester: Manchester University Press.

Whannel, G. (2002) *Media sport stars. Masculinities and moralities*. London: Routledge.

THE 'PALS', THE 'PROFESSIONALS' AND THE 'CONFORMERS': THE MEANING OF FOOTBALL IN THE LIVES OF WOMEN FOOTBALLERS IN SCOTLAND

Jessica Macbeth
International Football Institute
University of Central Lancashire

Introduction

There is little research on women's football in Britain that has related women's experiences to subcultural membership. The majority of research on women's football, with the exception of Williams (2003), has generally failed to consider the experiences of women footballers in Scotland. The subculture of women's football has yet to receive adequate representation in research on sport subcultures. A number of analyses of subcultures and sport subcultures have emerged that have the potential to inform an equivalent analysis of women's football. What follows then demonstrates a need for an interpretation of a subculture of women's football that is based on the meaning of football in players' lives, and informed by other research on women's football and sport subcultures.

As research on subcultures has evolved they have become seen as "micro-communities, groups within groups, who came to share similar felt and understood interests", including sport, "and a whole spectrum of embodied social practices" (Nayak, 2003: p. 14). This is a useful way to view the subculture of women's football in Scotland, which is identified in this research as comprising three 'interlocking group cultures' (Fine and Kleinman, 1979). This chapter focuses on the subculture of women's football based on player's experiences and the meanings they attach to football in their lives. There are several underlying aims. First, to offer an interpretation of the subculture based on an analysis of three interlocking group cultures within it. Second, to identify elements of subcultural capital and more specific elements of group cultural capital. Third, to explore how the nature and extent of a player's membership of these group cultures is based on the meanings they attach to football. Finally, to consider how the differences in meanings form potential sources of tension between group cultures.

Women's football in Scotland has developed into a competitive, structured and institutionalised sport, despite being subjected to a degree of hostility and subordination throughout its development.[1] Recent attempts to develop forms of professionalism are representative of its gradual incorporation into the dominant sport culture. Throughout its development, the subculture of women's football has acquired and is continually acquiring additional characteristics. Although football essentially brings players who share various ascribed and achieved characteristics together into this social space, the meanings attached to the place of football in their lives differ. These meanings tend to determine the nature and extent of their membership of the subculture as a whole and the interlocking group cultures within it.

Methods

This analysis is informed by evidence from a combination of quantitative and qualitative data obtained via a survey of 144 women footballers and 13 in-depth interviews and time-profiles. Questionnaires (n= 615) were distributed at a Scottish Women's Football League (SWFL) Club Secretaries Meeting in February 2002; 144 questionnaires were returned for a response rate of 23%. The questionnaire respondents represented a cross-ability sample of players who compete in the Premier Division (n=34), First Division (n=32), Second Division (n=37), and Third Division (n=41) of the Scottish Women's Football League (SWFL). The cross-ability sample of players meant the analysis could take account of different responses that might be attributed to ability level.

Semi-structured interviews were conducted between November 2002 and June 2003 with a total of 13 players representing three clubs within the SWFL. Five players represented a Premier Division team, four players represented a team recently promoted from the Second to the First Division and the remaining four players represented a team struggling at the bottom of the Third Division. Club secretaries were contacted and asked to recruit willing participants from their club, and preferably players who had previously completed the survey and were therefore familiar with the focus of the research.

My own position in relation to the research context is as follows. Apart from brief spells with a First Division club in 2000 and a Premier Division club in 2002, I was not a registered member of any SWFL club during the research. Both spells with the clubs were too brief for me to become socialised from a relative outsider to an established club member. My own experience as a member of the subculture of women's football is based on an immersion in the women's university football scene in Scotland, playing for Stirling University Ladies Football Club (SULFC) for six years (including two years whilst conducting this research), as well as my limited participation, as described above, in the SWFL during 2000 and 2002.

The 'pals', the 'professionals' and the 'conformers'

The meanings players attach to football and the importance of the sport in their lives were explored in both the survey and interviews. From the players' responses to a number of questions relating to their experiences and views about playing football and being a club member, three distinct but overlapping group cultures within the subculture were identified. The following offers a brief account of the typical characteristics of each of these group cultures.

The 'pals'

This group culture generally consists of players who consider the social aspects of being part of a football club as particularly important. Despite the majority taking their football relatively seriously, they accept that they are not likely to make a living out of football. The 'pals' tend to emphasise the social rewards of being a member of a club including friendship, enjoyment, and 'having a laugh'. As one player from the Third Division generalises, "... for all teams, having a laugh and you know, getting on with the people they're playing with, things like that, makes all the crowd go back every week" (Interviewee L, 27). Many of the 'pals' have a social life that revolves around friends from their team, or are involved in football outwith their team (e.g. previous teams) and the social lives of some of the 'pals' are often dependent on their involvement in football. A player from a Premier Division club explains how her social life revolves around football-related friends in such a way: "when I think about the things I do and who I do them with then it's all through football really that I do them, nearly always" (Interviewee A, 31).

'Pals' are also characterised by their attitudes towards club loyalty. Some 'pals' stress that they would find it very difficult to leave their existing club due to the various social rewards accrued. Such social rewards tend to be considered by the 'pals' as more important than ambitions to play at a higher level, as encapsulated in the following quote:

> It's a football team yeah, but it's also a big circle of friends. So therefore I'd find it hard to leave the team ... I was asked in the summer to leave the team and go and play football for another team ... But I thought yeah, I might get on better playing football with that team but I couldn't leave my pals, leave my mates ... so it wasn't an option really ... It's not as if you leave football and that's it, it would be too easy to leave then ... there's the huge social thing there that would make it hard to leave. (Interviewee B, 27)

One of the 'pals' described how she would probably stop playing if she moved away from the area of her current club. This player suggested she would prefer to retire from playing football rather than forsake her established social status within her current club and begin the process of socialisation into a new club setting without her accrued social rewards.

The 'pals' also tend to express disappointment if they miss any social club events. Participating in such events is a greatly valued aspect of club membership and attributed a relatively high priority. This group is defined by the value the 'pals' give to belonging to the club and its off-the-pitch activities. In summary, in terms of the meaning of football in their lives, the 'pals' consider social rewards to be a particularly important aspect of being a member of a football club. Consequently a number of players have formed important friendships with players within, and sometimes outside of, their own club. Friendships within the club and within football form a large proportion of their friend base and an integral part of their social life.

The 'professionals'

Players who take their football very seriously have been categorised as the 'professionals'. This is not due to professional status, since the vast majority of women footballers compete in Scotland on an amateur basis, but is a reflection of their professional attitude towards football. The 'professionals', while acknowledging a social element associated with being a member of a club, emphasise that this is not necessarily important to them. The meaning of football in their lives relates almost exclusively to the individual rewards accrued from playing football, illustrated by the following quote from an experienced Premier Division player:

> I like the game ... I'm maybe not one of those players who particularly plays for the social side, that doesn't mean that I don't get on with the team mates or anything like that, I do, but the reason I play is, I play for the game. (Interviewee E, 26)

One player exemplifies how the 'professionals' tend to differentiate themselves from other players who they consider to take their football less seriously, explaining that "I see myself as having a different attitude towards my football, I'm a competitive person, I'm basically there for my football's sake. I'm not there for social reasons" (Interviewee F, 21).

Players within this group culture tend to be either young players who believe in the possibility that they might make a future living out of playing football, or more experienced players who have played and still play at a high level and approach their football with very professional attitudes. The 'professionals' also have ambitions related to their football per-formance, as a young Premier Division player expresses, "I enjoy it a lot, I've always enjoyed it and I want to be a professional one day" (Interviewee D, 17). This prioritising of performance over friendships means that the 'professionals' tend to have friend-bases outside of football. As a result their fellow club members are treated primarily as footballers as opposed to a potentially prominent group of friends. This results in the social and football dimensions of their lives being separate rather than, as is evident amongst the 'pals', inextricably linked.

The ambitions of the 'professionals' include being involved in playing football for as long as possible and they expect it to play an important part in the rest of their lives, or even careers. Indeed most of the 'professionals' are already, and consider that they will continue to be, committed to football in some form after they have terminated their own participation, e.g. coaching or focusing their career around football. The commitment of the 'pals' is often based on the subsequent social rewards of participating, whereas the 'professionals' show particularly intense commitments to football based on individual rewards and potential future material rewards. One extreme example is offered by a 'professional' who hires a personal fitness instructor on the three days of the week when she is not involved in club training or matches. A significant proportion of her spare time (on 6 days of the week) is devoted to football-related activities aimed at improving her performance, demonstrating a particularly professional attitude.

Due to the significant time commitment the 'professionals' dedicate to football and its dominant place in their lifestyle, the prospect of being injured or not being able to play again has severe implications, with players suggesting that they would be at a complete loss. In summary the most defining characteristic of the 'professionals' is that they exhibit a very professional attitude towards their participation in football. There is a tendency to differentiate themselves from other players who they believe take their football less seriously. Their serious attitude results in the 'professionals' committing a significant amount of time to football and other activities related to improving their performance.

The 'conformers'

The term 'conformers' is used to represent a group of players who conform to a lesbian 'stereotype' and form part of a lesbian cultural element within the subculture of women's football in Scotland. The use of the term 'conformers' is not attached with negative connotations but simply acknowledges that the 'stereotypical' image of women footballers as lesbians is to some extent a legitimate one to which a proportion of women footballers in Scotland conforms. Through her research with women footballers in England and Wales, Caudwell (2002: p. 30) goes as far to suggest that, not only is there an indication that "the lesbian stereotype has real currency", but it may in fact "work to displace notions of dominant heterosexuality". It is necessary to distinguish between simply a lesbian presence and the extent to which there actually exists a gay cultural element, in order to justify the inclusion of the 'conformers' as one of the interlocking group cultures within the subculture of women's football in Scotland. The analysis of the 'conformers' is somewhat problematic in the sense that interviewees did not willingly represent the voice of lesbians. As an outsider to this particular cultural element of women's football in Scotland, and since experiences of sexuality were not a central research focus, it was not a priority to discover willing informants to explore these issues exclusively. This section of the analysis is based therefore on the views and opinions of interviewees and survey respondents on the existence of this cultural element within women's football.

The questionnaire included an optional question regarding players' views on whether they considered there to be a high proportion of lesbian/ bisexual women who play football in Scotland. Although the question was optional 76% of players answered: 92% of those respondents considered there to be a 'high' proportion of lesbian/bisexual women playing football in Scotland. The second part of the same question asked players to offer reasons for their response of 'yes' or 'no'. The majority who answered the first part chose to offer reasons, some of which were fairly extensive. Reasons included the possibility that being involved in women's football offers an acceptable environment in which women feel comfortable express-ing their sexuality, demonstrated by the response from a First Division player: "It's a good way to socialise and meet people, you can relax and be yourself" (Survey, F8).

Further investigation suggests that not only is there a lesbian/bisexual presence within the subculture of women's football, but the meaning of football in the lives of lesbian/bisexual players ought to be considered as culturally significant. One indication that the 'conformers' can be con-sidered as a group culture is the assertion that, aside from actually parti-cipating in football, the lesbian/bisexual presence is a significant reason for some players becoming club members. One player suggested that "the opportunity to mix/socialise in an all-female environment is part of the reason many get involved" (Survey, S34).

A number of responses indicate that the meaning that football has in the lives of some players is related specifically to the lesbian/bisexual cultural element. The survey data also tends to suggest that this cultural element can be identified as more prominent within certain clubs. A further indication of the 'conformers' representing a cultural element is the existence of a relatively overt lesbian identity and a social network amongst this group culture. One player in particular, through her experiences within a club where a lesbian/bisexual element is particularly prominent, suggests that she, as a heterosexual, often feels like an 'outsider', particularly socially:

> I think there is an identity ... at my club especially. I've never said this to anybody but I'm kind of like an outsider. Like the way they all go out to Glasgow to their gay clubs and all that kind of thing. At my club it used to be, well nobody was like that, but now that's like the majority going to Glasgow ... Honestly, a lot of people are like that ... so they're kind of like a wee group. I think there's a lot of them in football teams, either all, or the majority of them are like that, and they all kind of stay together ... But I don't have that actual identity with my team. (Interviewee F, 21)

In summary, the survey and interview data offer evidence that a lesbian/bisexual presence is perceived within women's football in Scotland. This is not simply that there is a presence of players who happen to be lesbian/bisexual, but there are various cultural elements associated with this presence. These findings indicate that associating women's football with a lesbian culture is not just a simple stereotype but an actual reality for some players. The existence of this cultural element as a source of conflict between group cultures is discussed below.

Subcultural capital and individual membership

Having identified the typical characteristics of the interlocking group cultures, this section explores three main overlapping themes. First, the identification of elements of subcultural capital that transcend group cultures. The term 'subcultural capital' is adopted from Thornton's (1995) analysis of (dance) club cultures, which will be considered more fully in the discussion section of this chapter. Second, the variation of individual membership to the subculture as a whole, and to group cultures. Third, how elements of subcultural capital differ across group cultures, suggesting that more specific elements of group-cultural capital exist. Individual membership of subcultures generally falls within the continuum of 'core' members to 'outsiders'. The extent to which an individual is a 'core' member or an 'outsider' to the subculture as a whole, and to group cultures within it, depends on their possession of various elements of subcultural and group cultural capital.

Subcultural capital transcending group cultures

Several clear interlinked elements of subcultural capital transcend group cultures. Resembling the factors that Donnelly (1981) identifies as resulting in the stratified nature of individual membership to subcultures, they include: a player's commitment to subcultural activities, the status they have within it, and their possession of knowledge and information regarding the subculture.

Commitment to subcultural activities

There are various forms of commitment to subcultural activities. First there is a commitment to primary subcultural activities directly related to the act of playing football, such as attending club training and matches, which forms a basic feature of subcultural membership. Secondary subcultural activities also require commitment. These activities relate to football, involve other subculture members and might include being involved in coaching other women's teams, administrative duties, writing match reports for newspapers, organising and attending social events and more informal forms of interaction and communication. A third level of commitment that is more indirectly related to tertiary subcultural activities can be identified: for example, being committed to additional personal fitness training outside of the club environment or being involved in coaching outside of women's football, such as coaching youth teams.

Player status

Some players, generally those relatively experienced players who have made friends and acquaintances through football over years of involvement, refer to an established network of players. Those players who recognise such a network identify themselves and other players as having a certain status within this network. There are various ways and contexts in which an individual might gain status. In particular, an individual's commitment to general subcultural activities is likely to enhance their status within the subculture, while commitment to more specific subcultural activities can gain status within particular group cultures.

Possession of information and knowledge

A third element of subcultural capital that transcends group cultures relates to an individual's possession of information and knowledge regarding the subculture. This element is clearly interlinked with the two other elements. The potential for an individual to possess information and knowledge is typically dependent on an individual's commitment to subcultural activities and their status within the subculture. Similarly, an individual's commitment and status will require some degree of information and knowledge regarding the subculture. The possession of information and knowledge relies heavily on the communication network within the subculture which has emerged, and will continue to develop, through direct and indirect interaction amongst members.

Individual membership

'Core' member and 'outsider' were the terms most commonly used by interviewees when discussing their own identity in relation to the sub-culture of women's football in Scotland. They also reflect those used by Wheaton (2000) in her analysis of membership to the windsurfing subculture. The extent of an individual's membership is based on her/his acquisition of subcultural capital. 'Core' members typically possess high, and 'outsiders' low, degrees of subcultural capital. In other words, commitment, high status and a good knowledge of the subculture define 'core' members. Conversely, 'outsiders' are less committed, possess little knowledge and information about the subculture and have a relatively unrecognised status.

What seems clear from the survey and interview evidence is that there are two main contributory factors to an individual's potential to acquire subcultural capital, and group cultural capital (discussed below). These factors are the duration of their membership of the subculture, and the level at which they compete. Interview data in particular revealed that those players who consider themselves to be established 'core' members of the subculture have competed within the SWFL for a number of years. They suggest the number of years of experience bring more direct and indirect contact with a wide network of players and result in more commitment, status, and knowledge and information about the subculture.

In contrast, the interview and survey data revealed that less experienced players, or those who have been involved for a short duration of time, are less likely to identify themselves as 'core' members of the subculture. One player from a relatively 'new' team in the Third Division suggested that she has not yet experienced a sense of being part of a network of players within the subculture and expects this to develop with involvement over a longer period of time. Although the players from this team share cultural characteristics typical of the 'pals' they are generally outsiders in relation to wider networks outside of their own club. This could largely be attributed to the fact that they are a relatively new club (two years old), but it is also important to consider the influence of ability level.

Survey data supports a relationship between ability level and the extent to which players have the potential to acquire elements of subcultural capital. The data identifies a difference between ability levels as those competing at a higher level generally attend more hours of training than those at lower levels. Spending more time at training and involved in other subcultural activities fosters the potential to acquire a higher level of subcultural capital. Time spent with other club and subcultural members outside of training and matches should also be considered as similarly significant in offering opportunities to acquire subcultural capital. The analysis did not reveal any correlation between ability level and time spent with club members outside of training and matches.

The survey explored the extent to which players are familiar with other aspects of the subculture outside of their own club: in particular, the extent to which they form part of the wider network of players. When asked to what extent they agreed with the statement 'I only really know players in my own club', there is a general trend towards players in lower divisions agreeing more strongly. In response to the statement 'I am friends with women who play for other clubs', there is a general trend towards players in higher divisions agreeing more strongly. The findings suggest that being involved at a higher ability level, which tends to also result in committing more time to primary subcultural activities, contributes to increasing a player's potential to acquire elements of subcultural capital.

Using the Third Division club as an example, some players may be considered 'outsiders' to the subculture as a whole but 'core' members within the context of their own club. Although they may attach similar meanings to football as other players, as a new team and with some beginners, they have not yet built up a high level of subcultural capital, in particular, they have not yet built up status or possess a high degree of information and knowledge outside of their own club. It seems that the combination of a long duration of subcultural membership and being involved at a high ability level provide the optimal conditions for players to acquire a high level of subcultural capital and become recognised as 'core' members of the subculture.

A final important point to stress is that the nature of an individual's membership of the subculture as a whole, and group cultures within it, is by no means static but can change. This dynamic nature of individual membership to the subculture might be exemplified by an 'outsider' gradually acquiring a higher level of subcultural capital and becoming a 'core' member. In contrast, the opposite might occur. On a more subtle level, the nature of individual membership and a player's identity as a 'core' member or an 'outsider' can be emphasised or diminished in various situations and contexts. An example is offered by an interviewee who was eight months pregnant at the time of the interview. Despite being unable to participate, the player explained how she continued to attend training sessions and matches to reduce the potential of feeling like an 'outsider' and maintain a feeling of being part of the group.

Group cultural capital

Certain elements of subcultural capital are considered more important amongst some group cultures than others. Not only do elements of subcultural capital exist, but elements of group cultural capital can be identified. Thus, individual membership to the subculture becomes more complex than simply having 'core' or 'outsider' status in relation to the subculture as a whole. Commitment to certain subcultural activities, various aspects of a player's status and an individual's possession of knowledge and information about certain aspects of the subculture are likely to be considered as important depending on group-cultural context. The 'pals' tend to consider commitment to organising and taking part in social activities, a player's reputation as 'one of the pals', having a sense of humour, and possessing knowledge and information regarding the social network of women footballers as constituting group-cultural capital. The 'professionals' consider a commitment to training, a commitment to fitness outside of training, a player's football ability, international caps, possibly even an avoidance of social aspects such as drinking, and possession of knowledge and information regarding the aspects of the subculture directly related to playing the game as important. The 'conformers' might deem a commitment to organising and taking part in social activities specific to this group culture, and a player's knowledge of the gay scene and other members of this group culture, as important elements of group-cultural capital. What constitutes group-cultural capital, is directly related to the meaning of football to individuals within each group culture.

Discussion

This analysis of the subculture of women's football in Scotland raises issues that warrant further discussion, particularly in relation to previous work on subcultures. These issues include individual membership of sub-cultures, notions of subcultural and group cultural capital, and power struggles within the subculture. The analysis of this subculture suggests that previous models of subcultural membership are in need of development. Donnelly (1981: p. 571) suggests that "a subculture may be pictured as a series of concentric circles". This horizontal stratification of subcultural membership into levels 1, 2, 3, 4 and 5 corresponds to 'principal members', 'auxiliary members', 'associate members', 'marginal members', and 'occasional participants', respectively (Donnelly, 1981: p. 572).

In his model, Donnelly (1981: p. 573) asserts that "subcultures are clearly stratified in terms of the amount and type of information in posses-sion of the various members, the level of commitment to the subculture in terms of the allocation of resources, and the degree to which the subculture is a dominant aspect of the life cycle of its members". However, this analysis of the subculture of women's football in Scotland would suggest that the stratified nature of individual membership of a subculture is less clear. Donnelly's (1981) model fails to account for the differences in meanings attached to subcultural membership by its members and how this complicates individual membership to subcultures beyond the notion of horizontal stratification. As Wheaton (2002) similarly discusses, one limitation of a model that recognises only the horizontal stratification of subcultural membership is that it struggles to appreciate that "lived experience is infinitely more complex and fluid than any rigid application of a model of identity positions would suggest" (p. 253). Any model of identity positions therefore needs to be less rigid and sensitive to the more complex nature of individual membership to a subculture. This analysis develops Donnelly's (1981) view of concentric circles representing levels of subcultural membership in order to account for varying extents of individual membership to, not simply the subculture as a whole, but to the three interlocking group cultures within it.

A model of individual membership of interlocking group cultures develops Donnelly's (1981) model in line with what Thornton (1997: p. 202) considers to be a particular strength of "Bourdieu's schema" by locating "social groups in a highly complex multi-dimensional space rather than on a linear scale or ladder". The adaptation of Donnelly's (1981) model allows for multiple identities and individual membership, to varying extents, of one or more of the interlocking group cultures. An individual might exhibit 'core' membership of one or more of the group cultures and 'outsider' membership to another. It is useful to adopt the term 'associate member' from Donnelly (1981) in order to represent subcultural membership between the extremes of 'core' and 'outsider', at which level an individual would acquire a medium level of subcultural and group cultural capital. Although this discussion seems to imply a relatively crude positioning of individuals and rigid horizontal stratification within group cultures, this is simply a limitation of attempting to categorise levels of individual membership. In reality, the boundaries between 'outsiders', 'associate members' and 'core members' are more subtle, as are the boundaries between the 'pals', the 'professionals' and the 'conformers'. In other words, over time and depending on certain contexts and personal situations, an individual's identity position might shift relatively freely across the subculture. For example, an individual's identity as a 'core pal' and an 'outsider' to the 'conformers' and 'professionals' at a particular moment can change, although such changes tend to be relatively subtle rather than drastic. They will inevitably occur over time as sub-cultural characteristics and individual situations and contexts develop and change.

This chapter has identified not only elements of subcultural capital that transcend group cultures, but also elements of subcultural capital that are specific to group cultures. In a similar fashion to Wheaton (2000), this analysis of the subculture of women's football is informed by Thornton's (1995) examination of "the ways subcultural groups distinguish themselves against others, as well as differentiate among themselves, creating internal hierarchies of participation, knowledge, and taste" (Wheaton, 2000: p. 258). Just as Thornton (1997: p. 201) criticised the Birmingham tradition of subcultural studies on youthful leisure for ignoring the "subtle relations of power at play within it", a similar criticism could be made against studies of women's sports. Whilst relations of power between various subcultures of women's sports and the dominant sports culture have been considered, studies have rarely been developed into examinations of the relations of power within subcultures. In order to compensate, Thornton (1997: p. 208) advocates a perspective that "rather than characterising cultural differences as 'resistances' to hierarchy or to the remote cultural dominations of some ruling body, ... investigates the micro-structures of power entailed in the cultural competition that goes on between more closely associated social groups". In relation to research on women's football, only Caudwell (2002) has so far revealed evidence of power struggles within the subculture and this emerged from research focusing specifically on experiences of sexuality within the context of women's football in England and Wales. This research on women's football in Scotland reveals evidence of the interplay and power struggles between such closely associated groups, in particular, between the 'pals' and the 'professionals' and between non-conformers and the 'conformers'. The scope of this chapter precludes a full analysis but these two examples illustrate the implications of power struggles for women's football in Scotland.

Discussions of players' own identity, based on the meanings they attach to football and the elements of subcultural and group-cultural capital they consider as important, reveal the possible tensions between members of group cultures. Tension between the 'pals' and the 'professionals' centres on how the 'professionals' view players who take their participation in football less seriously. There is evidence that the 'professionals' make some attempt to detach themselves from other players who they consider to be there primarily for the social aspects of club membership and do not take football as seriously. Some of the 'professionals' suggest that in order for other players to be able to compete at a higher level they will need to approach their participation in football with a more professional manner. There is also disapproval amongst the 'professionals' of players who prioritise the social aspects of club membership over optimising their potential performance for their club. In contrast, some of the 'pals' suggest that there are players who take their football too seriously, and members who do not become involved in the social aspects related to club membership might find it difficult to fit in and may in fact upset the group dynamics within a club. At a more developmental level, there is a concern, particularly amongst the 'professionals', that clubs need to adopt a more professional approach in order to ensure the positive development of women's football. Certain social aspects of club membership, particularly heavy drinking, are viewed as detrimental to the image of the sport.

The image of women's football is behind the most explicit tension amongst group cultures: that between non-conformers and the 'conformers'. This tension is almost exclusively uni-directional and is rooted in the views of some non-conformers towards the 'conformers'. It is recognised by Melling (2002: p. 328) that "from the 1960s onwards, gay women have indeed become increasingly involved in women's football", and that "it has not been uncommon for confrontations to arise between the heterosexual majority and the gay minority". But the extent to which there is a heterosexual majority and a gay minority in women's football is unclear. This research, like Caudwell's (2002), suggests that the lesbian image associated with women's football is not necessarily an inaccurate 'stereotype', but is actually a relatively accurate interpretation of reality. There is evidence of non-conformers displaying an overt detachment of themselves from lesbian 'stereotypes'. Both interview and survey data reveal a consistent identification of 'them' or the 'others' as distinct from 'us' by players whom it must be assumed are heterosexual. Some non-conformers express how they are offended by the association of 'butch' and 'lesbian' stereotypes with the game. Caudwell (2002: p. 41) also reveals that "there is evidence of conscious marking of self and space as heterosexual", the implications being that "such a strategy alludes to the fragility of [hetero] sexual identity, and therefore exposes heterosexuality as delicate and vulnerable" (Butler, 1990 cited in Caudwell, 2002: p. 41).

A number of players explain how they have to contend with stereo-typical assumptions regarding sexuality and that, to some individuals, such assumptions may have discouraged participation. More controversial tensions regarding the attitudes of some non-conformers towards the lesbian cultural element within the game are also revealed. In particular, some players consider there to be a predatory element associated with the lesbian culture within women's football. These findings are consistent with those of Caudwell (2002: p. 38) who views the "notion of the predatory lesbian" and the "positioning of lesbianism as licentious and lascivious" as a regulatory practice which protects heterosexuality. Many of the interviewed players suggest that stereotypes regarding sexuality are relatively old-fashioned and are likely to diminish with the emergence of more young girls taking up football. Such views are based, however, on the relatively naive assumption that the young players are heterosexual and therefore would not conform to the stereotype. The research reveals that, on two levels, attempts are made to diminish attention towards the stereotype, possibly forcing this cultural element to become more residual in nature. On one level, the ruling bodies are reluctant to draw attention to a lesbian presence and the associated cultural element within women's football. On another level, among non-conformers in particular, there is the insinuation that the 'lesbian stereotype' is inaccurate, unfair and gives women's football a bad name.

Concluding remarks

Women footballers in Scotland are not simply an homogeneous group; indeed there is evidence of multiple and sometimes conflicting identities. This chapter has identified that the subculture of women's football in Scotland is made up of three interlocking group cultures. The nature and extent of individual membership of these group cultures depends on the meaning of football in a player's life. Several elements of subcultural capital that transcend group cultures can be identified. The extent to which elements of subcultural capital are considered to be important is different for each interlocking group culture, suggesting that more specific elements of group-cultural capital exist.

In her discussion of subcultural capital, Thornton (1997: p. 208) makes the extremely pertinent point that "the social logic of subcultural capital reveals itself most clearly by what it dislikes and by what it emphatically isn't". It is evident that a common tendency for members of group cultures within women's football is to confirm or emphasise their own identity, and in some cases the collective identity of their club, by distinguishing what they are *not*. In the context of this research, Thornton's (1997: p. 208) notion can be adapted to suggest that the social logic of group cultural capital within the subculture of women's football reveals itself most clearly by what it dislikes and by what it emphatically isn't. The differences in meanings that players attach to their participation in football and the importance of elements of subcultural capital form the basis for tensions between group cultures. The two examples of tensions between the 'pals' and the 'professionals' and between non-conformers and the 'conformers' reveal how, as the subculture continues to develop, subcultural characteristics are continually negotiated and power struggles emerge between dominant, emergent and residual elements of culture that are similarly dynamic in nature.

There is evidence of an emergent professional culture that is compatible with the desired dominant image promoted by the ruling bodies. The extent to which the organisation and structure of women's football in Scotland can accommodate, eventually recompense, and then sustain a professional culture remains to be seen. The most explicit tension within women's football however is between non-conformers and the 'conformers'. There is strong evidence to suggest that although a lesbian culture exists within women's football its existence is considered, particularly by non-conformers, as a potential hindrance to the development of the sport. If attempts to diminish attention to the lesbian cultural element continue, the extent to which it becomes a residual element of the subculture remains to be seen.This chapter has shown how the desired subcultural image that the ruling bodies attempt to create is currently somewhat different from reality. The meanings players attach to football and the power dynamics between group cultures themselves, and between group cultures and the ruling bodies of women's football in Scotland, influence how subcultural characteristics are continually negotiated and modified as well as the future development of the subculture.

Note

[1]   The development of women's football and the emergence of the subculture of women's football in Scotland is examined by Macbeth (2004).

References

Bourdieu, P. (1984) *Distinction: A social critique of the judgement of taste*. London: Routledge & Kegan Paul.

Butler, J. (1990) *Gender trouble: Feminism and the subversion of identity*. Routledge: London.

Caudwell, J. (2002) 'Women's experiences of sexuality within football contexts: A particular and located footballing epistemology', *Football Studies* Vol. 5, No. 1: pp. 24–45.

Donnelly, P. (1981) 'Toward a definition of sport subcultures', in M. Hart and S. Birrell (eds) *Sport in the Sociocultural Process* (3rd Edition). Iowa: Wm. C. Brown, pp. 563–587.

—— (1993) 'Subcultures in sport: Resilience and transformation', in A.G. Ingham and J.W. Loy (eds) *Sport in social development: Traditions, transitions, and transformations*. Champaign, Illinois: Human Kinetics: pp. 119–145.

Fine, G. A. and Kleinman, S. (1979) 'Rethinking subculture: An interactionist perspective', *American Journal of Sociology* Vol. 85: pp. 1–20.

Macbeth, J. L. (2004) *Women's football in Scotland: An interpretive analysis*. Unpublished Ph.D Thesis. University of Stirling, United Kingdom.

Melling, A. (2002) "Women and football", in R. Cox, D. Russell and W, Vamplew (eds) *Encyclopaedia of British football*. Frank Cass: London: pp. 324–329.

Nayak, A. (2003) *Race, place and globalization: Youth cultures in a changing world*. Oxford: Berg.

Thornton, S. (1995) *Club cultures: Music, media and subcultural capital*. Cambridge: Polity Press.

—— (1997) 'The social logic of subcultural capital [1995]', in K. Gelder and S. Thornton (eds) *The subcultures reader*. London: Routledge: pp. 200–209.

Wheaton, B. (2000) "Just do it': Consumption, commitment, and identity in the windsurfing subculture', *Sociology of Sport Journal* Vol. 17: pp. 254–274.

—— (2002) 'Babes on the beach, women in the surf: Researching gender, power and difference in the windsurfing culture', in J. Sugden and A. Tomlinson (eds) *Power games: A critical sociology of sport*. London: Routledge, pp. 240–266.

Williams, J. (2003) *A game for rough girls? A history of women's football in Britain*. London: Routledge.

FOOTBALL FANDOM AND THE 'TRADITIONAL' FOOTBALL CLUB: FROM 'COCKNEY PAROCHIALISM' TO A EUROPEAN DIASPORA?

Jack Fawbert
De Montfort University

Introduction

It is no accident that almost all football clubs in Britain are named after places. Ever since the late 19th century when the working class appropriated the game from the public school 'gentleman elite', clubs have overwhelmingly 'represented' *local* pride in very specific working-class communities (Armstrong & Giulianotti, 2001; Clarke, 1976; Giulianotti, 1997; Holt, 1986; Hughson, 1997; Mason, 1998: p. 118; Mellor, 2000: p. 158; Taylor, R., 1992; Walvin, 2000). The notion of the football club acting as a metaphor for pride in the local working-class community was passed down through successive generations of male progeny and so became deeply embedded in the identities of football fans. Indeed, 'local pride' and 'family' are still by far the biggest reasons given in surveys about why fans support particular football teams (www.le.ac.uk/snccfr/resources/factsheets/fs3.html).

The East End of London: the 'ideal typical' traditional heartland of football?

The constituency within which West Ham United are situated was described in the last National Fan Survey by the Sir Norman Chester Centre for Football Research as one of the "... more traditional working-class footballing enclaves ..." (Williams & Neatrour, 2002: p. 5). More recently, the

99

West Ham United manager, Alan Pardew, has said:

> The power of this club is the supporter and it always has been. We
> are a working-class kind of club and we have to work hard. I expect
> my players to work as hard as our punters do when they go to work
> — they want to see that on a Saturday. (www.whufc.com)

The constituency of West Ham United is the East End of London. For
more than a century it was the archetypal working-class community,
described by Young and Willmott as "… a vast one-class quarter" of London
(Young & Willmott, 1957: p. 93). It was founded on the biggest docks complex the world has ever known (half the world's shipping used to come
through the docks in East London). In the 19th and early part of the 20th
century the development of a network of ship repair yards and engineering
workshops drove out pockets of affluent residents, both eastwards and
northwards. Social class homogeneity was reinforced as jobs and trades,
for men at least, were 'passed down' from generation to generation. Strong
bonds of working-class solidarity were forged not only in the workplace
but also in the myriad of East End communities as a defence against the
repressive apparatuses of the state and the local landlord class. For
example, it was very common for families to 'take in' other families who
had been evicted (O'Neill, 2001).

The people of the East End, thus, developed a culture that not only
consisted of a keen sense of "territoriality" and a "fierce local pride" but
also one that valued loyalty and comradeship (Belton, 1998: p. 11; Korr,
1986). The club literally emerged from the shipyards (Steele, 2003; Moore,
1989) as a works teams and has, for over a century, become a metaphor
for "the East End family" and for pride in the local working-class community (Belton, 1998: p. 11; Brooking, 2000: pp. 24–25; Brooking, 1981: p.
48; Korr, 1986; Lyall, 1989: p. 57; Taylor, M., 1994: p. 44).

'The great exodus'

After World War II, successive governments embarked on major house
building programmes that saw most of the slums of the East End that
hadn't been demolished by the Luftwaffe's V1 bombs, or 'doodlebugs' as
they were commonly known, finally torn down. Rather than re-build in

the area, the London County Council and its successor, the Greater London Council, decided to re-house the East End population on 'green field' sites like South Ockendon and Harold Hill and in New, 'over-spill', Towns such as Basildon in Essex, Harlow in Hertfordshire and Thetford in Norfolk.

This policy of resettlement continued right up to the 1980s when the anti-welfarism of the Thatcher years brought it all to a grinding halt. Nevertheless, what had become known locally as 'the great exodus', continued. 'Pathfinders' were often followed by extended kin searching for better homes with 'all mod cons' and gardens in what were considered better environments for raising children. Later still, the 'privatisation' of Council housing and the hegemonic invocation to 'buy, buy, buy!' (private, good; public, bad!) 'encouraged' many cockney émigrés to buy up, sell up and move on upwards and outwards.

Many of these ex-cockneys were more geographically mobile as a result of the greater upward social mobility that they had experienced as a consequence of the 1944 Education Act. A Grammar school education had provided many with an 'escape route' out of the working class (Greenslade, 1976; O'Neill, 2001; Southerton, 2002; Young & Willmott, 1957; Young & Willmott, 1960). However, for the majority for whom the tripartite system of education had provided nothing more than a confirmation of failure, 'push' factors were rather more dominating than 'pull' factors. The restructuring of capitalism in the late 20th century led to the destruction of much of the industry in the East End and destroyed the strongly integrated communities associated with capitalism's more organised 'Fordist' phase (Lash & Urry, 1987; Crow & Allen, 1994; Massey, 1994). 'Containerisation' and the dispersing of dock work across Britain, coupled with the break-up of traditional craft workshops associated with the docks, 'pushed' many of the old, white working class out of the area.

At the same time as this was going on, capitalism was relocating its control functions into the East End of London. Large parts of the East End became prestige locations for offices and expensive riverside apartments for the people working in them. The Docklands Development Scheme in particular became "the largest example of this process of gentrification in the world" (Morris & Morton, 1998: p. 65). The important point here is that, because the local population rarely had the skills and experience necessary for such work, the majority of the new jobs and, as a consequence, the new residences created by these developments went to middle-class 'outsiders' (Deakin & Edwards, 1993).

Pockets of the East End that have not been *gentrified* have been colonised over the last 30 years or so by new waves of immigrants from the Indian sub-continent, Eastern Europe, Somalia, the Balkans and Afghanistan. West Ham United's ground is situated in an area, Newham, which in the 2001 Census had the distinction of being the first Census district in Britain to have a majority of its population, 59%, from minority ethnic groups. However, these are not the West Ham United *nouveau passione*. Less than 1% of West Ham United season ticket holders are from minority ethnic groups (Williams & Neatrour, 2002b) and it seems likely that only a fraction of the East End's new middle-class actively support West Ham United as their primary leisure pursuit. Yet, average attendances at Upton Park have continued to grow in recent years. This is despite the fact that the club haven't won a major trophy since 1980 and, at the time of writing, were languishing in the Coca-Cola Championship after being relegated from the Premier League in the 2002/2003 season. So, where are all these new fans coming from? Or, are they 'new' fans at all?

West Ham United and the 'cockney diaspora'?

A few residual enclaves of the traditional East End working-class remain as the bedrock of support for West Ham United, but as long ago as 1981 West Ham's Trevor Brooking was commenting that:

> West Ham supporters come from all over the South-East of England. Our catchment area extends to Hertfordshire in the north-west and to Southend in the east. (Brooking, 1981: p. 54)

By 1997, research showed that West Ham, like other London clubs, had fewer 'local' fans than other Premier League clubs (Williams *et al.*, 1997: p. 53). By 2001 only three Premier League clubs— Tottenham Hotspur, Manchester United and Chelsea— had lower percentages of fans living within 10 miles of their respective grounds and only those clubs had a higher percentage of fans spending more than an hour travelling to home games (Williams & Neatrour, 2002a: pp. 13–14). In other words, West Ham had "... a much stronger regional fan core than is nationally the case" (Williams & Neatrour, 2002a: pp. 1–2).

But, as cockney émigrés have spread further and further afield, so the West Ham United constituency has spread much further than the region. By 1997, 36% of supporters lived more than 50 miles from Upton Park (Williams *et al.*, 1997: p. 53). By the end of the millennium there was a Northern Hammers group established that now has over 250 members spread from Carlisle in the North to Nottingham in the 'South' and from Hull in the East to Liverpool in the West. The slogan on the masthead of their web site reads: "You can take the boy out of the East End, but you cannot take the East End out of the boy" (www.hammernorth.demon.co.uk). This suggests that West Ham United is, for many fans at least, a means to a "magical recovery of community" (Clarke, 1976; Robins & Cohen, 1978; Hughson, 1997); a "proxy home offering a sense of belonging to a family with all its tribulations" (Vamplew *et al.*, 1998: p. 57).

The fortnightly ritual of flocking to the Boleyn Ground is a way of recapturing a lost heritage. Like Muslims on a pilgrimage to Mecca they are 'United' once more. Robson observes a similar phenomenon with regard to Millwall fans who have moved out of South London when he says, "such ritual visits to symbolically charged ancestral stamping grounds resonate with the voices and atmosphere of the past" (Robson, 2000: p. 149). Likewise, Hornby commented some years ago with regard to Arsenal fans that:

> ... because their occupation ... has removed them far away from where they belong or where they came from ... football seems to them a quick and painless way of getting back there. (Hornby, 1992: p. 186)

However, what this ignores in the case of West Ham United fans is the fact that only about 45% of Northern Hammers members are cockney émigrés, with 55% being "... born and bred Northerners who just love the Hammers" (www.whufc.com). How on earth did these fans come to support a struggling Coca-Cola Championship League side who haven't won a major trophy for nearly 25 years? Well, 85% of Northern Hammers fans have supported the club for more than 20 years (author's own unpublished research) and adopted West Ham United identities when it was a much higher national media profiled club who were winning trophies and were renowned for their stylish football.

'Europeanisation' and West Ham United fandom

In terms of the *Europeanisation* of football fandom, Manchester United might be regarded as the exception, or at least as 'exceptional' in that they have large fan bases throughout Europe. However, other less 'glamorous' clubs situated in 'traditional' working-class communities may soon begin to 'catch up'. Over the last few years the fan base of West Ham United has begun to spread to continental Europe. In terms of organised independent supporters groups alone there are now Hammers fans in Sweden, Norway, Denmark, Finland, Germany, France, Italy, Northern Ireland, Eire, Belgium, Cyprus, Iceland, Malta and Serbia. One of the oldest is the *Scandinavian Hammers* group that was formed way back in 1988 and now has over 400 members (www.whufc.com). They organise regular trips to Upton Park, West Ham's ground, to see matches and they help members who travel on their own with ticket information, hotels and so on. Like the majority of the Northern Hammers group, these supporters are not cockney émigrés. Expatriate cockneys are more likely to be found inhabiting the warmer climes of the Iberian peninsula.

So, in examining the spread, albeit fledgling, of West Ham United's support across Europe, one has to be very careful not to generalise. One needs to be sensitive to local traditions and cultures, specific histories and recognise that this spread of support is more a case of what I would term *Eurolocalisation* rather than *Europeanisation*. For example, there is a very long history of long-distance support for 'traditional' English football clubs like West Ham United in Scandinavian countries (Hognestad, 2003). This *anglophilia* has many causes. The relative 'classlessness' of the football experience in most Scandinavian societies means that many fans are attracted to the 'working-class experience' of British football fandom. Also attractive is the *jouissance* associated with the more *carnivalesque* nature of football fandom in Britain, founded as it is on the bitter rivalries and conflicts inherent in the English game. The consequent liminal experiences and identities is something that is not experienced in Scandinavian societies in general, let alone at Scandinavian football matches. The perceived 'joke' status of Scandinavian club sides in comparison to English teams and, not least, the introduction of live televised English League Saturday games as long ago as 1969 (Hognestad, 2003: p. 105) have also contributed to the phenomenon of Scandinavian support for British teams. Consequently, the *Supporterunionen for Britisk football* which was established in Denmark as long ago as 1985 now has a total membership in excess of 55,000 (Hognestad, 2003: p. 105).

In contrast, the tradition of support for English teams in Malta is founded on the basis that, unlike with Scandinavian fans, most of them, because of the specific history of the island, are of English descent (Armstrong & Mitchell, 1999: p. 103). In this respect, West Ham United supporters in Malta, though few in number, are mostly expatriate cockneys.

West Ham United fandom: new community or new communities?

The development of the Internet has enabled the spread of support to escalate across all parts of Europe and rekindled an interest in support for clubs like West Ham United. It is only since the mid-1990s that the Internet has really taken off as a way of creating and sustaining viable European cyber-communities (www.zakon.org/robert/internet/timeline. html). By 2001, 20% of English football fans were using the Internet on a daily basis to access general football information (Williams & Neatrour, 2002a: p. 29) and there is no reason to doubt that similar patterns are emerging in other European countries. More specifically, 42% of West Ham United supporters use the club's web site either daily, a number of times a week or at least once a week (Williams & Neatrour, 2002b: p. 81). Amongst Premier League club fans only Charlton Athletic and Chelsea supporters use their clubs' web sites more. It seems that for fans at the furthest reaches of the West Ham United European diaspora, the Internet provides the greatest means of connectivity to the club and other supporters.

The first question this raises is whether or not this 'virtual' community is a community at all in the usual sense of the word. It is important to ask this question as the answer has so many implications for the future, particularly for a club whose raison d'etre, to a large extent, is bound up with 'representing' a very specific 'community'. Sociologists used to assume that 'community' was in decline because of rapid increases in geographical and social mobility. Cohen (1985), however, argued that 'community' is not something that is necessarily bounded by clearly recognisable geographical limits but is bounded by the degree of 'communion' or 'shared meanings' inherent in the relationships between participants of a social group. Cohen argued that 'community':

> · ... exists in the minds of its members, and should not be confused with geographic or sociographic assertions of 'fact'. By extension, the distinctiveness of communities, and, thus, the reality of their boundaries, similarly lies in the mind, in the meanings which people attach to them, not in their structural forms ... This reality of community is expressed and embellished symbolically. (Cohen, 1985: p. 98)

For cockney émigrés this is completely apposite. When they moved from the East End ex-cockneys did try to retain a culture of 'East Endedness' (Young & Willmott, 1960). As the old East End was "... physically sub-merged and ... boundaries ... obliterated ..." it tended to "... live on in people's minds" (Young and Willmott, 1957: p. 111). As each new gener-ation has moved further and further from the communal roots they have tried ever more desperately to cling to the culture and values of their roots and to seek a surrogated expression of them through support for West Ham United. In a post-modern situation of existential doubt, uncertainty and ontological insecurity West Ham United have provided a communal shelter that at times, other than match days, consists of nothing more than a *cosa mentale*.

However, the fledgling, virtual West Ham United community that is beginning to grow across Europe includes many for whom support for West Ham United does not at first glance seem to be related to an imagined East End community or communities. What are these *nouveau passione* like and do they share commitments to the club and a culture similar to those of 'traditional' West Ham United fans? It is argued that *nouveau fans* in general are much more consumerist in their orientation. They regard football clubs as 'products' to be 'consumed' (Kearns & Philo, 1993; King, 2002) and are much more likely to express their support through the purchase of merchandise. This is particularly true of *nouveau fans* at a geographical, social and cultural distance from 'traditional' supporters.

For some time now some clubs have tended to encourage 'day trippers', or 'tourist reds' as traditionally local Liverpool supporters call them, recognising that such 'fans' are likely to spend more on merchandise in club shops (Greenfield & Osbourne, 2001: p. 64). For example, Manchester United tried to increase the capacity of their ground for 'members' as opposed to 'season ticket holders'. This was because the former, who are predominantly non-local fans, who can or only want to attend infrequently are likely to spend more money on the club's merchandise in the club mega-store (Lee, 1998: p. 39; Lee, 1999; King, 2002: pp. 159–60). Similarly, Nash, in a study of Scandinavian Liverpool FC supporters, found that 84% of them bought merchandise from Liverpool's shop (Nash, 2000: p. 6). And, like Manchester United, Liverpool now have a 'European' dimension to their marketing of merchandise, through mail order, but more particularly through on-line sales.

Marketing West Ham United in the 'new European' markets

In its merchandising activities West Ham have an annual turnover of between 3 and 5 million pounds. Revenue from sponsors brings in about another one million pounds, as does revenue from their kit suppliers. The biggest single item that makes up these incomes is replica shirt sales[1]. Depending on what point in the 'kit cycle' one takes, the club sells between 26,000 and 41,000 replica shirts a year. Sales to fans in other parts of Europe are as yet small. Currently mail order and Internet sales account for 12–15% of all sales, 18% of which are overseas: still less than 3% of total sales. However, Stuart Ryan, West Ham's Commercial Director, claims that "sales are switching to the Internet" (Interview with author, 8 April 2003) as overseas business is beginning to expand. This may be very good news for West Ham because as Pat Thomas at West Ham's kit supplier's, *Reebok* says:

> ... the Internet is fantastic ... for a lot of smaller clubs to reach their markets .... Smaller clubs ... haven't got what [Manchester] United have got ... distribution of sports shops across the world ... .
> (Interview with author, 19 September 2003)

However, in their marketing activities West Ham United should caution against regarding the 'European' supporters groups as yet largely untapped and fruitful constituencies to be targeted in their marketing activities. Firstly, if we are witnessing the emergence of a West Ham supporter base that is not ascribed by class, place of birth or geographical proximity to the club, such fans' support for the club may be much more unstable, fickle and ephemeral. Greater 'freedom of choice' as to which football team to support also means having greater freedom to make other choices later on.

Well, what evidence there is suggests that, far from being more fickle and ephemeral, support from the *nouveau passione* is just as stable, long-term and deep as that of 'traditional' local fans. In fact, it is often more so, as support for clubs that represent very traditional working-class enclaves seem to indicate an even more desperate search for what I would call a *"magical discovery of community"*. My own research shows this to be the case with regard to *Northern Hammers* members who are not cockney émigrés and research by others (Hognestad, 2003; Nash, 2000) shows this to be the case with regard to fans of English clubs in general from continental Europe. They seek the 'authentic' in the culture, values, concerns and lifestyles of 'traditional' supporters as opposed to what they regard as the more commercialised 'inauthentic' versions of fandom promoted by many clubs.

But this raises another problem. If such fandom proves to be more enduring, there is a danger in concentrating more on merchandising to this market. As new fans become old fans, whether or not their connections to the club are through 'traditional' routes or not, they may become more like 'traditional' fans. Nash found that:

> The more experienced element [of Scandinavian Liverpool FC fans] were contemptuous of the 'tourists' focus on buying official new merchandise, and would often not wear any club colours ... There is a clear sense of a progression, where ... official merchandise is fine for the novices, but the more experienced ... transcend such fripperies ... (Nash, 2000: p. 15)

Like 'traditional' supporters, what the experienced Scandinavian Liverpool fans were seeking was 'authenticity'. They wanted to learn more about the traditional working-class community from which Liverpool FC emerged;

they wanted to know about the local pubs, the local culture and the local traditions rather than establish a producer-consumer relationship with the club. In other words, they sought *communitas* and wanted to be part of the 'real' community.

Nevertheless, many of the overseas sales of replica shirts at 'glamour clubs' like Manchester United and Liverpool have been to 'fans' on the basis of "fashion" or wanting to be associated with a "successful brand". In comparison to other clients such as Bolton Wanderers and Crewe Alexandra, Pat Thomas at *Reebok* (Interview with author, 19 September 2003) described Liverpool as a "global property". However, long-standing fans, whether 'local' or 'long-distance', want to distance themselves from 'glory hunting johnny-come-latelies'. But, the fickleness of such fashion trends may not be such a problem for 'less glamorous clubs' like West Ham United. Unlike at Manchester United, Stuart Ryan says that the biggest consumers of West Ham United replica shirts are season ticket holders (Interview with author, 8 April 2003). Consequently, as Ryan said:

> ... as we have only sold kits to true supporters and not secondary fans who have bought shirts due to the success of clubs or because of star players we do not expect to experience the same level of drop off [in sales].

Perhaps there is a veiled reference here to the once seemingly ubiquitous number 7 'Beckham' Manchester United replica shirt that proliferated after the 2002 World Cup but seemed to disappear without trace just as quickly after Beckham's transfer to Real Madrid; a frippery if ever there was one?

Nevertheless, there does seem to be a more cautionary approach by the club. Stuart Ryan still regards their main catchment area as:

> ... London's East End, Essex, Hertfordshire and the South-East region in general. This informs our retail strategy of having stores in *Bluewater, Lakeside* [both large retail parks], Ilford [all within 10 miles of the ground] etc. We concentrate on our main catchment area and work with sponsors/partners on other overseas initiatives. (Interview with author, 8 April 2003)

With regard to the last sentence it does seem to be the case that sponsors and other partners do have a rather less parochial attitude to sales. Pat

Thomas at *Reebok*, for example, doesn't:

> ... want to keep it too localised ... Think big when you know there are West Ham supporters in ... Spain ... if you just think that West Ham is localised ... then how will you ever get past ... Basildon and Romford and Essex ... maybe America is pie in the sky but at the same time who is to say that they can't get somebody in Luton ... [or] Northampton and ... extend the boundaries that way. (Interview with author, 19 September 2003)

But there was also less of a concern shown by Pat Thomas to targeting 'authentic' supporters, suggesting that sales could be 'globalised' by appealing to the 'fashion-conscious' who may associate what is 'cool' with what 'stars' (not necessarily football stars at that) are wearing. He suggested that sales may be 'globalised' by what amounted to 'product placement' of West Ham replica shirts on celebrities in America and elsewhere. This would certainly seem to be appealing to a much more volatile market and certainly would be more dependant on the vagaries of the 'fashion' industry (and when was claret and blue ever 'fashionable'?).

When it comes to particular designs of replica shirts it is also important to take the fledgling *Eurolocalisation* of support for West Ham into account. In Nash's research on Scandinavian Liverpool supporters he found that, in their search for 'authenticity', experienced Scandinavian supporters would prefer to wear 'retro' or 'heritage' Liverpool shirts — that is, if they wore any club merchandise at all. In this respect, all three respondents in my interviews did seem to be very well-attuned to the importance of 'tradition' in the design of West Ham replica shirts. The fashion designer Sarah Moulds, who designed all the West Ham replica kits for *Pony* and *Fila* from 1993 until 2003, emphasised that "the home kit always had to be in keeping with the tradition of the club" and that the club's corporate image was "tradition and heritage, projected in colour usage, badge design and quality in the make up and fabric used in the kits" (Interview with author, 22 October 2003). Indeed, Stuart Ryan said that, "the home kit is modelled on a heritage shirt and the design team at *Fila* were given this as a brief" (Interview with author, 8 April 2003).

Ryan went on to say that, "over the last few years we have respected some of the fans' favourite shirts of old and used these designs as the base on which to design more up-to-date versions". Now *Reeebok* have succeeded *Fila* as kit suppliers, they are acutely aware of the likely popularity of providing more up-to-date versions of favourite shirts from the past. In 2004 West Ham launched a new away kit that was deliberately reminiscent of the shirt worn by West Ham in their highly successful European Cup Winners Cup campaign in 1976 (they lost in the final). For the reasons given earlier, evoking memories of past glories in this way is likely to resonate very well with West Ham supporters' 'European' contingents. It is far from coincidental that the one fan that *Reebok* consulted more than any other about previous kit designs was a Swedish fan who collects West Ham replica shirts! He was described by Pat Thomas as "a key fan" for putting the supporters' point of view about the design of the new kit for the 2003–4 season (Interview with author, 19 September 2003).

'Eurolocalisation' and the future of club/fan relationships

It seems that the *Eurolocalisation* of West Ham fandom will remain small and will grow only slowly in the immediate future. However, should promotion to the Premier League and possibly winning a place in a European competition in the not too distant future be realised, it could have a rather more dramatic impact. Such an impact is even more likely now because of the expansion of the EU, the greater 'opening up' of English teams to European 'markets' at the same time as all Europeans are becoming more affluent, more 'connected' through television and the Internet and more used to budget airline travel. It could be that 'traditional' clubs like West Ham could benefit as much, if not more, from these developments as the so-called 'glamour clubs'.

West Ham's current strategy of relocating merchandising and other commercial activities at the club itself may pay dividends in the future, especially with regard to long-distance continental European fans who may travel to see games at Upton Park more frequently in the future. After incorporating a big new 'mega-store' into the building of the new *Dr. Marten's* stand, Stuart Ryan told me that:

Before the stadium redevelopment and as *Fila* did not supply *JJB Sports*, we developed stores [within a 20 mile radius] to take the brand to the people as there were very few reasons for people to visit the Boleyn Ground on non-matchdays. Now we have a 70 bedroom hotel facility, a museum, conference and banqueting facilities etc. More people visit the stadium, so shopping habits and patterns have changed. (Interview with author, 8 April 2003)

It is unlikely that long-distance continental European fans would have travelled out to stores at Bluewater, Lakeside and Ilford when travelling to Upton Park, but they are certainly much more likely to use the new facilities at the ground.

Since the greater commercialisation and *commodification* of football in general over the last decade, the club has tried to strike a balance between its traditions and its new role as a 'business'. It seems to be trying very hard to ensure that it doesn't alienate its core fans in the way that it did in the early 90s with its ill-fated Bond Scheme (Campbell & Shields, 1993: p. 95; Dempsey & Reilly, 1998; Taylor, 1995) at the same time as trying to compete in football's 'new marketplace'. Stuart Ryan expressed this potential dichotomy well when he said that, "the club moved from being purely a football club to having broader brand activity with the opening of the hotel, museum and other facilities ..." yet felt compelled to add that, "...the club is [still] very much family and community based..." (Stuart Ryan interview). This dichotomy may come into sharper focus if and when the *Eurolocalisation* of West Ham United fandom reaches more impressive proportions.

We all follow 'United'?

In the new football 'market' the so-called 'glamour clubs' like Manchester United are bound to do well. They may have always 'represented' working-class districts of Manchester and, despite popular myths and jibes by rival fans, their core 'live' support from the working-class districts of Manchester is still greater in numbers than their local rivals Manchester City (Brown, 2002). However, like other clubs in the North-West, they have drawn heavily on support from a 70-mile radius as long ago as the 1920s. By the late

1950s and early 1960s they were already drawing large support from across the whole country and had many fans who travelled to see their games on a regular basis from Ireland (Mellor, 2002). The number of 'supporters' of Manchester United in Britain alone is now estimated to be about three million (www.le.ac.uk/so/css/resources/factsheets/fs8.html).

Their status as a European post-modern 'super-club', drawing on support from across Europe, has a history which pre-dates The Champions League and non-terrestrial television. It was forged in the period between the Munich air disaster in 1958 and their European Cup triumph in 1968. Their status as a glamorous European 'super-club' was elevated by the 'superstar' status of many of their players during this period, most notably, George Best. After 1968 they had fan groups in France, Spain and most other Western Europeans countries (Mellor, 2000). Their fan base has since expanded and been cemented in more recent years because of their seeming omnipresence in televised European football and because of their global marketing strategies which are now finely tuned.

However, as I hope has been shown in this chapter, other 'less fashionable' clubs like West Ham United who are now expanding their fan bases into Europe would be well-advised to be very cautious about trying to follow the Manchester United model of 'selling' the game and its accompanying merchandise to their fans. They must always be conscious about their specific histories, cultures and fan bases.

General conclusions: a 'nouveau passione'?

From its earliest days the establishment of football teams was generally characterised by *toponymy*; that is, concerned with 'representing' specific places. Moreover, for fans, a number of writers have emphasised how associations and identifications were always characterised by *topophilia*: i.e. a 'love of place' (Bale, 1988; Bale, 1991; Bale, 1992; Bale, 2000; Bale & Moen, 1995; Vamplew *et al.*, 1998). This *topophilia* was overwhelmingly a love of working-class 'places'. Now, it is easy to get carried away with the idea that post-industrial football fandom is more likely to be informed by a sense of 'placelessnesss' and 'classlessness'. Changes to British society over the last 50 years have certainly served to undermine the traditional, local working-class attachments to football clubs. The break up of many of the old working-class communities of Britain upon which the *topophilia* of football fandom was based and the scattering to the four winds of those communities were important developments. Better public transport networks, but more especially, the massive increase in car ownership and the building of better motorway systems then enabled football supporters to be more geographically mobile. As working-class Britons became more affluent, package holidays took them to new climes. More recently this has encouraged many of them to settle elsewhere in Europe. Expatriate communities now appear to be springing up all over Europe. More lately, the advent of low cost budget airlines has enabled fans, both expatriate and non-expatriate, to travel to and from other European destinations.

So, greater geographical mobility has fuelled, and has been fuelled to some extent by, post-war working-class affluence and an increase in intergenerational upward social mobility in both Britain and the rest of Europe. Hognestad's survey of Norwegian fans of English clubs found that "... every Norwegian fan travels on average approximately twice a year and spends up to £1,000 for each trip, all expenses included" (Hognestad, 2003: p. 105). Intergenerational upward mobility has, thus, also been partly responsible, it is claimed, for the gradual *gentrification* of football fandom (Robson, 2000: p. 35; Williams & Neatrour, 2002a: p. 7). It is also claimed that this isn't just because the old fans have been upwardly mobile. Those running the game have tried to change its image by disproportionately targeting recruitment of new fans from the ranks of the higher classes.

In addition, the 'de-localisation' and creeping *Europeanisation/Eurolocalisation* of football fandom has been aided by saturation coverage of football matches in broadcast media (Hognestad, 2003: p. 105). This had been identified as an issue on several occasions in official reports over the last forty years (Mellor, 2000). Whilst television coverage of the game only gradually increased after the BBC broadcast the World's first live television football match in 1938 (Barnett, 1990: p. 7), it has increased much more rapidly in the last ten years. Perhaps the most significant event came in 1992 when the satellite channel, *Sky Sports*, signed an historic deal with the new FA Premier League to screen live matches. By the late 1990s the beaming and screening of British football matches and matches involving British clubs across Europe became commonplace, especially following the advent of The Champions League and the UEFA Cup. Digital television has greatly increased audiences for non-terrestrial broadcasting and increased the more regular availability of *pay-per-view* of one's favoured team. However, the time/space compression of European football by satellite television has also contributed to a reduction in the identification of fans with their local clubs (Barnett, 1990: p. 1; Giulianotti & Williams, 1994: p. 13; Taylor, I., 1995: pp. 27–8).

Indeed, the *Europeanisation* of televised football may have contributed towards the creation of a new kind of fan who consumes football in a cultural and geographical void in the manner of extreme commodity fetishism ("Eat football, sleep football, drink Coca-Cola" as the slogan goes!). Whereas fans once had a more 'organic' relationship to football clubs, now, as the argument goes, relationships are based more on what they 'consume'. Not only is this 'new fandom' more consumer orientated but also it is more middle-class than the traditional working-class football fan community (Taylor, I., 1995).

The 'new consumer fans' (King, 2002) are 'freer' to pick and choose which club to support on bases other than class and propinquity. They are said to exhibit all the characteristics of the *neo-tribe* (Bauman, 1988; Bauman, 1992; Maffesoli, 1996; Hetherington, 1998; Bennett, 1999; Hughson, 2000). The *neo-tribe*, *post-tribe*, or *tribus* as Maffesoli calls it, are groupings "... based around interests and outlooks not determined by one's class [or geographical] background" (Hetherington, 1998: p. 7). The puissance of the neo-tribe is said to be 'choice' rather than class or territorial ascription. Many proponents of the concept of the *neo-tribe* use fans or supporter groups of sports clubs as exemplars (Shields in Maffesoli, 1996: p. ix; Hetherington, 1998: p. 57; Hughson, 2000).

However, as the evidence on the Europeanisation/Eurolocalisation of West Ham United fandom has suggested, clubs need to caution against marketing to a supposed new fan base that they assume is *atopophilic* and *neo-tribal* in character. The cultures of class, geography, life-long commitment and a yearning for a lost or never-realised *gemeinschaft* are not so easily dispensed with by the propagators of a 'market-orientated' football 'industry'.

Note

1   Extensive interviews were carried out with three key respondents involved in the design, manufacture and marketing of West Ham United replica shirts. These interviews were with:
Sarah Moulds, fashion designer, who designed all the West Ham United replica kits for *Pony* and *Fila* from 1993 until 2003. The interview took place on 22 October, 2003.
Pat Thomas, Development Manager for football at West Ham United's current kit supplier *Reebok*. The interview took place on 19 September, 2003.
Stuart Ryan, Commercial Director of West Ham United. The interview took place on 8 April, 2003.

Bibliography

Armstrong, G. and Giulianotti, R. (eds) (2001) *Fear and loathing in world football.* Oxford: Berg.

Armstrong, G. & Mitchell, J. (1999) 'Making the Maltese cross: Football on a small island', in G. Armstrong and R. Giulianotti (eds) *Football cultures and identities.* London: Macmillan.

Bale, J. (1988) 'The place of "place" in cultural studies of sport', *Progress in Human Geography* No. 12.

——— (1991) 'Playing at home: British football and a sense of place', in J. Williams S. Wagg S. (eds) *British football and social change: Getting into Europe.* Leicester: Leicester University Press.

——— (1992) *Sport, space and the city.* London: Routledge.

——— (2000) 'The changing face of football: Stadiums and communities', in J. Garland *et al.* (eds) *The future of football: Challenges for the twenty-first century.* London: Frank Cass.

Bale, J. & Moen, O. (eds) (1995) *The stadium and the city.* Keele: Keele University Press.

Barnett, S. (1990) *Games & sets: The changing face of sport on television.* London: BFI.

Bauman, Z. (1988) *Freedom.* Milton Keynes: Open University.

——— (1992) *Intimations of postmodernity.* London: Routledge.

Belton, B. (1998) *The first and last Englishmen.* Derby: Breedon Books.

Bennett, A. (1999) 'Subcultures or neo-tribes? Rethinking the relationship between youth, style and musical taste', *Sociology* Vol. 33 No. 3 pp. 599–617.

Brooking, T. (1981) *Trevor Brooking: An autobiography.* London: Pelham.

——— (2000) 'United for change', *Soccer and Society* Vol. 1 No. 3 pp. 24–29.

Brown, A. (2002) *'Do you come from Manchester?' A postcode analysis of the location of Manchester United and Manchester City season ticket holders, 2001.* Manchester: Manchester Metropolitan University.

Cohen, A. (1985) *The symbolic construction of community*. Chichester: Ellis Horwood.

Clarke, J. (1976) 'The skinheads and the magical recovery of community', in S. Hall & T. Jefferson (eds) *Resistance through rituals: Youth subculture in post-war Britain*. London: Hutchinson.

Crow, G. & Allan, G. (1994) *Community life: An introduction to local social relations*. Hemel Hempstead: Harvester Wheatsheaf.

Deakin, N. & Edwards, J. (1993) *The enterprise culture and the inner city*. London: Routledge.

Dempsey, P. & Reilley, K. (1998) *Big money, beautiful game: Saving football from itself*. London: Nicholas Brealey.

Giulianotti, R. (1997) 'Enlightening the north: Aberdeen fanzines and local football identity', in G. Armstrong & R. Giulianotti (eds) *Entering the field: New perspectives on world football*. Oxford: Berg.

Giulianotti, R. & Williams, J. (1994) *Game without frontiers*. Aldershot: Arena.

Greenfield, S. & Osborn, G. (2001) *Regulating football: Commodification, consumption and the law*. London: Pluto Press.

Greenslade, R. (1976) *Goodbye to the working class*. London: Marion Boyars.

Hetherington, K. (1998) *Expressions of identity: Space, performance, politics*. London: Sage.

Hognestad, H. (2003) 'Long-distance football support and liminal identities among Norwegian fans', in N. Dyck & P. Archetti (eds) *Sport, dance and embodied identities*. Oxford: Berg.

Holt, R. (1986) 'Working-class football and the city: the problem of continuity'. *British Journal of Sports History* Vol. 3 No. 1.

Hornby, N. (1992) *Fever pitch: The best football book ever written*. London: Victor Gollancz.

Hughson, J. (1997) 'The bad blue boys and the "magical recovery" of John Clarke', in G. Armstrong & R. Giulianotti (eds) *Entering the field: New perspectives on world football* Oxford: Berg.

——— (2000) 'A tale of two tribes: expressive fandom in Australian soccer's A-league', in G. Finn & R. Giulianotti (eds) *Football culture: Local contests, global visions*. London: Frank Cass.

Kearns, G. & Philo, C. (1993) *Selling places: The city as cultural capital, past and present*. Oxford: Pergamon Press.

King, A. (2002) *The end of the terraces: The transformation of English football in the 1990s*. Revised edition, London: Leicester University Press.

Korr, C. (1986) *West Ham United: The making of a football club*. London: Duckworth.

Lash, S. & Urry, J. (1987) *The end of organised capitalism*. London: Polity

Lee, S. (1998) 'Grey shirts to grey suits: the political economy of English football in the 1990s', in A. Brown (ed) *Fanatics! Power, identity and fandom in football*. London: Routledge.

Lee, S. (1999) 'The BskyB bid for Manchester United plc', in S. Hamil, J. Garland, D. Malcolm and M. Rowe (eds) *The business of football: A game of two halves*. Edinburgh: Mainstream.

Lyall, J. (1989) *Just like my dreams: My life with West Ham.* London: Viking.

Maffesoli, M. (1996) *The time of the tribes.* London: Sage.

Mason, T. (1998) *Sport in Britain.* London: Faber & Faber.

Massey, D. (1994) *Space, class and gender.* Cambridge: Polity Press.

Mellor, G. (2000) 'The genesis of Manchester united as a national and international "super-club", 1958–68', *Soccer and Society* Vol.1 No.2 pp. 151–166.

—— (2002) 'Local and global football clubs in the north-west of England', Paper presented at *Association football: British game, global passion* conference, University of Central Lancashire, National Football Museum, Monday 25th March 2002.

Moore, B. (1989) *West Ham United: The official history.* Watford: Video Collection International [Video].

Morris, A. & Morton, G. (1998) *Locality, community and nation.* London: Hodder & Stoughton.

Nash, R. (2000) 'Globalised football fandom: Scandinavian Liverpool FC supporters', *Football Studies* Vol. 3 No. 2 pp. 5–23.

O'Neill, G. (2001) *My East End.* London: Penguin [Audio].

Robins, D. & Cohen, P. (1978) *Knuckle sandwich: Growing up in the working class city.* Harmondsworth: Penguin.

Robson, G. (2000) *"No one likes us, we don't care": The myth and reality of Millwall fandom.* Oxford: Berg.

Southerton, D. (2002) 'Boundaries of "us" and "them": Class, mobility and identification in a new town', *Sociology* Vol. 36 No. pp. 171–193.

Steele, P. (2003) *When West Ham built battleships.* Pamphlet produced to accompany tour of West Ham United museum.

Taylor, I. (1995) *It's a whole new ball game,* Unpublished paper, Salford: University of Salford.

Taylor, M. (1994) 'Ethnography', in P. Banister *Qualitative methods in psychology.* Milton Keynes: Open University Press.

Taylor, R. (1992) *Football and its fans: Supporters and their relations with the game 1885–1985.* Leicester: Leicester University Press.

—— (1995) *Kicking and screaming 6: Whose game is it anyway?* London: BBC2 [VHS].

Vamplew W., Coyle J., Heath J. & Naysmith B. (1998) 'Sweet FA: fans' rights and club relocations', *Occasional Papers in Football Studies* Vol. 1 No. 2 August pp. 55–68.

Walvin, J. (2000) *The people's game: A social history of British football revisited.* Edinburgh: Mainstream.

Williams, J. (2002) 'Sociology and the World Cup', *Sociology Review* Vol.12, No.2.

Williams, J. *et al.* (1997) *FA Premier League national fan survey 1996: general sample report.* Leicester: Sir Norman Chester Centre for Football Research.

Williams, J. & Neatrour, S. (2002a) *The FA Premier League national fan survey 2001: summary report.* Leicester: Sir Norman Chester Centre for Football Research.

———— (2002b) *The FA Premier League national fan survey 2001: West Ham United supporters.* Leicester: Sir Norman Chester Centre for Football Research.

www.hammernorth.demon.co.uk [Accessed 08/07/04].

www.le.ac.uk/snccfr/resources/factsheets/fs3.html [Accessed 08/07/04].

www.le.ac.uk/snccfr/resources/factsheets/fs8.html [Accessed 08/07/04].

www.whufc.com [Accessed 08/07/04].

www.zakon.org/robert/internet/timeline.html [Accessed 08/07/04].

Young, M. & Willmott, P. (1957) *Family and kinship in East London.* Harmondsworth: Penguin.

———— (1960) *Family and class in a London suburb.* Harmondsworth: Penguin

'NO SCOUSE, PLEASE. WE'RE EUROPEANS': LIVERPOOL FC AND THE DECLINE OF THE BOOT ROOM MYSTIQUE

Stephen Wagg
Roehampton University, London

'As with cockney, scouse has acquired metaphoric force in hostility to modernity.' John Belchem[1]

'Chairman Mao has never seen such a show of red strength as this.' Bill Shankly to crowd gathered to celebrate winning of the FA Cup, St Georges Hall, Liverpool, May 1974

This chapter focuses upon a particular period in the recent history of Liverpool Football Club, spanning the installation of Roy Evans as manager of Liverpool in 1994 and his subsequent departure from the club in November of 1998. This departure seems to have been a watershed moment in the history both of the club and of English football and it is the management and the meanings of Evans' coming and going that are the central subject of the chapter.

But it will also discuss a couple of paradoxes.

Liverpool have been the most successful British club in the history of European inter-club competition. But for most, perhaps all, of the period of their domination they were perceived to be *in* Europe, but decisively not *of* it. They were European victors, but remained obstinately local. They conquered Europe apparently by being unalterably themselves, powered always by a no-nonsense folk wisdom incubated in a small room within the bowels of Anfield, expounded at the Melwood training ground and, equally importantly, drawing apparent affirmation from the terraced streets, the council estates and the satellite towns of Merseyside itself.

This links to a second paradox. The club has a powerful sense of tradition, which has few, if any, parallels in English football. This sense of tradition invariably takes the form of a dialogue with the ghost of the club's most charismatic figure, Bill Shankly (see, for example, Bowler, 1996; Kelly, 1996). Shankly was a Scot. He came to Liverpool only in 1959, he managed the club for fifteen years until his retirement in 1974 and he died over twenty years ago, in 1981. But the memory of Shankly survives in Merseyside football culture in a way that is perceptibly stronger than, say, the sense of Matt Busby in Manchester. Shankly is associated with a vivid sense of the common people and their relationship to football. This relationship now seems more historically specific than ever. But anyone planning to reform Liverpool Football Club must deal successfully with the Shankly legacy and its current interpreters. Shankly remains, for many, particularly those of and above a certain age, a powerful icon of social class and class relations on Merseyside. It is difficult to address these questions and not conclude that they are, in some sense, a manifestation of historic Merseyside exceptionalism and otherness (Belchem, 2000).

This chapter took me back to some arguments about football management presented in my first book *The Football World* (Wagg, 1984). This book discussed the strangely Goffmanite world in which people seek to 'know' football management — whether as managers themselves or as people who hire or in some way judge football managers. This world of cast-iron uncertainty has, in my view, not changed in its fundamentals. But it has, expectably, been modernised and the chapter, latterly, discusses this modernisation.

In summary, the argument will be as follows. Liverpool Football Club, while patently the most successful English football club in European competition, nevertheless represented an entrenched localism in English football culture which, by the 1990s, stood in the way both of the commercialisation of the club beyond English national boundaries and of the purported modernisation of its coaching staff. This localism drew on an historic local identity — the sense on the part of Liverpool people that they and their city were exceptional — and, within this, a populist sense of social class on Merseyside. This sense of class was embodied, in particular, by Liverpool's most famous manager Bill Shankly, and the cultural resistance to commodification of the club and to the European-isation of its coaching staff was bulwarked by the fact that the club's greatest successes had apparently been achieved through Shankly, his lieutenants and expressed ethos. The famous 'boot room' at Liverpool's Anfield ground was the key motif of this Shankly myth. A small room beneath the stand, where players' boots were kept and where visiting coaches were invited for a drink after games, the boot room came to represent the mystical and unelaborated 'Liverpool way', devised, apparently, by Shankly and his staff. The room remains symbolically at the heart of Liverpool football culture. At least one book has been written specifically about this room (see Kelly, 1999) and a Liverpool F.C. website (http://www.lfcbootroom.net/) bears its name. This site, in turn, is linked to separate sites dedicated to the room's most celebrated occupants: Shankly himself (www.shankly.com), Bob Paisley (www.bobpaisley.com), Joe Fagan (www.joefagan.com), Ronnie Moran (www.ronniemoran.com) and Roy Evans (www.royevans.net).

In the mid-1990s the club dallied for the last time with the Shankly myth by appointing Roy Evans, the one remaining representative of the 'Shanklyist' tradition, to manage the side. This move may have been borne of a belief that Shanklyism remained the only way to procure football success at Liverpool FC. More importantly, it was based on a realisation that any significant reforms of the club would have to be successfully reconciled with 'Shanklyism' — if possible, to be seen as an authentic manifestation of it. Thus, when Evans lost the sole managership of the team in 1998, he carried on in tandem with a new appointee (Gerard Houllier) who, though French, was successfully defined, by the club and by supportive local media, as a scouser-in-spirit. Evans later departed, not wishing, as he put it, to be a 'ghost on the wall' — the title of his recent biography (Dohren, 2004). The chapter concludes by suggesting that, despite the influx into English football of European coaches/team managers and the changed criteria for appointing them, the way in which football managers are ultimately 'known' and judged has not altered in its fundamentals.

Football, British culture and the idea of Europe

After World War II, two major political developments dominated British cultural life: the dismantlement of the British Empire and the coming of the Cold War. Both of these developments had huge reverberations in the realm of sport and popular culture. In the wake of the British Empire new ways were sought in which the 'Great' in Great Britain might be affirmed. Newspapers and commentators looked with greater expectation to national sports teams, who had now to achieve what had previously been taken for granted. Football has felt the weight of this mediated sense of national longing more keenly than other sports. The defeat of the English football team at Wembley in 1953 was rendered as a national disgrace by the tabloid press and as a call to modernisation by the more forward thinking elements in the English football world. Similarly, virtually every man charged with the job of coaching the England football team in the thirty five years or so that followed its victory in the World Cup of 1966 could at some stage expect vilification in the popular press for failing to retrieve the supposed glories of the national football past (Wagg, 1991).

The Cold War, of course, gave an extra edge to the confected hue and cry over the Hungary defeat — Hungary was a communist country — and it coloured thinking about 'Europe' among British football people. During the Cold War popular commentary rendered teams from behind Churchill's rhetorical 'Iron Curtain' as a series of 'dour Eastern European outfits' rolled off some totalitarian assembly line by state-appointed 'football commissars'. In this discourse, coaching equalled regimentation. Similarly, the countries of western mainland Europe were often seen as places where dwelled various breeds of plainly un-masculine footballers who cheated, wore cut-away boots without toe caps and fell at the slightest physical contact with their opponent.

But, most importantly, Europe became in the mid-1950s a place where leading British clubs might like to do business. By the end of this decade, more and more clubs, their supporters and the national sports press were talking about 'getting into Europe'.

This followed the inauguration of the European Cup for national club champions in 1955, a competition which, along with the Eurovision Song Contest begun in 1956, formed a purported cultural accompaniment to the growth of the European free trade area, or Common Market. This market was formally established under the Treaty of Rome in 1957. The treaty was in part dedicated to the 'closer union' of European nations. It should not be assumed, though, that the growth of political and economic cooperation in Europe brought with it any significant surge of cosmopolitanism in British football. The American novelist John Updike once referred to "that mostly imaginary activity termed 'cultural exchange'" (Updike, 1972: p. 12) and the writer Martin Jacques argued only recently that, globalisation notwithstanding, Britain has remained a doggedly parochial society (Jacques, 2004). Certainly this was reflected in British football culture up to the 1970s, characterised as it was by a What-Do-They-Know ideology (Wagg, 1984) which worked to exclude all amateurs, coaching theorists and, by extension, foreigners. Europe, in this culture, was for the most part there to be conquered, but not to be embraced or understood.

Shanklyism, the Boot Room and Liverpool in Europe

Bill Shankly came to Liverpool Football Club in late 1959, when they were still in the Second Division. He'd previously managed Carlisle United (1949–51), Grimsby Town (1951–54), Workington Town (1954–55) and Huddersfield Town (1956–59). Under his management Liverpool were promoted as Second Division Champions in 1962 and won the League two seasons later. They won the FA Cup in 1965 and, that same year, were European Cup semi-finalists. There were further European semi-finals in 1966 and 1971 before victory in the UEFA Cup Final — their first European trophy and their only one under Shankly's management. Liverpool's greatest triumphs in Europe, which collectively established the club as Britain's most successful club in European competition, came after Shankly, but they were achieved, in a sense, in his name and were rendered widely as a manifestation of his philosophy. Under Durham-born Bob Paisley, a former player and physiotherapist with Liverpool, the club won six league titles, three European Cups, one UEFA Cup and three League Cups between 1974 and 1983. Then in 1984, the management job went to Joe Fagan, Paisley's assistant and, like Paisley, strongly associated with the 'boot room', the club's fabled inner sanctum beneath the stand where Shankly's coaching staff had liked to talk football. The club now took the League title, the League Cup and the European Cup in a single season. When Fagan retired in 1985 the managership passed to Kenny Dalglish. Dalglish was still a Liverpool player at the time and Graeme Souness who took over from Dalglish in 1991 had also played for the club. But neither Dalglish nor Souness is generally seen as being part of the 'boot room' tradition. Far from it: when Roy Evans, signed by Shankly as a schoolboy and part of the coaching staff for most of his many years at Anfield, succeeded Souness in 1994, the appointment was generally rendered as a *return* to the traditions of the boot room.

The mystique of this boot room, like the mystique that still surrounds Bill Shankly, is rooted in ideas of social class. Shankly was managing Liverpool at a time when Britain was establishing a global reputation for a popular culture that had clear roots in the working class. The most overtly regionalised elements in this culture centred on Merseyside and Liverpool and Everton football clubs shared in the vibrant sense of the city conferred by the 'Mersey Sound' (Russell, 1997: p. 205; Williams, 2001: p. 101). But, whereas The Beatles, plainly the flagship for this new global visibility of Mersey culture, bought mansions in the Home Counties, Shankly and Paisley remained in their humble semi-detached houses in the heart of the city. "I'm one of the people", said Shankly. "I'm just one of the people that stands in the Kop" (McIlvanney, 1997).

In this regard, Shankly and Paisley, whether they knew it or not, were embracing longer established local identities. The historian John Belchem has convincingly argued that 'scouse' — a specifically Liver-pudlian way of talking and thinking about Liverpool — emerged in the nineteenth century as a response to the city's growth as a port and commercial centre based on Irish and Welsh migration. This was the basis of Liverpool's exceptionalism. As a city its identity was founded on trade, and not on industry like much of the rest of the North West (including Manchester) and on migration from further afield than its own hinterland. Popular culture played a big part in the elaboration of a 'scouse' identity which came in the twentieth century to encompass an ironic sense of humour that drew on the city's economic decline (Belchem, 2000: pp. 31–64). There's little doubt that the city's working-class people saw themselves as a special fraction of British working class as a whole.

Shankly corroborated for a section of this regional working class —
one, it's reasonable to assume, that stretched beyond the immediate
constituency of his own club — and for other local people besides, a sense
of themselves and of their place that was passionate, communitarian and
sufficiently ill-defined for them to unite around it. His emotional appeal
to the city in some ways recalls the relationship between Juan Peron and
the people of Argentina: he was for the people, but against politics. Shankly
conveys this in conversation with John Keith, a sympathetic interviewer,
in 1975, the year after his retirement:

> Shankly: ... "team spirit" is a form of socialism. I'm my own politics
> — I don't go for politics. But that kind of forms a camaraderie, as
> you say, and it's a basis for socialism. And when you hear people
> running down fellers that are socialists I think they're wrong. They
> don't know what they're talking about. I'm not talking about militant
> people at all ... .who go and try to destroy everything ... .
> Keith: 'As a code of life ... ?
> Shankly: 'I'm talking about life. I'm not talking about politics in the
> true sense of politics .... I'm talking about humanity. People dealing
> with people, and people helping people. (Keith, 1998: p. 103)

As one of Shankly's biographers has suggested:

> At a time when [John] Lennon was saying that the Beatles meant
> more to people than God, in the red half of Liverpool, Bill Shankly
> meant more than the Beatles. (Bowler, 1996: p. 175)

Shankly's mystic bond with the city's people underpinned, and was in
turn strengthened by, his notions of the game of football itself. The way
that Liverpool played was happily rendered as a relatively simple matter.
Shankly interviewed Prime Minister Harold Wilson on Liverpool's Radio
City in the mid-1970s and repeated then his often-stated belief that 'football
is a form of socialism' (Keith, 1998: p. 192). But he frequently dismissed
the idea that this football-socialism might have a rational or technocratic
dimension. He was particularly contemptuous of the FA's coaching centre
at Lilleshall:

It was an education because everything they did, I did the opposite. I heard some expressions, 'workrate', 'blind side running', 'peripheral vision', 'environmental awareness', 'working off the ball'. God Almighty! I could have written a comic cuts book about it! They were trying to tell me that you could make football players! They had a set plan all the time ... We're not too fond of coaching. Coaxing is a better word. (Bowler, 1996: p. 181).

People who came in increasing numbers to Liverpool's training ground at Melwood in search of the secret to the club's success came away none the wiser. Beyond his avowed collectivism, Shankly, ambiguous as ever, preached simply — simplicity (Hopkins, 2001: pp. 78–9).

Ironically, Shankly did on occasion allow that 'the Liverpool way' had actually been borrowed from Europe: "The basic system is what we call collective play. It is very simple but very effective. It is something we learned from the continent — a cat and mouse game that calls for patience and improvisation" (Bale, 1996: p. 116). Of course, in these more parochial times, nobody thought to acknowledge this cultural borrowing as 'hybridity' (Giulianotti, 1999: p. 24), and, in the main, Liverpool's success in the 1960s has been attributed to Shankly's eccentric genius (Bale, 1996; Bowler, 1996; Keith, 1998; Ward, 2001) and to the various football strategies thought to have been concocted by his lieutenants, sipping tea in the club's mystical boot room.

At Shankly's retirement in 1974 the club clearly felt that, whatever might be the source of the club's recent success, it could be found on the premises. There seems to have been little inclination to go outside the club to replace Shankly and Bob Paisley, Shankly's assistant, who took over, now presided over even more success than Shankly had. Similarly, Joe Fagan, another Anfield veteran who'd been assistant to Paisley, had three trophies to show for his first season as manager (1983–4). During this ten year period, then, between 1974 and 1984, the boot room mystique seems to have received its most powerful affirmation. The mystique was rooted in particularism. Paisley and Fagan, it was assumed, were 'Liverpool, through and through'. They knew the club, its ways and its cultural power. They were, moreover, keepers of a specific flame and could not necessarily be expected to procure these successes for any other club. A blissfully contradictory aura hung around Anfield: the boot room was full of secrets, but there was, in the final analysis, no secret (see for example, Kelly, 1999). Just good, homespun commonsense expounded by decent, unassuming working-class blokes. They knew a thing or two but, ultimately, their wisdom was the wisdom of the people: the Kop spoke through them, just as it had through Shankly.

And this wisdom, of course, had, apparently, conquered Europe. Shankly had, it seems, been as suspicious of 'Europe' as he had been of Lilleshall coaching courses. While not averse to pinching a European idea or two, Shankly later confided to John Keith that he'd found Europeans 'devious': "...knowing everything's strange across there and you can expect anything to happen at all" (Keith, 1998: pp. 108, 110). Paisley, somewhat in contrast, has been more celebrated in recent years as a tactician and as the quiet counsel behind Shankly's throne (Hopkins, 2001; Kelly, 1997). Importantly, though, he too remains quintessentially the unspoiled working-class male, padding quietly along in flat cap and carpet slippers, or sat with a modest whiskey in some sumptuous continental hotel (Hopkins, 2001: p. 84) tending quietly to a European Cup winning football team, as he might a prize marrow or a hutch full of racing pigeons.

What would Shanks have wanted?: The 1990s

By the 1990s a number of important changes had occurred at in the English football world, sufficient to crack the proud proletarian cultural edifice that was seen variously as the Shankly/Paisley/Fagan/Boot Room legacy.

Firstly and perhaps most importantly, as Anthony King has recently argued, the structure of European football in the 1970s and 1980s that had clearly sustained Liverpool in their parochialism was dismantled in the 1990s. The 'Bosman ruling', the growing volume and importance of TV revenue and the abandonment of the knock-out format all favoured the big city clubs in Europe. Footballers began to move across Europe for huge fees and/or salaries and Liverpool, who in their heyday had recruited players largely within the British Isles and the south of Ireland, found it hard to compete. King goes on to argue that the particularist identities recently developed by Manchester United supporters are different in kind from those generated on Merseyside, the former being less atavistic and more European (King, 2003).

Secondly, players' expectations of management were almost certainly changing. With more money coming into the clubs through sponsorship, footballers, including Liverpool's, were on big money and perhaps less susceptible to the often military disciplines of the boot room regimes. The sergeant-major figure of Ronnie Moran, another boot room veteran, became increasingly archaic in the years preceding his retirement in 1998.

Thirdly, and related to this, players wanted more detailed tactical preparation than had been countenanced in the 'golden years'. This expectation would now, on occasion, be specifically European in origin. The Dane Jan Molby, for example, came to Anfield from Ajax of Amsterdam in 1984: "At Ajax and Denmark we had 45-minute, perhaps hour long, meetings before games. But not at Liverpool. I said to Joe Fagan 40 minutes before the game, 'What do you want me to do?' He said, 'Listen, we've signed you because you're a good player, just go and show us what a good player you are, whatever you want to do'" (Kelly, 1999: p. 169).

Fourthly, while detailed preparation was more likely to come from Fagan's successors Kenny Dalglish (1985–91) and Graeme Souness (1991–94), these two managers, while both of them ex-Liverpool players, were now wealthy men with expensive tastes. Unlike Shankly, Paisley or Fagan, who'd played their football under the maximum wage, Dalglish and Souness had earned well in the more moneyed 1970s. For a section of Liverpool's earnest football public, this was discomfiting. On the Kop Souness was known as 'Champagne Charlie' (Kelly, 1999: p. 197) and he had, in any event, inspired widespread feelings of betrayal on Merseyside when, in 1992, he had sold the story of his heart operation to the *Sun* newspaper, still largely boycotted in the city for accusing Liverpool supporters of robbing their own dead after the Hillsborough disaster of 1989 (http://www.soccerphile.com/soccerphile/archives/wc2002/ne/rd3.html). If the team prospered, these factors might be overlooked, but if it didn't the disinclination of either Dalglish or Souness to live in a semi-detached house in the city might count against them. There might be calls for people who 'put the club first'.

Fifthly, in the late 1980s the club stopped winning trophies. It's remarkable, perhaps, that the power of the boot room mystique was still such that, in 1994 when Souness' management was deemed to have failed, the board of the club should think of re-embracing it.

Part of the reason for this is that football discourse in the city of Liverpool itself was still strongly coloured by evocations of 'Shanks', Paisley and the boot room. The popular fanzine *Through the Wind and Rain*, has in recent times retained a strongly boot room paradigm and football commentary in the *Liverpool Echo* during the 1990s was dominated by men such as Tommy Smith who, as readers were frequently reminded, had played under Shankly and Paisley.

In January of 1994, with Liverpool having just incurred a humiliating FA Cup defeat at home to Bristol City, the front page of the *Echo* announces that Souness has agreed to go. Elsewhere in the paper, Smith, perhaps with an inkling of what is now to happen, calls Souness "aloof and distant", accusing him of hurting "the club that I know and love". "You are nothing", writes Tommy, "without the total support of the people" (*Liverpool Echo* 28th January 1994 pp. 6–7). The following day's edition discloses on page one that "Bootle-born Roy Evans has emerged as favourite to become the Reds' ninth post-war boss".

Evans, signed by Shankly as a 16 year old in 1965, had played fitfully for Liverpool between 1969 and 1974, but, following Shankly's retirement, he'd become a full time coach at the club at the very young age of 25. Born in one of the most disadvantaged districts of a working-class city, he had therefore been at the club for nearly thirty years, twenty of them in the fabled boot room. All this is cited to the Liverpool public in the *Echo*'s presentation of Evans, following his appointment as manager on 1st February. Staff reporter Ian Hargreaves reports that:

> ... a beaming [chairman] David Moores welcomed long-serving coach Roy Evans to the managerial hot seat ... Evans, a quiet-spoken, greying 45-year-old wearing a track suit, looked as far removed from the flamboyant Souness as one could imagine ... A Liverpudlian through and through who has been with the club in one capacity or another for more than thirty years, and was given his first backroom role by Bill Shankly, he did not really need to state either his credentials or his priorities ...

On the same page, Tommy Smith declares that "Roy's the right choice for the Reds". He elaborates:

> Congratulations to Roy Evans on being appointed the new manager of Liverpool. I've had a couple of good nights' kip knowing the club is back on the rails and in the hands of a man who I believe is right for the job ...The club is in his blood and he will now set about the rebuilding job, not in his own image, but in the style of famous predecessors like Shankly, Paisley and Fagan ... He will have Ronnie Moran at his right hand in the first instance. And while Bob Paisley is not well, Joe Fagan will be only too ready to offer support if asked. (*Liverpool Echo,* 1st February 1994: p. 46)

Two pages further on, Evans is reported to have insisted that "he won't be a high-profile, jewellery-jangling manager".

The rhetoric here is unmistakeable. In an uncertain world there will now be a return to the localised, class-based verities of the 1960s and 70s. The man now in charge touches that era and these verities in every important particular: he's local; he's from within the club; he was appointed by Bill Shankly, founding father and focal point of the club's powerful populist ethos; he's a veteran of the boot room; he's an ordinary man, not 'flash'. Moreover, in keeping with Shankly's professed scorn for formal certification and training, he has no coaching qualifications (Jewell, 2004: p. 20). Here, symbolically, it seems that the club rediscovers its own beating heart.

Evans' undoing was, in a sense, contained in this hopeful, atavistic presentation: his teams were measured against the achievements of his mentors, and although performing respectably, failed to recapture past glories. The influential fanzine *Through the Wind and Rain* meanwhile constantly summoned up the ghosts of Shankly and Paisley through the 1990s, calling both the club's administration and its team management to account. As Keepers of the Flame the journal's writers, in the name of the heroes of the past, attacked both the commercialisation of the club and its football shortcomings. "Over the past few years", wrote Dave Usher in 1998:

> ... the club has been criticised for not doing enough to honour the memory of great men such as Shankly and Paisley. This criticism

was, and in my opinion still is, fully justified. If the powers that be think the 'Paisley Gates' and a statue of Bill are enough to appease the fans they are very much mistaken. I for one will not be satisfied until both of these great men have stands named after them. The most sickening sight at Anfield these days is that huge ugly "Macdonalds Family Stand" sign at the back of the Kop. This stand is famous throughout the world, and for LFC themselves to cheapen it in this way is criminal. (Usher, 1998: p. 38)

But while the club was rebuked for its commercial exploitation of its global image and its desecration of the club's heritage, Evans, one of the few remaining links with this heritage, albeit with no League championships and no European trophies in the club's cabinet, now found that his local identity and apparent rootedness now counted against him. A cartoon late in 1997 has a photograph of Evans looking at a map of Europe; a bubble coming from his mouth asks: 'Laffinstock? Is that in Russia?' (*Through the Wind and Rain* 37 (Winter) 1997: p. 23).

Jeu sans frontières? The coming of Gerard Houllier

By the late 1990s players born on the continent of Europe, or beyond, were commonplace at the higher levels of English football and a number of leading clubs had begun to appoint European coaches as their managers. In 1990 Aston Villa had gone for Josef Venglos, who had just taken Czechoslovakia to the quarter finals of the World Cup in Italy, the Dutch international Ruud Gullit took over as player-manager at Chelsea in 1996, Arsenal employed Frenchman Arsène Wenger also in 1996 and the Swiss coach Christian Gross became Tottenham's manager the following year. It was therefore becoming expectable for a top English club to consider looking to Europe, rather than the lower English leagues, for their manager. Yet when Liverpool reconsidered the management of their team in the summer of 1998 they opted to try to reconcile tradition with modernity and persuaded Evans to become joint manager with Gerard Houllier, lately in charge of the French national football academy. Several pages of the *Liverpool Echo* were now given over to leading spokespeople to try to square this cultural circle. Houllier, while on the one hand presented as a global figure (being given much of the credit for France's recent World Cup win in Paris), is at the same time established as a man with local associations: a friend to the city. He once lived in Liverpool, readers are told, taught French at a local school (Alsop Comprehensive in Walton) in the 1960s and even stood on the sacred Kop. "I have a Red heart!" he tells his inaugural press conference (*Liverpool Echo* 16th July 1998: p. 1). Staff writer Ric George adds that Houllier's period of teaching in Liverpool was "during the Shankly days" (p. 91) and Vice Chairman Peter Robinson calls up the ghost of Shankly in support of the appointment: "Bill was never averse to change and innovation and he would have been very happy" (p. 66). On page 63 another reporter, Philip McNulty, similarly tries to reconcile the memory of Shankly with football practices that Shankly, for what it's worth, had openly repudiated:

> The cynics labelled it the kindest sacking in soccer history. The optimists hailed the following winds of French revolution blowing through Liverpool Football Club. It is the partnership that mixes the Liverpool tradition of Evans with the vision of Houllier, a man in the Arsène Wenger mould with no playing career to boast about but coaching credentials to place alongside the best.

It is also a recognition that Liverpool, even Liverpool, must move with the times. Peter Robinson said Bill Shankly would have approved and who are we to argue?

> ... Liverpool's players will also feel the winds of change blasting through Melwood. The replacement of the retiring Ronnie Moran, the archetypal up-and-at-'em coach who wouldn't know airs and graces if they bit him on the backside, with a French coaching guru is some culture shock. It is also the answer to a groundswell of unrest among Liverpool fans who feared they were on the brink of being marginalized by Manchester United, Arsenal and Chelsea.

Robinson explains the club's need to act, significantly citing the club's global, and not local, contingent of supporters:

Shortly after the end of last season we took a firm decision to strengthen our management team, in a determined effort to return Liverpool Football Club to its proper place at the very highest level of the game. We owed this to our thousands of fans throughout the world ... Gerard is generally acknowledged as one of Europe's finest coaches. (p. 5)

Elsewhere a more cautious Evans says: "There will be some problems, that is for sure, but ... we both share the same philosophies on football" (p. 5). Talking to Chris Bascombe, he acknowledges the European dimension that the job now carries, while trying, like other commentators, to marry new exigencies to the club's previous ethos:

We'll organise things between us, but that's nothing new. It will be no different to the days of Shankly and Paisley.

Many observers are surprised that the Reds have broken with tradition to appoint an 'outsider' to the coaching staff, but Evans insisted it was vital to the club to match the vast European knowledge boasted by some of their chief rivals:

It's always helpful to have the experience of European football. Gerard has a great knowledge and great contacts. He will also bring with him different training methods and techniques. It's the case of the boot room being modernised. The concept of two managers working together like this might be seen as radical, but there's nothing new in the idea of everyone working together as a team. To be honest, when people talk about the 'traditional' boot room a lot of rubbish is said. It was just a room where we chatted about football. It became legendary as a think-tank because we kept on being successful and buying good players. It was great to sit there with a beer and a cup of tea, but in the end it was a mutual thought society. The relationship between Gerard and myself will be no different ... (p. 66)

Taken together, this torrent of rationalisations is essentially about representing a break with the past as a continuation of it. Two days on and former Liverpool player Phil Thompson speaks more bluntly:

> It's sad, in a way, to say goodbye to the Boot Room days. But foot-
> ball moves on and I think most Reds' fans will welcome Houllier's
> appointment. Arsenal and Chelsea have shown the way by bringing
> in coaches from abroad and I'm sure their success has had a
> bearing on Liverpool's move to recruit Houllier. Only results will tell
> if the Reds have made a good decision. For now, I'd like to think
> that we have taken a good step forward. (*Liverpool Echo*, 18th July
> 1998: p. 7)

Meanwhile, on the pages of *Through the Wind and Rain*, the editor uses
irony and self-mockery to negotiate this increasingly acknowledged rupture
with the boot room heritage:

> Bonjour, mon ami — comment allez vous? Yes folks, it's French
> week in TTW&R. Gerard's arrival will no doubt see dollops of this
> kind of franglais that was never very humorous in the first place,
> but since not being funny never stopped us before (I have turned it
> into a personal ethos) expect beaucoup de bon mots Francaise
> encore. Et maintenant (*oh stop it* — readers). (Editorial No. 39,
> Summer 1998: p. 9)

This, in one possible reading, is an Everybody's-Doing-It nod toward the
tabloid press. It hints at a discomfiture with the taking on of a European
manager and a brittle-jokey unease with European-ness itself, and it does
so by imputing it to others. There are no simple answers here, politically.
Through the Wind and Rain is broadly progressive and devoutly 'Shanklyist'.
The defence of the Shankly tradition is in some sense the defence of notions
of class and community, but also of parochialism and a suspicion of
'foreign'. The embrace of a French manager is an embrace of cosmopolitanism and anti-racism, but also of the commercial globalisation (the de-
localisation) of the club: here Houllier and Macdonalds become rendered,
ultimately, as part of the same process.

Four months later, Roy Evans resigned his joint managership and
left Liverpool Football Club for good, saying that he didn't want to be 'a
ghost on the wall at Anfield'. Houllier now became manager and Phil

Thompson his assistant, with chairman Moores offering the rather clumsy explanation "We don't want to go completely foreign" (*Liverpool Echo* 12th November 1998 p. 1). Evans may not have wanted to be a ghost on the wall but the city's most familiar ghost was once again conscripted in support of the new moves. "While feeling a genuine sadness for Evans", wrote *Echo* sports editor Ken Rogers:

> ... a man who went so near ... to reviving the glory days, my first thoughts are with Houllier. This is nothing to do with taking sides. I admire Roy Evans both as a football person and [as] a man who was steeped in the down-to-earth traditions of the club he served man and boy. He was — and is — a genuinely nice man. No, my Houllier thoughts are more to do with aligning myself with a couple of Anfield sayings that seem more important than ever today.

> The first is ... *no man is bigger than the club*. Legends have stepped aside in the past with those on the inside, including Roy, chanting loudly from the Liverpool Book of Quotations: *"The King is Dead. Long Live the King"*.

> Secondly Liverpool have never been a club for looking back. I quote from the little red book of Bill Shankly: *"The most important thing is the next game"*.

Rogers' headline advises readers to "Pull Up the Drawbridge and Back Houllier". The column also contains a distinctly ambivalent reflection on the historic boot room by photographer Stephen Shakeshaft. Entering it, he says, "was almost an anti-climax", while adding the mandatory "if walls could talk what tales they would be able to tell ... ." (p. 94). A still colder judgement follows 24 hours later from Ric George:

> Houllier's partnership with Roy Evans didn't work. Not through a clash of personalities, but a clash of philosophies, a clash of cultures ... Liverpool are where they are because they have stood still for years, stuck in a time warp and wrapped up in their traditions. As a result, dramatic change is required ... Liverpool, remember, is the most traditional of English clubs, their policy tending to be to appoint only their own. Now we have an outsider in

charge — and a foreigner to boot! (*Liverpool Echo* 13th November 1998: p. 72)

On the next page George's colleague Philip McNulty insists, with yet another invocation of Shankly, that Evans had to go:

> Moores made the move he never wanted to make because to do otherwise was asking mediocrity to walk through the Shankly Gates. And he could never have lived with that. (p. 73)

In conclusion: Shanklyism, football management and modernity

This has been the story, in outline, of an extraordinary conjunction of the local and the global in the English football. What Bill Shankly and his associates and successors represented was a kind of cultural resistance — albeit partial, symbolic and incoherent — to changes in the class relations of the football world. This was possible largely because these reluctant heroes of the club's boot room were so very successful and wielded such emotional power in a city accustomed to economic hardships (Williams, Hopkins and Long, 2001: pp. 4–8). Bill Shankly managed Liverpool during a time when, as a big city club, it began to realise its market potential. The club was in the Second Division when he arrived; it is unlikely to occupy a lower division ever again. Shankly's regime, like many at League clubs in the 1950s and 60s, was incipiently modernist, but swathed in the particularist mystique of British working-class football people. He favoured fitness and some notion of tactical preparation while insisting that only he and people like him, who'd been through the fire and water of the professional game, could do the things that he did. By the 1990s clubs the size of Liverpool had ceased to be clubs in the established sense and were now seeing themselves as brands (Williams, Hopkins & Long 2001). But those policy makers at Liverpool FC who have wished to pursue new strategies of modernisation and commercialisation since the 1980s and 90s have known that they must do so in negotiation with the (not necessarily reactionary) elements of ancestor worship that characterise Anfield football culture. This has led them and the local football media into an often queasy and unpersuasive dialogue with the ghost of Bill Shankly. Similarly their opponents, in the fanzines and elsewhere, have pressed their case extravagantly in terms of Shankly and of What-He-Would-Have-Wanted.

But it would be wrong to see this as simply a fascinating and anguished study in corporate public relations — although it clearly is that. It's also a study in the modernisation of the vocabulary of football management. Moreover it's a study that shows how, while some things have changed, others have remained essentially as they were. There was scarcely such a thing as 'football management' in England before World War II. Up to the 1950s football managers wore waistcoats and watch chains and were seldom seen. In the 1960s and 70s, like Revie, Ramsey, Shankly and Stein, they sported tracksuits and communed with their players, creating sometimes intense family atmospheres while disdaining anything very academic. By the 1990s the leading managers were often everything that had previously been disdained in English professional football culture: a coach with an intellectual aura, who happily gave and attended seminars, worked often with short contracts, wore the air of a disinterested professional and was very likely a non-British national. By 1998, in England, Arsène Wenger was the model of the manager which clubs now sought to employ and, notably, he is mentioned several times in the *Liverpool Echo*'s welcome of Houllier in July of that year.

But judgements on football managers remain unalterably circumstantial. Football managers are still found, in general, by identifying successful teams and working backwards to locate the man in charge of them. In the 1950s, 60s and 70s manager-less First Division clubs usually looked down the leagues to see the currently best sides and then enquired about their managers. Some helpful football journalist would confirm that X or Y was, indeed, one of the most promising young managers around. This is how Liverpool acquired Shankly in 1959. But by the 1990s clubs were looking to international tournaments and enquiring who were the masterminds behind the success of this or that nation/foreign club. Even Wimbledon, an English club with a sense of localism to compare with Liverpool's, was moved in 1999 to approach the Norwegian coach Egil Olsen, once he had coached Norway to the World Cup Finals of 1994 and 1998. Houllier came to Liverpool credited, through his work at the French national academy at Clairefontaine, with bringing the World Cup to France. He left the club in the summer of 2004 with Liverpool in fourth position in the Premier League, the same position they'd finished in under Evans in 1998. Most careers in football management still end in failure. In general most winning teams still, by definition, have good managers and failing teams have managers who have erred and must therefore expect to clear their desks some time soon. It is simply the terms in which we seek to make sense of football management that have changed. Liverpool were probably the last major club to embrace this new vocabulary. And it's possible — even likely — that the Liverpool board believed everything they said about Shankly, about the boot room, about the possibility of marrying supposed European sophistication to Anfield folk wisdom. After all, W. I. Thomas' famous dictum — "If men define situations as real, they are real in their consequences" (Thomas, 1928: p. 257) — still holds true, and nowhere more so than in the realm of football management. But, by the autumn of 1998, even Liverpool directors seemed to have accepted that, in the words of Mark Twain, "an expert is always from out of town".

Acknowledgements

I'd like to thank Jonny Magee, Stephen Hopkins and Terry and Greta McManus for help in the preparation of this chapter. Alan Bairner, Stephen F. Kelly, Martin Johnes, Jonny Magee and John Williams helped me improve it following its first airing.

Note

1   John Belchem's observation quoted at the beginning of the chapter is taken from his *Merseypride* (Belchem, 2000: p. 53). Bill Shankly's exclamation appears in Andy Ward and John Williams' chapter 'Bill Shankly and Liverpool' in *Passing rhythms* (Williams, Hopkins and Long, 2001: p. 72). It can also be found in John Keith's *Shanks for the memory* (Keith, 1998: p. 146).

References

Bale, B. (1996) *The Shankly legacy*. Derby: Breedon Books.

Belchem, J. (2000) *Merseypride: Essays in Liverpool exceptionalism*. Liverpool: Liverpool University Press.

Bowler, D. (1996) *Shanks: The authorised biography of Bill Shankly*. London: Orion.

Dohren, D. (2004) *Ghost on the wall: The authorised biography of Roy Evans*. Edinburgh: Mainstream.

Giulianotti, R. (1999) *Football: A sociology of the global game*. Cambridge: Polity Press.

Jacques, M. (2004) 'Our problem with abroad', *The Guardian* 21st August: p. 17.

Jewell, A. (2004) 'Ghost story' [Profile of Roy Evans] *LFC Official Magazine* No. 104, 3–9 (August): pp. 19–25.

Keith, J. (1998) *Shanks for the memory*. London: Robson Books.

Kelly, S. E. (1996) *Bill Shankly: It's much more important than that*. London: Virgin.

––––––– (1999) *The Boot Room boys*. London: CollinsWillow.

Kelly, S. (1997) 'Forgotten Man (Again)', *Through the Wind and Rain* 37 (Winter): p. 39.

King, A. (2003) *The European ritual*. Aldershot: Ashgate.

McIlvanney, H. (1997) *Arena*, 'Busby, Shankly and Stein: The football men', Programme Three 'The Price of Glory'. BBC2, 30th March.

Russell, D. (1997) *Football and the English: A social history of Association Football in England 1963–1995*. Preston: Carnegie Publishing.

Thomas, W. I. (1928) *The child in America*. New York: Knopf.

Updike, J. (1972) *Bech: A book*. Harmondsworth: Penguin.

Usher, D. (1998) 'There used to be a football club over there' *Through the Wind and Rain* 38 (Spring): pp. 38–9.

Wagg, S. (1984) *The Football world*. Brighton: Harvester Press.

––––––– (1991) 'Naming the guilty men: The popular press and the England football team', in J. Williams and S. Wagg (eds) *British football and social change*. Leicester: Leicester University Press.

Ward, A., with J. Williams (2001) 'Bill Shankly and Liverpool', in J. Williams, S. Hopkins and C. Long (eds) *Passing rhythms: Liverpool FC and the transformation of football*. Oxford: Berg, pp. 53–75.

Williams, J. (2001) 'Kopites, "Scallies" and Liverpool Fan Cultures: Tales of Triumph and Disasters' in J. Williams, S. Hopkins and C. Long (eds) *Passing rhythms: Liverpool FC and the transformation of football*. Oxford: Berg, pp. 99–127.

Williams, J., S. Hopkins and C. Long (2001) Introduction to J. Williams, S. Hopkins and C. Long (eds) *Passing rhythms: Liverpool FC and the transformation of football*. Oxford: Berg, pp. 1–14. http://www.soccerphile.com/soccerphile/archives/wc2002/ne/rd3.html (Accessed 17th November 2004).

FOOTBALL AND THE BASQUES:
THE LOCAL AND THE GLOBAL

John K. Walton
University of Central Lancashire

Introduction

The Basque Country of northern Spain and south-west France offers inter-esting opportunities for research into contested relationships between sport and identity. It is a classic example of a 'nation without a state', with a distinctive politics of linguistic and cultural nationalism which has gathered momentum in conflict over the proper relationship between the Basques and the French and Spanish states, especially but not solely since the late nineteenth century. The roots of the current manifestations of Basque nationalism can be traced back to the 1890s in Bilbao[1], when the foundation of Sabino Arana's *Partido Nacionalista Vasco* (Basque Nation-alist Party: PNV) was closely followed by the emergence of Athletic Club de Bilbao, whether we take 1898 or 1901 as the 'authentic' foundation date of the latter (Ball, 2004). This marked the origins of association football as an organised sport in this part of Spain, though there had been earlier stirrings elsewhere in the country, wherever British influences (directly or at a remove, usually through Switzerland and especially Neuchâtel) were significant. Football was a foreign import associated with the global-izing influence of the British Empire and with the economic transformation of Bilbao and its region through overseas trade and industrialization, in ways that generated extensive migration from other parts of Spain to fuel rapid urban growth and challenge the ideals of rural innocence and religiosity on which early Basque nationalism was founded. It therefore sustained for several decades an uneasy relationship with those aspects of Basque culture that the nationalists espoused. This applied especially to the 'traditional' Basque sports like pelota, in its various forms, and the rural and maritime tests of strength and endurance that the nationalists sought to revive and promote, preferably shorn of their strong associations with betting. Football was at first seen as a competitor with Basque sports, and by pitting villages, towns and provinces against each other in fierce and well-supported combat it tended to divide the emergent nation rather than uniting it. This was so especially in the absence (most of the time: see below) of a 'national' team like those that represented the nations without a state within the United Kingdom. It was not until the 1920s and especially the 1930s that mainstream nationalists embraced football as compatible with Basque virtues, and Athletic Bilbao laid disputed claim to representing the Basque people on the playing fields of Spain and further afield (Díaz Noci, 2000).

Anatomy of the Basque country

This chapter focuses on the Spanish side of the national boundaries in this 'nation without a state', and on the emergent relationships between football and Basque identities before the Spanish Civil War. The tensions between the local (and, increasingly, the provincial), the 'Basque national' and the Spanish national were all becoming increasingly evident within the Basque provinces of Spain at this time. Despite the growing nationalist insistence on Basque unity and distinctiveness, and the relatively compact area and small population under consideration (there were still only 1,237,000 inhabitants of the four Basque provinces within Spain in 1930, half a million of whom lived in the most industrialised province, Vizcaya), there were many different versions of Basqueness on offer (De Pablo, 1995: p. 9). The three core provinces of Vizcaya, with its capital Bilbao, Guipúzcoa (San Sebastián/Donostia) and Alava (Vitoria/Gasteiz) had distinctive economic, cultural and political profiles. The fourth province, Navarra (Pamplona/Iruna), was identifiably Basque in the 'montana' of the north and west, towards the Pyrenees, while the overwhelmingly Spanish-speaking 'ribera' of the south and east looked towards the neighbouring provinces of Aragón and La Rioja and was much more readily assimilated into the

Castilian Spain of Madrid and the high tableland of the *meseta* (Castells and Walton, 1998; Castells and Elorza, 1999). Within the Basque country, too, there was a systematic contrast between the maritime economy and the inland agricultural economy. The former was outward-looking, in touch with a variety of different cultures through fishing and overseas trade, and with its own distinctive social organizations and cultural practices. The latter was more inward-looking and self-sufficient, basing itself more on networks of isolated farmsteads than on concentrated urban communities, but seeing its traditional characteristics coming under challenge from the spread of railways and the growth of industrial towns, often in symbiosis with an increasingly market-oriented agriculture. The two economies were not sealed off from each other, of course, but the contrasts were marked and persistent, expressing themselves in (for example) contrasting traditions in cookery and other patterns of consumption (Kurlansky, 1999).

Vizcaya, which likes to present itself as the cradle and the heartland both of Basque identity and of Basque football, experienced the most dramatic transformations within its borders. Since the 1870s, with gathering momentum, parts of the province had experienced rapid industrialization, based on iron mining, steel, engineering and shipbuilding; and Bilbao had become an international port, trading extensively with British ports like Cardiff and Liverpool as part of a much wider pattern of activity, and adopting English middle-class customs, conventions and consumption patterns, from gentlemen's clubs to suburban architecture, and emphatically including sport. The Nervión estuary, from Bilbao itself to the open sea, became a polluted monument to carboniferous capitalism (González Portilla, 2001; Beascoechea, 1995; Castells, 1999). But industry also spread into the heart of the Vizcayan countryside, as small towns like Durango and Guernica developed their own manufacturing identities in the early twentieth century, while the fishing ports also began to organise on a novel scale and develop fish preserving and canning plants, as the spread of the railways enabled them to reach new markets for their fresh products (Delgado, 2005).

Guipúzcoa, the other coastal Basque province within Spain, to the east of Vizcaya and stretching up to the French border, followed a different pattern of development, although the small manufacturing towns that developed in the upland valleys close to the provincial boundary shared a great deal in common. Eibar, for example, which specialised in small arms manufacturing, is just on the Guipúzcoa side of the border but developed industrial links with Guernica in Vizcaya in the early twentieth century; and from the 1890s the two provinces were linked by a narrow-gauge railway network (Delgado, 2005). The industries of Guipúzcoa spread up the valleys behind San Sebastián, and the combination of water power and the lack of usable mineral wealth produced a focus on papermaking and related industries in small manufacturing centres, although railway rolling stock manufacture developed at Beasain. It was significant that the main international rail route to the west of the Pyrenees between Madrid and Paris passed through the province, stimulating economic development along its route. Here as in Vizcaya the rise of industry reduced the isolation of agriculture, but there was nothing to match the industrial juggernaut of the Nervión valley below Bilbao (Luengo, 1991). As in Vizcaya, the provincial capital provided a focus for economic and cultural interchange with the wider world. San Sebastián, however, followed a distinctive trajectory as an international sea-bathing resort, with its more conventional manufacturing industries (cement, especially) banished to the urban periphery, and its international seaport function displaced to Pasajes, a few kilometres to the east. San Sebastián became the summer seat of government and (until 1929) of the royal family, the resort of the Madrid aristocracy and upper middle classes, and the glamorous holiday location of choice for the aspiring middle ranks of (by the 1920s) provincial capitals all over Spain. This gave the town an affinity with central government and the Spanish monarchy, which cut across its Basque identity as Donostia, although this was more of a problem for some inhabitants than for others (Artola, 2000; Larrinaga, 1999; Garate and Martín, 1995; Walton, 2000). Where Bilbao looked to England for external inspiration, San Sebastián looked more to France. Where Bilbao's industrial and growth threatened the rustic Basque cultural and ethnic integrity that Sabino Arana and his cohorts idealised by attracting miners and industrial workers from other parts of Spain, San Sebastián's tourism-based economy undermined the preferred vision of the Basques as tough, dour, honest, hard-working exponents of the hard masculine rural virtues. Its economy offered work in hotels, bars, shops and domestic service, presenting a hospitable, friendly but more conventionally civilised, even feminised face of Basque identity (Walton, 2000). We should not over-simplify: there was plenty of unambiguously 'masculine' work in building and related industries, and the 'old town' near the harbour was a stronghold of Basque-speaking fishing families who provided strong support for the PNV as it gathered momentum during the first third of the twentieth century (Castells, 1987; Luengo, 1991; Rodríguez Ranz, 1994). But there were real contrasts, within a shared framework of Basque assumptions, between Guipúzcoa and Vizcaya, San Sebastián and Bilbao; and this was to have consequences for the development of Basque football.

The inland provinces were more purely agricultural and less in tune with external developments, whether emanating from Madrid or overseas. Vitoria, the capital of Alava, had no direct transport link with Bilbao, although it was on the main Paris-Madrid railway route, and remained a classic *ciudad levítica* (frock-coated city, connoting a closed and traditional urban society existing in old-fashioned insulation from the rest of the world), given over predominantly to servicing a rural hinterland, to pro-vincial administration and to garrison and ecclesiastical life (Rivera, 2002). Pamplona had similar preoccupations, constricted as it was behind the town walls until well into the twentieth century: it did not begin to develop significant manufacturing industries until the last quarter of the twentieth century. It was best known for the bull-running and associated revelry at the July fiestas, as communicated to the rest of the Western world by Ernest Hemingway (Ugarte, 1998; for an effective brief summary De Pablo, 1995: pp. 9–11).

Sport and identity in the Basque Country

The key point here is that every Basque province had its own traditions and identity, and the first loyalty of most Basques was to locality and province rather than to the imagined nation, even as the PNV and other advocates of distinctive Basque culture and virtues sought to promote the latter identity and give it political expression. Even the language, which was supposed to play a key role in setting the Basques apart and defining their claim to shared cultural and therefore political nationhood, had at least seven variants (depending on the classification system used) in different parts of the territory, and efforts to introduce a standard version were to serve only to complicate matters further (Castells and Walton, 1998; Kurlansky, 1999). The contrasts between different parts of the Basque country, entailing provincial rivalries that came to be focused through the flagship football teams of the provincial capitals, coupled with the prevalence of more local rivalries at village and small town level, ensured that sporting encounters would be hard-fought and have consequences beyond the immediate outcomes of individual games. This was an environment conducive to the development of a rich tapestry of sporting activity, under the umbrella of a shared overarching Basque identity which came to the fore when local pride was matched against powerful forces elsewhere in Spain, especially Madrid or Barcelona, or when a Basque international team took the field. This occurred six times in 1915–16, when a series of matches was played against Catalonia; twice again in 1930–1, on the same basis; eleven times during 1937–8, when a Basque national side went on tour in Europe, Mexico and Cuba after the Basque Country fell to Franco's forces in the Civil War; once (intriguingly) towards the end of the Franco regime, when a match against Catalonia was played in 1971; and several times between 1976 and 1980. Eventually a regular sequence of matches began from 1990 onwards, in which pride came to be taken in the capacity of the national side to fill San Mamés stadium.[2] Despite the emergence of the national side, and the development of a Basque championship and Cup competition under nationalist auspices between 1925 and 1935, relationships between football and Basque identities were enduringly complicated, especially in the light of the imported status of the game (Walton, 2001; Díaz Noci, 2000; Duke and Crolley, 1996; MacClancy, 1996).

Football entered a well-developed Basque sporting culture, with strong traditions of betting and professionalism in spite of the aura of traditional virtue that Arana's nationalists sought to attach to the established practices. Each provincial capital developed a flagship side that came to dominate not only the city but the province; and Athletic Bilbao, in particular, tracing its foundation date to 1898, laid claim to representing the whole of the Basque Country. Ball's account of Basque football tends to privilege Athletic, despite his understanding of the complexities of Basque football and identity (Ball, 2004). Athletic's claim did not pass unchallenged by Real Sociedad of San Sebastián, which emerged in 1909 as Club Ciclista de San Sebastián, despite Athletic's dominance of Basque football in terms of results and time spent in the top division of the Spanish League after its foundation in 1928 (Walton, 2001; Ball, 2004; Alonso, 1998; Leguineche *et al.*, 1998; Mandiola, 1979; Unzueta, 1999). Osasuna of Pamplona, and Alavés of Vitoria, were later developers and never matched the pretensions of the other provincial capital clubs; but they, too, became the acknowledged emblems of provincial pride, even for those who also had more immediate loyalties to their local clubs. Club Deportivo Alavés was founded in 1920 as Sport's Friends, changing its name to celebrate the province at the beginning of 1921. Osasuna, taking its name from a Basque word connoting health and strength, was also founded in 1920 from an amalgamation of two small existing clubs, making use of local political support to rise swiftly to a position of local and provincial dominance in a town of just over 40,000 inhabitants in 1930 (Caspistegui, 2001). This was part of a pattern whereby football grew impressively in popularity during the first third of the twentieth century, and especially from the 1920s to the outbreak of the Civil War in 1936; but it developed alongside a range of other sporting and commercial leisure activities, rather than replacing or overwhelming them (Walton, 1998; MacAlevey, 2001; Capistegui and Leoné, 2001).

Commercialised sport was developing apace across urban Spain from the later nineteenth century, and the Basque Country was no exception (Pujadas and Santacana, 2001: pp. 148–51). Under these conditions, the absence of overt professionalism in the imported game, until the 1920s (it was formally legalized in 1926) and especially the introduction of the national football league in 1928, together with the apparent lack of a betting culture, may have helped to ease the path to its acceptance in nationalist circles (Pujadas and Santacana, 2001: pp. 162–4). Basque sports provided alternatives that were culturally acceptable to the nationalists and, especially in the case of pelota, reached out to much wider constituencies. Pelota was already well established as a commercial spectator sport by the 1870s, and by the turn of the century it was spreading beyond its Basque roots across urban Spain, with a speculative boom in the provision of *frontones* (courts) with ample spectator accommodation to meet a burgeoning demand in Madrid, Barcelona and smaller cities throughout the country (Pujadas and Santacana, 2001: pp. 152–3). It provided ample opportunity for betting on the course of the game, mainly between individual spectators. From at least 1915 bookmakers employed by the management were facilitating bets for crowds that might easily reach four figures at week-ends in Bilbao or San Sebastián, or when particularly attractive players were performing. This was a sport for individuals or pairs, but it could still canalise hometown or village loyalties, especially as every village had its *frontón* and its eager amateur participants; and it remained the leading revenue-earning sport, week in, week out, right through into the 1930s. Its smaller daily crowds accumulated income for entrepreneurs more gradually and less conspicuously than the much larger fortnightly gatherings of football fans in the new purpose-built stadia that were constructed from 1913 onwards. Bilbao's San Mamés and San Sebastián's Atocha both opened their doors in that year, while Osasuna's Campo de San Juan was inaugurated in 1922 and Alavés's Mendizorroza followed two years later. All were soon capable of attracting crowds several thousand strong to attractive matches (Walton, 1998; MacAlevey, 2001: p. 107; Caspistegui and Leoné, 2001; De Pablo, 1995: p. 134; Gallop, 1930: pp. 230–48). But the evidence of the provincial entertainment tax suggests that in most of the Basque provincial capitals pelota remained much more popular than football. In San Sebastián it generated eight times the revenue of football in 1920, and more than twice as much in 1932, although a brief football boom in 1923–4 gave the imported sport a moment of narrow primacy in the latter year, when revenues were boosted by an international match (Walton, 1998: p. 48). In Pamplona the gaps were considerably wider, as pelota outscored football by more than twelve to one in 1921 and by more than two and a half to one ten years later (Caspistegui and Leoné, 2001, 65) Only in Bilbao was football consistently more popular than pelota after 1921, and here the statistics are based on tickets issued rather than revenue, removing football's competitive advantage (for these purposes) of higher entrance prices (MacAlevey, 2001: p. 101).

Local loyalties were also channelled in a maritime setting by the *regatas de traineras*, races between ocean-going rowing boats which represented the collective strength and pride of maritime communities, and which also generated substantial volumes of betting. These were passing through a difficult phase in Vizcaya by the 1930s, but they still retained great popular support in Guipúzcoa, where the annual grand final in San Sebastián saw the bay of La Concha thronged on all sides with enthusiastic spectators (De Pablo, 1995: pp. 133–5). Beyond this there were the more informal village sports, involving trials of strength between farmers, labourers and their animals, which were again closely associated with betting. They were occasionally brought into Basque festivals in the towns as part of the invention or reinvention of traditions that accompanied the diffusion of Basque nationalism as a political force (De Pablo, 1995: pp. 136–7).

Football also had to make headway alongside a variety of other sports and related activities that were imported or less specifically Basque. Culturally specific variants of road running and bowls sustained widespread interest into the 1930s, and boxing enjoyed a spell of popularity, fuelled by the success of the European heavyweight champion Paulino Uzcudun in 1933. Cycling also developed a strong following by the 1920s, with the inauguration of the Tour of the Basque Country in 1924, which anticipated the Vuelta de Espana by eleven years (De Pablo, 1995: pp. 131–2). Mountaineering and fell walking also had their clubs and devotees from the early twentieth century. They expressed what nationalists and others regarded as a characteristic Basque affinity for the natural world. They were also seen as being conducive to the health of the race, a specific against alcoholism and other vices (Ferrer, 1943; De Pablo, 1995: pp. 126–7). At a more elevated social level there was also an array of imported elite sports, such as golf, polo, tennis, horse racing, motor racing and yachting, whose exclusivity helped divert aristocratic attention from the more plebeian and democratic sport of football within the region, just as had been the case in Madrid at the beginning of the twentieth century (De Pablo, 1995: pp. 125–6; Bahamonde, 2002). And then there was bullfighting, a spectacle rather than a sport, which was viewed askance by nationalists as a vector for corrupting Basque morals by introducing alien Spanish culture into their midst, and by socialists for its cruelty and immorality. Even so, it persisted in attracting larger crowds and accumulating much more impressive entertainment tax revenues than either pelota or football (De Pablo, 1995: pp. 105–6). In San Sebastián bullfighting generated more than fifty times the tax revenues attributed to football in 1917, and although this multiple had fallen to less than 5 in the mid 1920s, it was back to around 8 by 1932 (Walton, 1998: p. 48). In Pamplona the bullfighting revenues generally eclipsed those from sports of all kinds, accounting for 35 per cent of entertainment tax income from all sources in 1918 as against 14 per cent for all sports, and 27 per cent as against 16.5 in 1936, although the figures for 1931 saw the roles temporarily reversed (Caspistegui and Leoné, 2001: p. 60). Bullfighting was an occasional spectacle, a few times a year, demanding elevated prices from the spectators (especially those in the best seats). Its popularity was boosted in San Sebastián by the holiday season (and by large numbers of French excursionists from across the border), and in Pamplona by the formidable popularity of the San Fermin fiestas. In Bilbao, where neither set of special circumstances applied, the contrast was never as striking, as the bulls were ten times as popular as football at the end of the World War I and just over twice as popular in the early 1930s. But this calculation is again based on number of tickets sold, and if the higher admission changes were taken into account the gap would be inflated considerably (MacAlevey, 2001: pp. 101). The belated emergence of something resembling a consumer society, extending beyond the traditional middle classes, in the Basque Country during the 1920s and 1930s brought swelling revenues to all sports and spectacles, including theatres, cinemas and dances. It also generated an increasing diversity of retail outlets and the spread of fashion consciousness through most of the population; and the growing popularity of spectator and participant sport needs to be seen in this broader context (Castells, 1999; Caspistegui and Leoné, 2001: pp. 57–62; Delgado, 2005).

Football and the Basques

But the growing popularity of football in the Basque Country during this period is nevertheless highly significant, not least for what it suggests about issues of identity. It developed slowly during the first two decades of the twentieth century, but then expanded rapidly, not only in the provincial capitals but also in the smaller towns and villages. The earliest stirrings were in Bilbao, under direct British influences, and in 1898 Athletic Bilbao was (on some showings) the second Spanish club to register its identity with the civil government, nine years after Recreativo Huelva in the far south-west, where there was also a strong British influence, in this case associated with the local mines. Over the next decade new foundations focused on Barcelona (1899), Madrid, Seville and the ports of the far north-west. It was not until 1909 that the club that was to become Real Sociedad registered in San Sebastián (it took the name, with the 'Real' prefix accorded by King Alfonso XIII, a regular visitor to the town, in 1910), along with Arenas Guecho, based in a suburban seaside resort on the right bank of the Nervión a few miles outside Bilbao (Pujadas and Santacana, 2001: p. 154). But football in San Sebastián had a longer pedigree, as in 1903 a local side had played against a team from the nearby border town of Irún, and a year later San Sebastián Recreation Club combined football with tennis and Basque sports. After internal conflicts San Sebastián Football Club emerged as a separate entity in 1905, playing against Athletic Bilbao for the first time in 1906. Meanwhile, football continued to develop in Irún, where the two leading sides joined forces in 1915 to form Real Unión. As we saw above, the emergence of Osasuna of Pamplona and Alavés of Vitoria took place a few years later, in the early 1920s, although the first Pamplona football club of which we have evidence was founded in 1907 (Walton, 1999: pp. 268–9; Caspistegui and Leoné, 2001: p. 71).

It took time for the flagship teams of the provincial capitals in Vizcaya and Guipúzcoa to affirm and consolidate their status. A handful of smaller teams in San Sebastián and district were unable to sustain effective competition with Real Sociedad, which developed privileged access to the new Atocha stadium and a useful array of contacts on the local authority. When the club's municipal lease on Atocha was renewed in 1923, after some debate that revealed tense relationships with the lesser clubs, Real's local dominance was assured (Walton, 1999: pp. 274–6). But the rivalry with Real Unión within Guipúzcoa province proved enduring, and it was not until the advent of full-scale professionalism in the 1930s, as the new national league became firmly established, that the club from the smaller town fell back into obscurity. Something similar occurred with Athletic Bilbao and Arenas Guecho: the latter was never able to command the crowds and weight of influence that Athletic quickly attained, but it remained a significant playing rival, with considerable competitive success, until the advent of full-scale professionalism. The smaller clubs of the industrial left bank of the Ría de Bilbao, such as Barakaldo and Sestao, both of which were founded during World War I, always lived in Athletic's shadow (MacAlevey, 2001: pp. 109–10; Beascoechea, 2002).

It was not until the early1920s that football became popular enough to start to challenge the hegemony of existing sports and pastimes and to become an attractive commercial proposition in its own right; and it is no coincidence that it was also at this point that the relationships between provincial and sporting identities became crystallised into particular clubs. The breakthrough years were very similar in all the Basque provinces that have so far attracted researchers: we still await a study of Vitoria and Alavés, although Santiago de Pablo of the Universidad del País Vasco is currently supervising a research project on this theme. The entertainment tax receipts for the Atocha ground in San Sebastián, which were dominated by the takings at Real Sociedad's home matches, quadrupled between 1920 and 1922, nearly doubled again in the following year, fell away slightly in 1924 and returned to hovering around the 1922 level for the next decade, as the advent of the national League failed to make an impression (Walton, 1998: p. 48). Athletic Bilbao more than quadrupled its tax yield between 1919 and 1921, adding another forty per cent to the total in 1923 before again falling back to the 1921 levels until 1927. In this case, however, there was a renewed surge in ticket sales with the advent of the League, returning to the 1923 level in 1928 and growing by a further 50 per cent at the start of the 1930s, to sustain a level more than double that of Real Sociedad (MacAlevey, 2001: pp. 101). In Pamplona the tax receipts from football rose from just under 8 per cent of the total for all commercial sport (excluding bullfighting) in 1921, to more than 25 per cent in 1930 and more than 47 per cent in 1936. At this point it overtook pelota, overwhelmingly its chief rival, temporarily in a year whose statistics were affected by the outbreak of the Civil War on 18 July. The number of tickets sold increased from 9,719 in 1921 to 40,634 ten years later (Caspistegui and Leoné, 2001: pp. 63–5). These developments reflected considerable investment in new or expanded stadia in the early 1920s, supported by the members of local elites who ran the clubs and by the municipalities who recognised the potential for promoting civic pride and external visibility through the promotion of a flagship club. In Bilbao and San Sebastián, at least, where international opposition had visited from the earliest days, the clubs set up a sustained programme of invitations to attractive foreign clubs (including, for example, Newcastle United) to come and display their skills against the locals. The high peak of popularity in the mid–1920s could not be sustained, but the gains of the early 1920s remained permanent and could be built on later; and there was an explosion of activity at small town and village level in the late 1920s as the league structure extended at lower levels within each province (Walton, 1998: pp. 30–1, : pp. 33–4; Walton, 1999: pp. 277–9, 282–4; Caspistegui, 2001: p. 78).

As the popularity of football expanded during this period, it came to be seen as an expression both of Basque identity and of identities within the Basque Country, as provincial, urban and parochial rivalries came to be expressed through football. Football became appropriated as Basque through a negotiation between the global (in the form of the version of globalization associated with the British Empire, formal and informal) and the local, which eventually appeased even the nationalists. The name of Athletic Club de Bilbao (using an English word rather than the Spanish Atlético: it mattered a great deal when the Franco regime imposed the alternative form) was rendered into a distinctive Basque pronunciation by omitting the 'th' and the 'c' in Athletic and the concluding 'b' in Club. Meanwhile the nationalist media were unwilling to use the English vocabulary of terms of art that dominated early descriptions of the game, but they were even more uneasy about adopting the Spanish equivalents that soon began to appear (MacAlevey, 2001: pp. 99, 113; Díaz Noci, 2000). Basque football journalism soon developed, first through expanding column inches in mainstream newspapers like the secular monarchist *El Pueblo Vasco*, which favoured cultural expressions of Basque identity without embracing nationalism. It later extended its influence through specialised sporting publications, beginning with *Excelsior* in 1924, a nationalist sporting paper whose appearance confirmed the reconciliation (and more) between the sophisticated nationalists of Bilbao's bourgeoisie and the imported English game (MacAlevey, 2001: p. 112; Díaz Noci, 2000; and compare Pujadas and Santacana, 2001: pp. 161–2).

It helped that it became possible to identify football with the promotion of health, strength and the future of the Basque race, as a healthy alter-native to spectatorship at the alien spectacles of bullfights or films; and the identification of a distinctive Basque playing style, powerful, forceful and robust, underlined its acceptability to nationalist ideals. Football could also be made to conform, at least rhetorically, to ideals of a classless Basque society in which shared racial and cultural characteristics transcended mere economic divisions, although crowds at the increasingly segregated grounds of the top teams remained predominantly middle-class, with a substantial lower middle-class element at least in Bilbao, and a larger female minority than was usually the case (Walton, 1998: pp. 42–3; MacAlevey, 2001: p. 105; Caspistegui and Leoné, 2001: pp. 66–70). These perceptions were conveniently reinforced by the Basque role in the Spanish national side's success in gaining a silver medal at the Antwerp Olympics in 1920, in the context of a deplorable overall performance by the Spanish athletes, which helped to encourage the wave of investment and popularity that followed (Caspistegui and Leoné, 2001: pp. 75–6). In this case the 'Spanish fury' which enabled the team to overpower the Dutch and Swedish sides was really 'Basque fury', with a prominent role ascribed to Rafael Moreno, 'Pichichi' of Athletic Bilbao, whose early death perhaps helped to cement his reputation as an 'epic hero' after whom the Spanish League's goal-scoring trophy was named in 1953 (MacAlevey, 2001: p. 114; Ball, 2004; Díaz Noci, 2000). This worship of power and strength carried over into representations of the Basque virtues of long-serving players in other teams and provinces, such as Patricio Arabolaza of Real Unión, who was described as noble, manly, vigorous and virtuous on his retirement from the game in 1923 (Walton, 1999: p. 285), or Martín José Muguiro of Osasuna, big, vigorous, self-sacrificing and prepared to play on through injury for the good of the side. The praise heaped upon him by the local media echoed a widespread Basque predisposition in favour of courage, virility and commitment rather than skill (Caspistegui, 2001: pp. 202–4). Contrasts were made between this Basque style of play and the delicate skills ascribed to the Andalucians of Seville in 1923, or the short passing and ball control skills that were associated with the Catalan game when identified with the Portuguese side Casa-Pia at San Sebastián in 1921 (Walton, 1999: p. 285). Even in San Sebastián, where the tensions between Basque, Spanish and cosmopolitan identities were at their most taut, and Real Sociedad changed its name to Donostia F.C., taking the city's Basque name as well as dropping the club's royal affiliation, at the start of the Second Republic in 1931, the shared perceptions of Basque footballing values were as strong as elsewhere (Walton, 1999: p. 288). By the 1930s, with the onset of professionalism, Basque footballers were plying their trade all over Spain, and the Pamplona press (for example) emphasized that the large number of Basque players in the Real Betis side from Seville had given it similar playing characteristics to those of Osasuna (Caspistegui, 2001: p. 213). The Basque diaspora is a strong and recurrent theme in Basque history, and here we find an early example of it in a football context, which was to recur across the ensuing decades.

Although there was general agreement across the Basque provinces about the distinctive virtues of the good Basque footballer, there were also endemic tensions within Basque football, which brought recurrent conflicts between clubs, and within and between regional and provincial associations. The journalism that nourished ideals about Basque football virtues also stirred up conflict and controversy about the outcomes of particular games, sometimes with enduring consequences. The robust Basque playing style sometimes degenerated into mayhem. During the years between 1916 and 1920 (but also previously and subsequently) pitched battles on the field, sometimes involving spectators as well as players, led to contested administrative responses, boycotts and suspensions, with decisions sometimes seeming to follow geographical loyalties rather than the letter of the law. These were endemic problems, fuelled by the fierce rivalry between provinces even more than between localities; and the occasional successful appeals for Basque fraternity to transcend such divisions, and for the national success of one Basque team to be celebrated by adherents of the others, proved to be only temporary reconciliations of the endemic tensions (Walton, 2001: pp. 124–6; Leoné, 2001: pp. 179–92). This applied particularly to Guipúzcoa and Vizcaya, and the enduring rivalry between Athletic Bilbao and Real Sociedad, which lasted until the latter were relegated in 1935 and resurfaced when they returned to the top division a generation later, remains the most significant division within Basque football. It can sometimes be friendly rivalry, open to mutual aid in time of crisis, but it is not to be taken lightly, fuelled as it is by Athletic's special claim to virtue in signing only Basque players (although the definition has become increasingly flexible) and to be the true representative of the Basque nation on the football field, thereby being entitled to cream off the best Basque players. This rivalry between clubs is also between cities and provinces, and it is a constant reminder of a key dimension of division beneath the façade of Basque unity. There are, of course, many others, not least on the political front (Walton, 2001; Ball, 2004).

Concluding thoughts

The developments treated here foreshadow the interesting current situation of Basque football, although a lot of work needs to be done on the neglected years of the Franco dictatorship. On the one hand, we have Athletic Bilbao cleaving to its now unique tradition of hiring only Basque players, although definitions of 'Basque' have shifted in recent years. Now that Yorkshire County Cricket Club have sold the pass this is perhaps the only remaining purist stance about the relationship between locality and sporting identity to survive at the highest levels of professional sport, however compromised it may be at the margins, and in spite of Athletic's long tradition of hiring foreign (and in the early days especially British) managers (Russell, 1996; Ball, 2004). On the other hand, we have Real Sociedad of San Sebastián, with its own tradition of hiring foreign players and managers, breaking very quietly in 2003–4 with its own practice of not signing players from the rest of Spain, although Boris sounded more like a Russian than a mercenary from Asturias. But the club then started the 2004–5 season with a new Basque manager, born in Bilbao, and a professed determination to focus more on players from the *cantera* (the 'quarry' of local talent), with the result that seven of the starting line-up in the first match of the season were Basque. The club website indicates that the squad soon after the start of the season included a Turk, a Russian, a Serb, a Frenchman, and two Brazilians, one of whom was in Brazil for the previous two seasons, the other, Rossato, newly signed from Porto by the new Basque manager, José María Amorrortu. Boris has been loaned out: he was a regular in the 2003–4 season, and an under-21 international, but it does not seem that the break with tradition was motivated by the need to sign an exciting prospect who could not be allowed to escape. Two South Americans and a Korean international were sent out on loan, and the Holland international Sander Westerveld went to Real Mallorca. Osasuna and Alavés trade globally too, and the Basque football diaspora continues, as Javier De

Pedro and Xabi Alonso left Real Sociedad for Blackburn Rovers and Liverpool, while Arteta has moved in the opposite direction, returning to his home town from Glasgow Rangers.

The ideas about football and Basqueness which have been discussed in this chapter were not the product of a fleeting historical moment: they are still with us, as are those divisions within Basque society that are expressed through football. The pecking order changes: Alavés have enjoyed a recent spell in the top division and Eibar, a modest small-town side founded as recently as 1944 and with a history spent mainly in third division and regional football, are currently challenging for promotion from a Segunda División in which they have survived doggedly on crowds of fewer than 2,000 since 1987 in a ground that holds just over 5,000. They have enshrined the classic Basque virtues of honest endeavour and rugged defending, and they would make a remarkable addition to a Primera Liga that already contains three Basque sides.[3] Football at the highest levels may have become a global game, but Athletic Bilbao continue to defy the implications of such a development, Real Sociedad negotiate with it in their own way, and the complex nature of the continuing relationship between football and Basque identity across the whole of this nation without a state continues to mount a challenge to easy notions about the globalization of football.

Notes

[1]   I have chosen to use the Spanish rather than the Basque versions of place-names throughout, simply because they are still likely to be more familiar and accessible to readers from outside the Basque Country (Euskadi).

[2]   For this see http://privatewww.essex.ac.uk/~mcruic/EUSKADI.htm, although this is not a complete record, and *El Diario Vasco*, 14 December 2004.

[3]   For Eibar see http://www.sdeibar.es

References

Alonso, J. M. (1998) *Athletic for ever! 1898–1998*. Bilbao: Coronet.
Artola, M. (ed) (2000) *Historia de Donostia/San Sebastián*. San Sebastián: Editorial Nerea.
Bahamonde, A. (2002) *El Real Madrid en la historia de Espana*. Madrid: Taurus.

Ball, P. (2004) *Morbo: The story of Spanish Football*. London: WSC Books, second edn., Chapter 3.

Beascoechea Gangoiti, J. M. (1995) 'Desarrollo urbano y urbanización en la Ría de Bilbao', Doctoral thesis, Universidad del País Vasco.

—— (2002) 'La ciudad segregada de principios del siglo XX. Neguri, un suburbio burgués de Bilbao', *Historia Contemporánea* Vol. 24: pp. 245–80.

Caspistegui, F. J. (2001) 'Osasuna y Navarra entre primera y segunda división', in Caspistegui and Walton (eds) *Guerras Danzadas*, pp. 193–214.

Caspistegui, F. J. and S. Leoné (2001) 'Espectáculos públicos, deportes y fútbol en Pamplona (1917–1940)', in Caspistegui and Walton (eds) *Guerras Danzadas*, pp. 51–86.

Caspistegui, F. J. and J. K. Walton (eds) (2001) *Guerras danzadas. Fútbol e identidades regionales y locales en Europa*. Baranain, Navarra: EUNSA.

Castells, L. (1987) *Modernización y dinámica política en la sociedad guipuzcoana de la Restauración, 1876–1915*. Madrid: Siglo XXI.

Castells, L. (ed) (1999) *El rumor de lo cotidiano*. Bilbao: Universidad del País Vasco.

Castells, L. and A. Elorza (1999) 'Una inmensa fábrica, una inmensa fonda, una inmensa sacristía. (El espacio urbano vasco en el paso de los siglos XIX al XX.)', in Castells (ed) *El rumor*, pp. 13–53.

Castells, L. and J. K. Walton (1998) 'Contrasting identities: North-west England and the Basque Country, 1848–1936', in E. Royle (ed) *Issues of regional identity*. Manchester: Manchester University Press, pp. 44–81.

Díaz Noci, J. (2000) 'Los nacionalistas van al fútbol. Deporte, ideologia y periodismo en los anos 20 y 30'. *Zer. Revista de Estudios de Comunicación* 9: pp. 367–94.

Delgado, A. (2003) 'Fishing industry and fishing "community" in the Basque Country: Bermeo and Lekeitio, Vizcaya, c. 1877–1920'. *International Journal of Maritime History* 15: pp.129–58.

—— (2005) *Gernika-Lumo (1876–1937). Una villa vizcaína entre dos guerras*. Gernika: Ayuntamiento de Gernika, forthcoming.

Duke, V. and L. Crolley (1996) *Football, nationality and the state*. Harlow: Longman.

Elorza, A. (2001) *Un pueblo escogido. Génesis, definición y desarrollo del nacionalismo vasco*. Barcelona.

Ferrer, A. (1943) *Cuestas del Duranguesada*. Bilbao: Imprenta Editorial Moderna.

Gallop, R. (1930) *A book of the Basques*. London: Macmillan.

Garate Ojanguren, M. and J. Martín Rudi (1995) *Cien anos de la vida económica de San Sebastián (1887–1987)*. San Sebastián: Instituto Dr Camino.

González Portilla, M. (ed) (2001) *Los orígenes de una metrópoli industrial: la Ría de Bilbao*. 2 vols., Bilbao: Fundación BBVA.

Kurlansky, M. (1999) *The Basque history of the world*. London: Jonathan Cape.

Larrinaga Rodríguez, C. (1999) *Actividad económica y cambio estructural en San Sebastián durante la Restauración, 1875–1914*. San Sebastían: Dr Camino.

Leguineche, M., P. Unzueta and S. Segurola (1998) *Athletic 100: conversaciones en La Catedral*. Madrid: El País-Aguilar.

Leoné, S. (2001) 'Fútbol e identidad local: las disputas en la Federación Guipzcoana de Fútbol, 1920–1928', in Caspistegui and Walton (eds) *Guerras Danzadas*, pp. 179–92.

Luengo, F. (1991) *La crisis de la Restauración. Partidos, elecciones y conflictividad social en Guipúzcoa, 1917–1923*. Bilbao: Universidad del País Vasco.

MacAlevey, W. (2001) 'Football and local identity: The case of Athletic Club de Bilbao as seen through the growth of its crowds, 1911–1932', in Caspistegui and Walton (eds) *Guerras Danzadas*, pp. 87–118.

MacClancy, J. (1996) 'Nationalism at play: The Basques of Vizcaya and Athletic Club de Bilbao', in J. MacClancy (ed) *Sport, identity and ethnicity*. Oxford: Berg.

Mandiola, J.R. (1979) *Casi un siglo de fútbol en Vizcaya*. Bilbao.

Pablo, S. de (1995) *Trabajo, diversión y vida cotidiana. El País Vasco en los anos treinta*. Vitoria: Papeles de Zabalanda.

Pujadas, X. and C. Sartacana (2001) 'La mercantilización del ocio deportivo en Espana. El caso del fútbol, 1900–1928', *Historia Social* Vol. 41: pp. 147–67.

Rivera, A. (2002) *La ciudad levítica. Continuidad y cambio en una ciudad del interior (Vitoria, 1876–1936)*. Vitoria.

Rodríguez Ranz, J.A (1994) *Guipúzcoa y San Sebastián en las elecciones de la II República*. San Sebastián: Instituto Dr Camino.

Russell, D. (1996) 'Sport and identity: The case of Yorkshire County Cricket Club, 1890–1939', *Twentieth Century British History* 7.

Unzueta, P. (1999) 'Fútbol y nacionalismo vasco', in S. Segurola (ed) *Fútbol y pasiones políticas*. Madrid: Debate.

Ugarte, J. (1998) *La nueva Covadonga insurgente. Orígenes sociales y culturales de la sublevación de 1936 en Navarra y el País Vasco*. Madrid.

Walton, J. K. (1998) 'Reconstructing crowds: The development of Association football as a spectator sport in San Sebastián, 1915–1932', *International Journal of the History of Sport* Vol. 15: pp. 27–53.

—— (1999) 'Football and Basque identity: Real Sociedad of San Sebastián, 1909–1932', *Memoria y Civilización* Vol. 2: pp. 261–89.

—— (2000) 'Tradition and tourism: Representing Basque identity in Guipúzcoa and San Sebastián, 1848–1936', in N. Kirk (ed) *Northern Identities*. Aldershot: Scolar Press, pp. 87–108.

—— (2001) 'Basque football rivalries in the twentieth century: Real Sociedad and Athletic Bilbao', in G. Armstrong and R. Giulianotti (eds) *Fear and loathing in world football*. Oxford: Berg, pp. 119–33.

—— (2003) 'Policing the seaside holiday: Blackpool and San Sebastián from the 1870s to the 1930s', in B. Godfrey, C. Emsley and G. Dunstall (eds) *Comparative histories of crime*. Cullompton: Willan Publishing, pp. 145–58.

PART TWO

FINANCES

PRESENT CHALLENGES AND FUTURE SURVIVAL IN THE ENGLISH FOOTBALL LEAGUE

Babatunde Buraimo and Jessica Macbeth
International Football Institute
University of Central Lancashire

1. Introduction

The English football sector, over the past 20 years, has gone through a series of changes. These changes have presented great opportunities for some football clubs, whilst for others they have presented arduous challenges. The challenges have stemmed from the eradication of cross-subsidisation and more recently the collapse of ITV Digital, a significant buyer of football rights in 2001–02. Added to this the poor financial performances of many English clubs have for some resulted in a spell of financial administration. Whilst analysis and examination at the institutional level can provide an institutional perspective, the consequence and impact for individual clubs is also important. This study provides an institutional perspective of the challenges and survival of clubs within the English football sector, with particular attention being placed on Burnley Football Club in Division One of the Football League[1]. The study therefore focuses on financial, economic and on-field performances of clubs, the relationship between these performances, and the implications for Burnley Football Club. The remainder of the paper is structured as follows. Sections 2 to 4 examine the sources of the challenges facing football clubs, particularly those in Division One of the Football League. Section 5 analyses and discusses the results of the study and assesses the implications for Division One clubs. This is achieved by first of all exploring, in some detail, Burnley Football Club, before then examining aggregate revenue and performance in Division One and the Premier League. The final section provides concluding remarks.

2. Structure and organisation

The structure and organisation of English football has gone through major changes over the past decades. Before 1992 English football was organised as a single league comprising of four divisions with movement between divisions organised through promotion and relegation for the best and worst performing teams respectively. In the lowest division, Division Four, poor performance meant relegation from the Football League and such clubs were duly replaced by the best performing clubs from a feeder league subject to certain criteria. In Division One, the best performing clubs were rewarded with entry into one of two European competitions, the European Champion Clubs' Cup and the UEFA Cup. A third European competition, the European Cup Winners Cup, was also available but was for clubs who had won their premier cup competition; in the case of English Football, the FA Cup. The organisation of English football as a single league meant that revenue generated by the league from a variety of sources including marketing, sponsorship and broadcasting were shared amongst all its members. Revenue sharing was effectively a means of cross-subsidising less profitable clubs. League authorities have generally used revenue sharing as a means of potentially addressing any competitive imbalance that may exist amongst teams. The extent to which it achieved its aim, however, has been debated. Fort and Quirk (1995), in their review of cross-subsidisation, conclude that cross-subsidising does not address competitive imbalance and this is more likely, under the current organisation of leagues, to be achieved through salary capping.

Whatever the intentions and achievements of cross-subsidisation in English football, the dominant clubs in Division One objected to the mechanism. The issues of cross-subsidising raised the serious threat of a breakaway league and to prevent this, the League agreed for those clubs in Division One to share 50% of the revenue generated by the league from marketing sponsorship and broadcasting, whilst 25% was shared by those clubs in Division Two. Clubs in Division Three and Four then shared the remaining 25%. The discontent, however, grew further and in 1992 the FA Premier League was established with 22 clubs[2] from Division One. The remaining three divisions of the Football League were renamed Division One, Division Two and Division Three and the system of promotion and relegation continued. The only real change to ensue was the cessation of cross-subsidisation between divisions. Revenue generated by the FA Premier League was now retained and shared by those 22 clubs. In addition to marking the end of cross-subsidisation, the FA Premier League also took advantage of the potential that existed in the broadcasting market (Dobson and Goddard, 2001).

3. The broadcasting market

Prior to 1992, live broadcasting of English football was limited. The broadcasting rights were sold to the state and commercial terrestrial broadcasters, BBC and ITV. The presence of competition in the broadcasting market however, did not result in competition for rights and, instead, BBC and ITV were able to establish a bilateral monopsony [buyer's monopoly] which suppressed the rights' value (Cowie and Williams, 1997). The two-year agreement in 1983 was for 10 live matches per year and was worth £5.2 million. The Football League, aware that the true market value of rights was being suppressed, failed to come to an agreement with the broadcasters for the renewal and during the first half of 1985, no live league football was broadcast. An agreement was eventually reached during the second half of the season and the rights were sold for £1.3 million. For the following two seasons, the rights value was increased to £6.2m, however, in real terms this was a reduction as price per match had reduced from £260,000 to £220,000 per match.

As with many cartels, agreeing a set of binding rules is difficult and in 1988, ITV negotiated a 4-year agreement with the Football League. The agreement was for £44m at an average cost of £610,000 per match but this, significantly, was at the exclusion of the BBC. The value of football rights was now beginning to reflect their market worth. Whilst rights' values were now increasing, the Football League, however, restricted the exposure of football on television. The key concern was that too much exposure on television might harm live attendances, the main revenue source for the clubs. The breakaway of the Premier League in 1992, however, tested this theory. BSkyB, a satellite broadcaster, acquired the rights to live Premier League matches at an unprecedented cost of £210m for five years. Whilst penetration within UK households was limited because of BSkyB's satellite platform, live televised football nevertheless increased from a modest 11 games per season between the 1988–89 and 1991–92 seasons to 60 matches per season between 1992–93 and 2001–02. The Football League's concerns of over-exposure were unfounded. Increased television exposure not only increased television audience ratings, but stadia attendances during this period also improved. Football clubs in the FA Premier League were and have since been faced with the problem of capacity constraint. Baimbridge, Cameron and Dawson (1996) analysed the impact of satellite broadcasting on football attendance during the 1993–94 season. Their results found that matches broadcast on Monday had the effect of reducing attendances by 15% whilst those broadcasted on Sunday had no effect on stadia attendances. An alternative and more likely interpretation of their results is that satellite broadcasting of football matches in the FA Premier League does not affect attendance and the changes in attendance that were reported are more likely to result from scheduling — matches schedule for weekday as opposed to weekend when leisure time is more abundant[3].

Since 1992, clubs in the FA Premier League have enjoyed levels of income which have not been afforded to those clubs in the Football League. Income from broadcasting has increased substantially and as a direct consequence of television exposure, marketing and sponsorship have also increased. Table 1 shows the increase in revenue in the FA Premier League from the 1992–93 to 2007–08 seasons.

Table 1   Rights fee for live televised football in the FA Premier League from 1992 to 2008

Contract Period	Number of live matches	Annual rights fee £m
1992–93 to 1996–97	60	38.3
1997–98 to 2000–01	60	167.0
2001–02 to 2003–04	66	343.0
2004–05 to 2007–08	138	341.3

Adapted from Baimbridge *et al.* (1996), TV Sports Markets (various issues)

Whilst FA Premier League clubs have benefited from increased broadcasting and marketing revenue, clubs in the Football League have collectively experienced reductions in match day and commercial revenue. For example, during the 1998–99 season, clubs in the Football League collectively generated £136 million and £110 million in match day and commercial revenue respectively. Notwithstanding increases during the intervening seasons, match day and commercial revenue reduced to £97 million and £80 million respectively in 2001–02. The decline in traditional sources of revenue and the success of televised football in the FA Premier League saw the Football League look to broadcasting as a solution.

The successful alliance between BSkyB and the FA Premier League provided the broadcaster with a significant volume of live football which attracted large audiences, however, the combination of only 60 matches and increased broadcast space meant that BSkyB was still willing to acquire sports rights for programme content and whilst live Football League games were not able to match the quality of those presented by the Premier League, it enabled the broadcasters to increase their portfolio of sports content. In 1996–97, BSkyB and the Football League entered an agreement to broadcast live matches, of which 55 were broadcasted in 1996–97 and 65 in subsequent seasons until 2000–01. The income from broadcasting, however, has not been to the same extent as that of the Premier League.

BSkyB dominance of live televised football had attracted the attention of other broadcasters. The state broadcaster, BBC, was not able to compete for live football and duly played a supporting role to BSkyB by broadcasting recorded highlights of matches. The two broadcasters also shared the rights to the FA Cup. And whilst ITV dominated the transmission of European football, it had been squeezed out of the domestic football market. In 2001–02 ITV embarked on a very aggressive attempt to acquire a share of the domestic football market. The alliance between BSkyB and the FA Premier League meant that the only domestic rights available to ITV were those of the Football League. The rights acquisition was reported to cost £315m over 3 years and gave ITV access to matches in all three divisions of the Football League[4]. The expansion of the broadcasting spectrum and the introduction of digital transmission meant that ITV would broadcast the majority of these matches on the newly established digital platform, owned by its subsidiary company ITV Digital (formerly ON

Digital). As with all non-terrestrial platforms with access charges, the greatest challenge facing broadcasters is market penetration. Whilst the entire UK population has free access[5] to the terrestrial platform, access to satellite and digital platforms is constrained by installation and subscription charges. It had taken BSkyB 10 years to improve its subscriber base from 2 million in 1992 to 10 million in 2002 and this was achieved with no competition in the pay-television market and exclusive access to live domestic football rights.

ITV Digital on the other hand faced competition from an already well-established pay-television operator, and had access to domestic football rights that were inferior to those of the FA Premier League. When transmission of Football League matches began in 2001–02, average audience ratings for matches broadcast in 2001–02 was 33,000 compared with BSkyB's average audience of 1.2 million in the same season. In fact the audience ratings for some matches were very poor. For example, the audience ratings for two matches, Sheffield Wednesday vs. Coventry City and Wolverhampton Wanderers vs. Manchester City, were so low that the British Audience Research Board's[6] measurements for both matches were zero. Given the annual cost of acquiring the rights, the cost per audience is an estimated £53,000. ITV Digital were quick to realise the consequence of paying over the market price for Football League matches and duly tried to renegotiate the agreement. The Football League rejected offers of renegotiations by the broadcaster and eventually ITV Digital went into administration before the conclusion of the 2001–02 season.

Member clubs in the Football League have managed and responded to the broadcasting crisis in different ways. For some clubs, the collapse of ITV Digital meant administration. Bradford, Ipswich and Leicester are examples of Division One clubs to have faced a spell in administration. The effects of spiralling debt and a loss of a major revenue source meant there was no alternative to administration, particularly since some clubs had effectively spent the ITV Digital revenue in full expectation of it being received. Others engaged in a cost-cutting exercise which saw the reduction of team squads and wages. The overall effect was a reduction in the ratio of wages to revenue. Buraimo, Simmons and Szymanski (2004) provide an account of the consequences and clubs' responses to the crisis. They report a downward adjustment in the ratio of wages to revenue from approximately 1 in 2000–01 to approximately 0.7 in 2001–02, a consequence of a loss in broadcasting revenue. The broadcasting market and the breakaway of the FA Premier League has put the Football League in difficulty and provided even greater challenges for its members. Whilst these external forces may be beyond the influence of the Football League, some of the challenges its constituent clubs face are internal and within their grasp. The following section examines these.

4. Managing football's resources

FA Premier League football has seen a significant increase in revenue, particularly from broadcasting. Added to this, clubs in the Premier League have also benefited from the increased attendances too. Since the advent of the League in 1992, attendances have risen dramatically that nowadays, demand for many Premier League matches outstrips supply; a problem of capacity constraint. The problem of capacity constraint can be addressed by either increasing prices to regulate and reduce demand to the same level as supply, or to engage in stadia development. The issue of price and price elasticity of demand has been researched extensively in the literature (Bird, 1982; Simmons, 1996; Forrest, Simmons and Feehan, 2002). Many of the studies have reported price elasticity to be inelastic as well as elastic. The dilemma with these assertions is that, given that football clubs are effectively monopolists, price elasticity should be (close to) unity. Forrest *et al.* (2002), using the travel cost approach, show that this is the case for some clubs. Their approach, unlike previous studies, includes not only the price of attendance but also the cost of travel. They found that price elasticity of demand for Premier League football was in fact closer to unity than previously thought. This suggests that management of price for some clubs in the FA Premier League is appropriate and informed. Similar questions should be asked of Division One clubs, both collectively and at the club level. The lack of research on price elasticity at this level raises questions on how decisions regarding ticket prices are actually made. Are pricing policies fully informed or are they ad hoc?

Similarly with wages, Hall, Szymanski and Zimbalist (2002) examine the impact of payroll on performance in Major League Baseball (MLB) and English football. Their study showed that whilst in MLB, causality ran in both directions — increases in wages caused performances to improve and improvements in performance caused wages to improve — causality ran from wages to performance in English football. Furthermore their study showed that the effect of wage increases on performance in English football was extremely high. Using end-of-season positions from 1974 to 1999, they provide an analysis of the relationship between team wages and team performance, and average team wages and average team performance. They report correlation coefficients of 0.74 and 0.94 respectively, providing strong evidence of the link between wages and performance. Hall *et al.*'s (2002) analysis of football was an aggregated response for all English professional football clubs. An appropriate question is whether the wage-performance relationships by division are similar or do some divisions extract better performances for their wages whilst others fail to do so.

The literature on professional team sport has also recognised that the market areas in which a club is based will have a significant influence on how well it performs. This is one of the key driving forces behind revenue sharing in North American professional team sports — the realisation being that if market forces were allowed to prevail, teams in small market areas with smaller opportunities to generate revenue will not be able to compete effectively with large market teams, who will use their market buying powers to acquire the best playing talents in the league and consequently destroy competitive balance (Zimbalist, 2002). Whilst small market teams in English football do not benefit from the same level of protection as their North America counterparts, the effects of market power in sport are not fully understood. For example, does having a monopolist within the local market actually benefit football clubs, or does the presence of other rival football clubs, in higher, lower or the same division, create positive or negative externalities; and how important is the concentration and composition of the population within a given area in improving revenue? Such questions have not been adequately addressed within the literature and an understanding of these issues can serve football clubs in improving their management decision-making. With regards to rival clubs, Baimbridge *et al.*'s (1996) analysis of attendance in the FA Premier League suggests that the presence of other rivals within the same market improves attendances for all matches by an average of 27%: however, it is unclear how they define rivals. For clubs in Division One, it would be particularly interesting to examine the impact of having other football clubs of the same divisional status, as well as higher and lower divisional statuses.

This section has highlighted three key issues relating to managing football clubs' resources — ticket prices, wages, and the market. It is these three issues that form the basis of our analysis and discussion in the context of Burnley Football Club.

5. Analysis and discussion

As noted earlier, and by way of an example of the challenges and the survival issues facing some clubs in the Football League, some of the analysis and discussions on attendances, performance and ticket pricing policy focuses on Burnley Football Club. The club was promoted to Division One of the Football League at the end of the 1999–2000 season. They have remained in this division since then but have suffered a gradual decline in performance. Similarly they have experienced a clear fall in home attendances over the last four seasons. The average home attendance for Burnley Football Club fell from 16,234 in 2000–01 to 12,520 in 2003–04. Figure 1 shows the rate of decline in average attendance compared with the increasing average attendances in Division One from the 2000–01 to the 2003–04 season.

Figure 1 [page following] clearly shows that the fall in average attendance of Burnley Football Club is contrary, and quite significantly so, to that of the average Division One club. The most logical reason for the fall in average attendances for the club is its declining performance in Division One during this period. Figure 2 [page following] shows that the decline in performance, as measured by the total points at the end of the season, mirrors the decline in average attendance to some extent.

The senior management team at Burnley Football Club recognised a number of more specific incidents during and after the 2002–03 season that led to their supporters becoming dissatisfied. Despite good performances in both cup competitions the climax to the season was worse than expected and Burnley Football Club finished 16th in Division One, compared to 7th in the two preceding seasons, resulting in a large

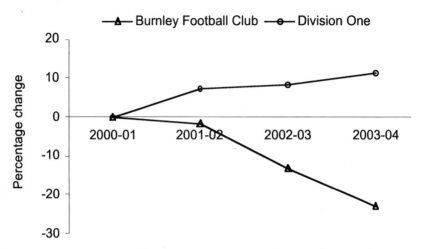

Figure 1   Percentage change in average attendances for Burnley
                Football Club and Division One clubs between 2000–01
                and 2003–04. Base year 2000–01.

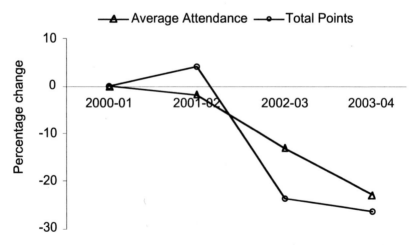

Figure 2   Percentage changes in average attendance and total points
                for seasons 2000–01 to 2003–04 for Burnley Football Club

group of supporters became disgruntled and dissatisfied (Abis, 2003). The crucial events in terms of supporter dissatisfaction occurred at the end of March 2003. After a run of poor results in the league, the management team admitted that any ambitions to reach the play-offs were not going to be realised and the season was effectively over. Supporters seemed even more pessimistic and began to fear a relegation battle despite having reached 49 points at this stage (Scholes, 2003). The following week saw the club loan out a key player to a fellow Division One club in order to cut costs. This activity on transfer deadline day angered supporters; and the announcement and nature of the club's new season ticket prices for the 2003–04 season the following day only served to increase their dissatisfaction (Scholes, 2003). It has since been revealed that due to this culmination of incidents, "season ticket sales were down 3,000 on the previous season" (Abis, 2003: p. 4).

Although it was anticipated that the club suffered a loss of 3,000 season ticket sales between the 2002–03 and 2003–04 seasons, the difference in average attendances between these seasons is less severe. Table 2 shows that average attendance fell by 1588 between the 2002–03 and 2003–04 seasons.

This suggests that despite the loss of season ticket sales not all of these supporters were necessarily 'lost'. Instead there was a partial switch from demand for season tickets to match-by-match demand, a switch that would not be in the interests of any football club. More information on the level of season ticket sales and their pricing policy would reveal a more thorough picture in order to advance this analysis. The club announced their season ticket package for the 2004–05 season in March

Table 2   Average attendances at Burnley Football Club
from 2000–01 to 2003–04

Season	2000–01	2001–02	2002–03	2003–04
Average attendance	16234	15948	14108	12520
Difference from previous season	3297*	−286	−1840	−1588

* This increase in attendance is more than likely due to promotion to
Division 1 the previous season.

2004 and it seems that efforts have been made to engage in discussion with supporters regarding some pricing issues (Burnley Football Club, 2004). As with many clubs, their pricing policy may not necessarily reflect a thorough knowledge and understanding of their market. The club is currently taking the first fundamental steps in market research in an effort to become more aware of the composition and concentration of their market, their supporters, and the nature of demand for season and match-day tickets. In doing so the club will be able to make more informed decisions regarding changes in pricing policy and, depending on the club's performance of course, should be in a better position to prevent dramatic falls in season ticket sales.

By way of contextualisation, this section has so far offered a brief exploration of attendances, performance and issues regarding ticket pricing policy for Burnley Football Club. In terms of performance, on face value a lower final league position or lower total points than the previous season represents a decline in performance, particularly as far as supporters are concerned. However, to offer a more complete examination of the performance of a club it is important to take the wage bill, and the degree to which wages are being managed effectively, into account. The remainder of this section does so first in order to compare Division One of the Football League with the Premier League and second, in order to locate the Burnley Football Club within Division One.

In examining the degree to which wages are being effectively managed by the constituent clubs of Division One, we construct an econometric model, details of which are shown in Appendix A. The model simultaneously analyses, firstly, the effects of an increase in wage on performances and, secondly, the effects of an increase in performance on revenue. During the first stage, the model enables an assessment on how management in different divisions are able to convert wages into on-field performances. At the second stage, the model addresses how on-field performances are being effectively converted into revenue. Are fans responding positively to performances by attending in greater number, buying more merchandising and is there an increase in non-gate revenue, such as marketing, sponsorship, advertising and corporate hospitality, as a consequence?

As a benchmark, two models are developed: one for the Premier League and one for Division One of the Football League. This allows for appropriate comparison of efficiency, i.e. the ability to convert wages into on-the-field performance, within the two leagues. The results are interesting for a number of reasons. At the first stage, team wage bill is a strong predictor of performance for both the Premier League and Division One. However, the effect is much higher in the Premier League, indicating that Premier League clubs are more efficient at extracting better on-field performances for a given wage. For example, if the wage bill (or more specifically playing talent) of a Premier League team was improved by one standard deviation at the average — equivalent to increasing the wage by 40% — this results in a marginal improvement of 0.15 point-per-game or an increase of 5.6 points in any given season (0.15 x 38 games). In Division One, an equivalent improvement in the wage bill improves end-of-season performance by 0.13 points-per-game or 6 points in 46 games. These measures indicate that Premier League clubs on average are 31% more efficient at converting wages into on-field performances when compared with clubs in Division One. At the second stage, the effect of on-field performance on club revenue shows that, in contrast to the first stage, the performances of clubs in Division One have a stronger effect on revenue than those clubs in the Premier League. The analysis shows that an improvement in performance by one standard deviation, or by 30%, improves revenue by 52%. Contrasting this with the Premier League, improvements in performance have no significant effect on revenue. The lack of significance in the Premier League can be explained by the fact that the majority of matches, irrespective of how well or how poorly the home team is performing, are at or nearing capacity.

For Division One clubs, an appropriate strategy to adopt is one in which the wage-performance relationship is improved — i.e. generating the same performance for reduced level of wage. This is in fact the situation at Burnley Football Club. During the three seasons in the sample period, the analysis shows that it outperformed the divisional average on two of these. This suggests that the club is more efficient than others in the Division. In contrast, however, the club is not as effective in generating revenue for a given improvement in performance when compared with the average club in the division. This is obviously an area that the management should review.

6. Conclusion

This study explores the current challenges facing football clubs outside the FA Premier League in England and the effects of a change in structure and organisation, broadcasting arrangements, management of wages and other resources. Much of the evidence explored shows that clubs in Division One of the football league are facing challenging issues which continue to affect future survival. This is particularly the case when the issues of wage, performance and revenue management are taken into consideration. Comparisons with the FA Premier League indicate that football clubs in Division One are not effectively managing their wage-performance relationship, and improvements should be sought at the league level.

With respect to Burnley Football Club, the evidence suggests that emphasis should be placed on effective management of pricing policy which, based on the information provided, could be improved to make better use of historical pricing data. Effective assessment of consumer response to price is necessary. With regard to the wage-performance relationship, Burnley Football Club outperforms the average of Division One and wages are not specifically a problem when compared with the Divisional average. More effective information on the impact of market effects and size is also needed. Such information will provide the club with better insight as to whether it is maximising the returns given the size and composition of its immediate market.

Notes

1   At the beginning of the 2004/2005 season Division One of the Football League was renamed the Championship; and Division Two and Division Three of the Football League were renamed as League One and League Two, respectively. This paper refers to league names as they were prior to the beginning of the 2004/2005 season.
2   The number of FA Premier League clubs was subsequently reduced from 22 teams to 20 in the 1995–96 season.
3   The actual scheduling of matches on weekdays is primarily due to broadcasting arrangements. The actual broadcasting of matches per se is therefore not responsible for reduction and the reduction can be attributed to scheduling rather than to broadcasting.

4   The agreement between ITV Digital and the Football League was for 65 Division One matches and 8–15 Divisions Two and Three matches along with Division Two and Three play-off finals.
5   All television owners have to purchase a licence; however, access to programme content thereafter is free.
6   The British Audience Research Board is an organisation jointly owned by the major broadcasters including BBC, ITV and BSkyB and is responsible for measuring audience ratings for programmes. Audience ratings are measured using panel households and establishment surveys. These are combined to provide an estimate of the number of household viewers. The measurements do not include viewers in public places such as public houses and bars.

References

Abis, E. (2003) Marketing research proposal — To identify whether the level of satisfaction of Burnley FC supporters is influenced more by the performance of the football team or by the service provided by its commercial staff, unpublished.

Baimbridge, M., Cameron, S. and Dawson, P. (1996) 'Satellite television and the demand for football: A whole new ball game?', *Scottish Journal of Political Economy* Vol. 43, No. 3: pp. 317–333.

Bird, P. (1982) 'The demand for league football', *Applied Economics* Vol. 14, No. 6: pp. 637–650.

Buraimo, B., Simmons, R. and Szymanski, S. (2004) *The financial crises in English Football.* Imperial College: Mimeo.

Burnley Football Club (2004) 'Burnley FC announce Season Ticket Package for 2004/05'. At http://www.burnleyfootballclub.premiumtv.co.uk/page/SeasonTickets/0,,10413,00.html. Accessed on 22 July, 2004.

Cowie, C. and Williams, M. (1997) 'The economics of sports rights', *Telecommunications Policy* Vol. 21, No. 7: pp. 619–634.

Dobson, S. and Goddard, J. (2001) *The economics of football.* Cambridge: Cambridge University Press.

Forrest, D., Simmons, R. and Feehan, P. (2002) 'A spatial cross-sectional model of elasticity of demand for soccer', *Scottish Journal of Political Economy* Vol. 49, No. 3: pp. 336–356.

Fort, R. and Quirk, J. (1995) 'Cross-subsidisation, incentives and outcomes in professional team sports leagues', *Journal of Economic Literature* Vol. 33: pp. 1265–1299.

Hall, S., Szymanski, S. and Zimbalist, A. (2002) 'Testing causality between team performance and payroll: the cases of Major League Baseball and English soccer', *Journal of Sports Economics* Vol. 3, No. 2: pp. 18–38.

Scholes, T. (2003) '2002/03 Review Part Six — It all comes to a sudden end', Clarets
    Mad. At http://www.clarets-mad.co.uk/news/loadfeat.asp?cid=ED14&id=
    105559. Accessed on 13 August, 2004.
Simmons, R. (1996) 'The demand for English league football: a club-level analysis',
    Applied Economics Vol. 28, No. 2: pp. 139–155.
TV Sports Markets (Various issues). London: Elman Publishing.
Zimbalist, A. S. (2002) 'Competitive balance in sports leagues: an introduction', *Journal
    of Sports Economics* Vol. 3, No. 2: pp. 111–121.

Appendix A

To model the relationship between teams' wage bills, performances and revenue, an
econometric model using Two Stage Least Squares is adopted. At the first stage, the
relationship between wage bill and performance is examined i.e. for a given
improvement in the wage bill, how much does on-the-field performances improve
by? At the second stage, the relationship between improvements in performance
and corresponding improvements in revenue are determined. These relationships
are shown in equation 1.

$$
\left.\begin{array}{l}
performance_{it} = f(wages_{it}) \\
revenue_{it} = g(performance_{it})
\end{array}\right\} \qquad (1)
$$

where $wages_{it}$, $performance_{it}$ and $revenue_{it}$ are the wage bill, end-of-season performance
and revenue of team i in season t. Given that the wage bills increase each season
by some inflationary measure, each team's wages is divided by the average for that
season in order to remove this inflationary increase. Therefore by construction, the
average wage bill in any given season is 1. Also to enable comparisons with teams
in the Premier League who play 38 matches per season compared with 46 in Division
One, end-of-season performances is taken as the ratio of points at the end of the
season to the number of games played. In order to linearise some of the relationships
between the variables and be able to report percentage rather than absolute changes,
the logarithm of revenue is used. This then provides us with equation 2.

$$
\left.\begin{array}{l}
performance_{it} = f(wages_{it}) \\
\ln(revenue_{it}) = g(performance_{it})
\end{array}\right\}
$$

or

$$
\ln(revenue_{it}) = g(performance_{it}(wages_{it})) \qquad (2)
$$

Fixed effects are used to capture and control for unobserved effects specific to each
club such as prices, income and market characteristics. Summary statistics for the
above variables are reported in Table A1 with the results of the model in Table A2.

Table A1:   Summary statistics

	Mean	Standard deviation	Minimum	Maximum
Variable	FA Premier League			
Revenue (£m)	34.3	30.2	4.5	181.0
$performance_{it}$	1.4	0.4	0.6	2.4
Absolute wage (£m)	16.7	13.0	2.7	70.0
$wage_{it}$	1	0.4	0.3	2.3
	Division One of the Football League			
Revenue (£m)	7.5	5.4	1.7	34.2
$performance_{it}$	1.4	0.3	0.7	2.3
Absolute wage (£m)	5.2	4.0	1.0	25.4
$wage_{it}$	1	0.5	0.3	3.1

Table A2:   Results

	Premier League		Football League Division One	
	Coefficient	Absolute t Statistic	Coefficient	Absolute t Statistic
Variables	First stage. Dependent variable			
$performance_{it}$	0.37	3.45*	0.26	3.76*
Constant	1.00	9.33	1.11	15.42
n	179		200	
Adjusted R^2	0.81		0.44	
F test for fixed-effects	1.60		1.75	
	Second stage. Dependent variable			
$performance_{it}$	0.78	1.04	1.74	2.82*
Constant	2.15	2.10	−0.59	0.70
n	179		200	
Adjusted R^2	0.45		0.32	
F test for fixed-effects	1.94		2.06	

* Significant at the 1% level

A CRITICAL ANALYSIS OF THE STATE OF SCOTTISH FOOTBALL: REASONS, EXCUSES AND SOLUTIONS[1]

Stephen Morrow
University of Stirling

Introduction

To remark that Scottish football has endured a difficult few years is something of an understatement. The experiment of employing a foreign coach for the national side ended in failure, resulting in the replacement of the former Germany manager, Berti Vogts, with Walter Smith, a man steeped in the Scottish game. Off the field, competent administration of one of the fundamental principles of sporting competition — promotion and relegation — seems annually to be beyond those charged with running Scotland's top division. More fundamentally, the very existence of many top clubs is uncertain. For several months during season 2003/04, three Scottish Premier League (SPL) clubs (Dundee, Livingston and Motherwell), a quarter of the league, experienced a spell in administration, while other clubs including Dunfermline Athletic[2] and Heart of Midlothian[3] were required to take or threaten drastic action in the form of wage cuts and asset sales to avoid a similar fate (Morrow, 2004).

Crisis? What crisis?

While it is true that individual clubs in Scotland have experienced financial crises on many occasions in the past, to many observers what was witnessed during season 2003/04 was akin to a systemic crisis in Scottish football: a common set of problems afflicting all clubs, with negative financial implications for all; the crisis in one club or group of clubs

183

threatening to damage the financial stability of other clubs (Rimini Group, 2004). Twelve months on, ostensibly the situation looks less severe. Certainly no club has actually gone out of business. That said, and despite avoiding the ten-point penalty that the SPL agreed to impose on any club that had not begun the formal process of coming out of administration by 31st May 2004, February 2005 sees Livingston still in administration as well as finding itself in bottom position in the SPL[4]. Elsewhere a rights issue at Rangers has displaced approximately £50m of debt from the club's balance sheet to the balance sheets of other companies controlled by the club's majority owner, David Murray. The most interesting developments have taken place at Hearts, where Lithuanian businessman Vladimir Romanov has effectively assumed control by acquiring the shares of former Chief Executive Chris Robinson, taking his stake to 29.9%. Already Romanov has withdrawn the club from an agreement to sell its Tynecastle stadium to Cala Management Limited for £22m (Robertson, 2005). Other plans apparently include inviting the Edinburgh business community to invest in the club and challenging the Old Firm of Celtic and Rangers, both on and off the field.

But one must be careful not to generalise from these one-off capital injections and ownership changes. In short, the financial outlook for Scottish football continues to look bleak. For example, despite extensive cost cutting, no SPL club reported a profit for 2003 and to date none has reported a profit for 2004. There remains little prospect of clubs trading their way out of their accumulated levels of debt. Even after the effects of the Rangers rights issue, the combined debt of the twelve SPL clubs is approximately the same as their combined turnover. The annual turnover of two clubs (Celtic and Rangers) equates to about 70% of the total turnover of the SPL. Unsurprisingly this dominance is also apparent on the field: no club outside the Old Firm has won the title since 1984/85.

The roots of the crisis

The very nature of competitive sport can encourage irrationality in business decision-making as directors and managers strive to reach 'the next level'. It is clear that the following sentiments expressed by Rangers Chairman, David Murray, are not peculiar to that club:

I think football has gone through a revolution financially and we as a club were obviously caught up in chasing a dream. Perhaps we spent too much money doing that, but we all bought into it at the time. (quoted in Halliday, 2004: p. 62)

The pressure for success placed on clubs is heightened by financial factors such as the scale of reward on offer to league winners (e.g. Champions' League qualification or promotion), the skewed mechanisms for distribution of revenue sources, and moves away from inter- and intra-league redistri- butive principles. For example, the last decade or so has seen greatly increased importance of television income. This has caused wider polar- isation of wealth, with leagues in larger television markets benefiting from substantially more lucrative television deals. But, within those leagues, much of that income then flows to that marketplace's major clubs. Such market differences have been exacerbated by decisions taken by football's governing body, UEFA, concerning the sporting and financial operation of its competitions (Morrow, 2003: pp. 22–27).

Certainly Scottish clubs have suffered as a result of factors outwith their control. Looking at clubs' cost base, one consequence of the *Bosman* ruling and subsequent modifications to the player transfer market has been to create something akin to a single European market in players (Morris *et al.*, 2003). Scottish clubs do not exist in a vacuum. The mobility of players has resulted in wages — the principal expense of football clubs — being influenced by wage rates in other countries. Hence, clubs in countries like Scotland are squeezed. Income levels are driven primarily by domestic factors; European or other international influences have an effect on the cost base.

That said, on the face of it the SPL's current financial predicament arises more directly from television arrangements demonstrably within the control of clubs themselves. For many observers, the decisions taken in 2001 that resulted in the SPL not renewing its deal with Sky Television and ending up instead with a lesser and shorter deal with the BBC — approximately £8.5m pa compared with £12m pa; two years compared with four — was the single most important explanation of the SPL crisis. In both deals the Old Firm share was approximately 35% of the total revenue, the remainder being divided among the other ten clubs. For clubs outwith the Old Firm there were other related financial consequences, most notably the drop in home attendances at matches shown live by the BBC.

But emphatically the fall in television income does not fully explain the present financial difficulties. For example, it is worth noting that the fall off in income experienced by Scottish clubs — £3.5m pa between the twelve clubs — was quite different in magnitude to that arising out of the collapse of the English Nationwide League's deal with ITV Digital which cost its twenty four clubs approximately £80m per season between them (Plunkett, 2002). It is also worth noting that the published accounts of the SPL clubs for the 2001/02 financial year, the final year of the previous deal with BSkyB, demonstrate that five of the twelve SPL clubs were already technically insolvent at that time — their liabilities exceeding their assets — with a further club, Motherwell, already being in administration (Pricewaterhouse Coopers, 2003).

More generally, football clubs are not the only organisations that exist in rapidly changing environments. One responsibility of any company's directors is to respond to alterations in market conditions and to manage their business risk. Many clubs have given the impression of disregarding financial consequences. Whether self-inflicted or otherwise, the duty of the directors was to respond appropriately to the changed financial circumstances. Instead some clubs have shown a disregard for financial common sense: continuing to live well beyond their means, their profit and loss accounts continuing to show a marked imbalance between income and expenditure.

The main explanation for the lack of profitability within the SPL has been the high level of wage costs (Pricewaterhouse Coopers, 2005). For example, wages represented 76% of turnover for SPL clubs in 2002 (75%, 2001), while three clubs had wages to turnover ratios in excess of 100% — Dundee (154%), Dunfermline Athletic (132%) and St Johnstone (112%). The most recent report on the finances of the SPL suggests that clubs are beginning to manage wages more effectively, noting both an absolute fall in such costs and a highlighting of the importance of the management of wage costs in clubs' annual reports (Pricewaterhouse Coopers, 2005). Despite this welcome trend, and notwithstanding that the fixed nature of players' contracts reduced the ability of clubs quickly to cut costs, it is apparent that cost cutting was not sufficiently aggressive at several clubs. For example, in full cognisance of the figures set out above for 2002, during the autumn of 2003 Dundee Football Club embarked on a high-profile recruitment strategy bringing players of the calibre of Fabrizio Ravanelli and Craig Burley to the club. Less than three months later, on 24 November 2003, Dundee applied to the Court of Session to be put into administration, with debts estimated at £20m. Elsewhere, again despite the figures set out above, Dunfermline Athletic continued to recruit players during the January 2004 transfer window. Three weeks later Dunfermline was forced to ask its players to take a sizeable pay cut to avoid administration.

Such examples do little for the credibility of football as a business. But more than credibility is at stake: one possibility is that the directors of SPL clubs in administration may be investigated for wrongful trading, i.e. where the directors allow a company to continue in business when they knew or ought to have known that there was no prospect of meeting the company liabilities as they fell due (s.214 Insolvency Act 1986). In the words of one expert in this area, "it is not enough for directors to hope that every cloud will have a silver lining ... the prospect of more generous TV viewing fees is not enough, seen in isolation" (Frier, 2004: p. 18). Furthermore, these examples do nothing to preserve the integrity of football competition. With SPL prize money awarded on the basis of final league position, clearly sporting and financial advantages may accrue to clubs that have recruited players they cannot subsequently afford — a point noted by the then Aberdeen Chief Executive, Keith Wyness in a television interview (Sportscene, BBC Scotland, 14 February 2004).

The inescapable outcome of consistently spending more than you earn is debt. Prior to the rights issue at Rangers, the debt of SPL clubs was approximately £190m, well up on the £144m reported at the end of the 2002 financial year (Pricewaterhouse Coopers, 2003) and markedly greater than the £12m reported five years ago at the end of the 1998 financial year (Pricewaterhouse Coopers, 1999). Of course, it is normal and desirable for companies to be funded partly by borrowings, but the debt must be appropriately structured in terms of timescale and its level proportionate to income and profit. The key factor is whether a company is in a position to comfortably service its debt. Questions have been raised about the role of the banks in Scottish football's financial crisis. But when one looks dispassionately at the levels of debt, the financial issue is not whether they should have intervened, but rather why did it take them so long to intervene?

It does not seem unreasonable to suggest that the banks should have been concerned not only with a profitable business opportunity but also with ensuring that its customers' prospective cash flows and profits were proportionate to the lending being provided. The banks must take some of the blame for the present situation, but it ill becomes football club directors to blame the banks for lending them the money in the first place. These directors are experienced businessmen, not individuals in chastened circumstances, forced into the hands of unscrupulous money lenders. Looking ahead, it is difficult to imagine that the banks will make the same mistake again in terms of their lending policies and subsequent monitoring.

Dealing with the crisis

The signing of a £35m four-year television deal beginning in season 2004/ 05 with the Irish broadcaster Setanta to broadcast 38 live matches has provided some respite for clubs (Broadfoot, 2004). Concerns were expressed initially both about the reliance on pay-per-view, a concept that to date has not performed well in European football, and about the financial position and performance of Setanta itself (see, for example, Wilson, 2004; Wilson and Murden, 2004). More recently the company's decision to provide new customers with free access to all games played in February 2005 has been construed by some as an indication of trouble. Such concerns are refuted by the company which maintains that it is "well on track to reach subscription targets [between 80,000 and 100,000 subscribers] set for the first season of our four-year commitment to the Scottish game" (*Daily Record*, 2005: p. 40).

While the new deal is welcome it is important to bear in mind that the annual payment of approximately £8.75m requires to be split twelve ways[5]. To avoid similar problems recurring in the future, clubs' emphasis must remain on the cost base, particularly player wage costs. As well as continuing to reduce the terms and conditions of future contracts, one way forward may be to encourage voluntary wage cuts or wage restraint agreements for players currently under contract, a policy adopted by

Dunfermline[6]. Understandably this may not look an attractive option to players or to the Scottish Professional Footballers' Association union, but it is probably preferable to dealing with the social and financial consequences of yet more clubs going into administration. That said, any such revised agreements would require the most careful professional scrutiny to ensure that they would be honoured in full, not simply postponing the administrative process[7].

Financial realism in clubs should also be demanded by those charged with regulating the game. While ultimately it is the responsibility of individual clubs to manage their business and sporting risks, some regulation of football finance and governance by the authorities is required. The UEFA Club Licensing System, which the SFA is charged with implementing in Scotland, is designed to ensure that the financial management of clubs is effectively monitored and regulated and sets out financial criteria that clubs must meet in order to be permitted to participate in European competitions (UEFA, 2002). National Club Licensing is seen by many, including the SFA, as a modern form of regulation (SFA, 2003). For SPL clubs to be granted a licence for a particular season there are four main requirements within the financial criteria:

- Provision of audited financial statements for the preceding season (para 8.1);
- Confirmation that the club has no overdue payments from transfer activities with other clubs affiliated to national associations and/or league, players or other third authorised third parties (para 8.5.2);
- Confirmation that the club has no overdue payments to employees (para 8.5.3);
- A letter from the club's auditor confirming the previous two points (para 8.5.4).

While a step in the right direction, arguably these requirements are not sufficiently demanding in the present financial climate. For example, clubs are encouraged to prepare budgets, to monitor liquidity, to ensure that they are in a positive equity or net asset position (SFA, 2003). Licensing could be broadened to make these requirements, as well as being introduced more widely. For example, the award of a licence to participate in the SPL could be made conditional on the prior agreement of a club's annual budget. Also, as noted by the Independent Football Commission, the independent regulatory body for the football business in England, in its 2003 annual report, a particular requirement could be placed on clubs to demonstrate their capacity to meet contractual salary costs over the length of a player's contract as well as any transfer fee (IFC, 2004); such a requirement would prevent player purchases of the type entered into by some Scottish clubs during the 2003/04 winter transfer window. Domestic licensing systems have existed for a number of years in other European countries, among them France and Germany, where regulatory bodies such as the Deutsche Fußball Liga (DFL) can impose sanctions, including points deduction and denial of promotion, on clubs which fail to comply with the conditions of the national licence (IFC, 2004). Furthermore, a call for domestic licensing was one of the recommendations made by the Westminster All Party Parliamentary Football Group in its report on English football (All Party Parliamentary Football Group, 2004).

Financial realism should also be demanded of those charged with regulating the game. Some welcome, if belated, progress is apparent in this respect. A decision taken by SPL members in June 2004 resulted in the rule requiring clubs to have a stadium with a capacity of not less than 10,000 before they were eligible for membership of the SPL (SPL, 2003) being replaced from season 2005/06 by the requirement for a stadium with a minimum of 6,000 seats. For the last two seasons the 10,000 seats rule has led to farcical scenes, involving first Falkirk and Motherwell and then Inverness Caledonian Thistle and Partick Thistle. Falkirk MSP, Denis Canavan, noted the irony that all three of the Scottish clubs in administration during season 2003/04 (Motherwell, Dundee and Livingston) voted against the promotion of the financially solvent 2002/03 champions of the First Division, Falkirk, to the SPL on the grounds that it did not meet the stadium criteria (Scottish Parliament, 2004). Twelve months on, before Inverness Caledonian Thistle — whose Caledonian Stadium at that time had a capacity of only 6,000 (2,200 seated) — could take its place in the SPL for season 2004/05, it had to overcome not only the other clubs in the Scottish First Division, but also the SPL's rule book, as well as the apparent inability of some administrators and members of the SPL to understand that rule book; and survive a legal challenge in the Court of Session brought by the club that finished bottom of the SPL, Partick Thistle. Promotion was only secured after agreeing to ground-share with Aberdeen at a cost of £30,000 per game, and a return journey of 200 miles for players, supporters and officials. Fortunately common sense has finally prevailed in this case. Inverness Caledonian Thistle was permitted to return to its own stadium for its home match against Dunfermline on 29 January 2005, that match marking the start of the second half of the SPL programme, after a remarkable 47-day building programme transformed the stadium, enabling it to meet the revised SPL stadium guidelines. The club drew a crowd of 5,449 for the game, more than 2,000 greater than its average attendance for its home marches in Aberdeen.

Scottish football also needs to refocus. The SPL is not and never could be a mark two version of the English Premiership: the financial rewards available in England, particularly from television, will always markedly outweigh those available in Scotland. This financial reality is inescapable. Hence, for the majority of its clubs, the way forward may be to refocus on their community positioning or role. The existing ownership model has demonstrably failed in most of our clubs. One way forward is to widen the ownership of club: for their stakeholder groups — supporters, the local community, local businesses, and local councils — to become more directly involved in the ownership, governance and management of the clubs. Initiatives like Supporters Direct and its encouragement to supporters to set up mutually structured Supporter Trusts to take a stake in their clubs have already shown their value, financially and otherwise, at many clubs (see www.supporters-direct.org.uk). Already there are trusts at 30 of the 42 senior Scottish clubs and this involvement offers some hope for the future of individual clubs. Looking longer term, it may be desirable for clubs to adopt more appropriate legal forms than the conventional limited liability model, which was never designed with the needs of small-scale community-based enterprises like football clubs in mind. In truth the conventional limited liability company only makes sense to many football club stakeholders if all / any profits are immediately ploughed back into the club. The recent creation of a new legal form for social enterprises, the Community Interest Company (CIC), presents an interesting opportunity for clubs, inevitably concerned with both financial and social objectives. What is envisaged is the establishment of firms that have the specific aim of benefiting the community, with any profits earned by the company being spent on community work rather than passed on to shareholders. In addition a CIC's assets are protected against distribution to members or shareholders, and it has increased requirements in terms of transparency and accountability — characteristics that are attractive to football stakeholders.

Irrespective of structure, in moving forward it will be essential that all stakeholders behave in a manner appropriate to football's changed financial circumstances. Key to this in the short term is realism about buying and paying players. Longer term, it is about recognising the need for change. Football's business significance arises out of the game's enduring communal and social appeal. But in the current financial situation there is little merit in blind defence of history or tradition if the consequence is the disappearance of the very thing you are trying to save. Quite simply, there is an urgent need for rational debate involving all of football's stakeholders, debate which must encompass economic and social issues, however immune to resolution these issues seem to be. At a European level this debate needs to be about issues like league restructuring (Moorhouse, 2004; Morrow, 2003). Competitive imbalance and polarisation of wealth within clubs are not unique to Scotland (Rimini Group, 2004). There is an urgent need for UEFA to lead a debate on cross-border initiatives like the Atlantic League or about clubs playing in leagues organised other than under the auspices of their home association. Increasingly it seems that solving the problem of Old Firm dominance would benefit not only those clubs but also all other Scottish clubs. At a domestic level, debate is required about initiatives like restructuring, ground sharing, relocation, involvement in broader multi-sport community complexes and so on; initiatives that might just ensure that football remains significant in Scotland.

Notes

1   This chapter is a development of a paper published in *Scottish Affairs* 'The financial crisis in Scottish football' (Morrow, 2004, No. 47: pp. 48–57). This chapter benefited from responses received to a presentation made at the *International Football Institute Conference*, held at the University of Central Lancashire, Preston in September 2004.

2   The playing staff at Dunfermline Athletic were obliged to accept substantial pay cuts to avoid the club being placed into administration.

3   The then board of Heart of Midlothian indicated that it was seeking to sell its stadium to meet its debts and avoid administration, moving its home matches (average attendance 12,521) to Murrayfield Stadium (capacity 67,500).

4   The Court of Session in Edinburgh granted approval to Motherwell to resume trading as a limited company in April 2004, while both Livingston and Dundee had posted Creditors Voluntary Arrangements before the 31 May 2004 deadline. The prospective owners of Livingston, the Lionheart Consortium, have not yet finalised the takeover of the club, resulting in it being required to apply to the court for a for an extension after being in administration for a year.

5   The first 50% of the revenues from the Setanta deal are split equally between the twelve member clubs. The remainder is divided up according to a club's final league position.

6   According to PKF's 2004 survey of football club finance directors, 83% of SPL clubs have discussed wage capping, with 60% believing it could be introduced effectively (PKF, 2004).

7   One positive feature of wage setting in the SPL is the use of performance related pay. All SPL respondents in the PKF 2004 survey of football club directors claimed to pay at least 10% of their salaries based on performance (PKF, 2004).

References

All Party Parliamentary Football Group (2004) *Inquiry football and its finances.*

Broadfoot, D. (2004) 'Setanta's sums add up to winning deal for SPL', *The Herald*, 27 February: p. 38.

Daily Record (2005) 'Setanta offer free February', *Daily Record*, 31 January: p. 40.

Frier, G. (2004) 'Professional brief', *The Herald*, 23 February: p. 18.

Halliday, S. (2004), 'Murray admits he made expensive mistake', *The Scotsman*, 2 September: p. 62.

IFC (2004), *Independent Football Commission annual report 2003*. Middlesbrough: IFC.

Moorhouse, B. (2004), 'Economic inequalities within and between professional soccer leagues in Europe: Sporting consequences and policy options', in Fort, R. and Fixel, J. (eds) *International sports economics comparisons*. Westport, Connecticut: Praeger, pp. 107–122.

Morris, P., Morrow, S. and Spink, P. (2003) 'The new transfer fee system in professional soccer: An interdisciplinary study', *Contemporary Issues in Law* Vol. 5, No. 4: pp. 253–281.

Morrow, S. (2004) 'The financial crisis in Scottish football', *Scottish Affairs* No. 47: pp. 48–57.

—— (2003) *The people's game? Football, finance and society.* Basingstoke: Palgrave.

PKF (2004) *Financing football — fit for business? The annual survey of football club finance directors.* London: PKF/AccountancyAge.

Plunkett, J. (2002) 'Sky steps into ITV football breach', *The Guardian*, Media (online), 5 July (at media.guardian.co.uk/digitaltv/story/0,12184,750093,00.html).

Pricewaterhouse Coopers (1999) *The Pricewaterhouse Coopers financial review of Scottish football 1997/1998.* Edinburgh: PWC.

—— (2003) *The Pricewaterhouse Coopers financial review of Scottish football 2001/02.* Glasgow: PWC.

—— (2005) *The Pricewaterhouse Coopers annual financial review of Scottish football 2002/03.* Glasgow: PWC.

Rimini Group (2004) *First report of the Rimini group: The financial crisis in European soccer* (at www.imperial.ac.uk/business/dynamic/other/RiminiGroup/index.htm)

Robertson, R. (2005) 'Hearts pull out of Tynecastle deal', *The Herald*, 9 February: p. 32.

Scottish Parliament (2004) S*cottish Parliament official report: football,* Cols 5695–5723 (at www.scottish.parliament.uk/plenary/0r–04/sor0211–02.htm).

SFA (2003) *National club licensing.* Glasgow: Scottish Football Association.

SPL (2003) *The Scottish Premier League handbook 2003/04.* Glasgow: Scottish Premier League.

UEFA (2002) *UEFA club licensing system — Season 2004/05.* Version 1.0 E — March. Nyon, Switzerland: UEFA.

Wilson, M.J. (2004) 'Setanta's ability to pay called into question by accountants', *The Herald*, 26 February: p. 34.

Wilson, M.J. and Murden, T. (2004) 'Royal Bank in talks over SPL television deal', *Scotland on Sunday*, Business, 22 February: p. 1.

SEE NO EVIL, HEAR NO EVIL — THE CRISIS
OF DOMESTIC FOOTBALL IN NORTHERN IRELAND

David Hassan
School of Health Sciences,
University of Ulster at Jordanstown

Introduction

This chapter examines the role played by Northern Ireland's senior football clubs in the creation of what is widely believed to be a state of crisis in the local game. Previous research in this area has focused almost exclusively upon the activities of the sports governing body in Northern Ireland, the Irish Football Association (IFA). Bairner (2004) claims that maladministration and institutionalised inertia within the IFA are two of the main reasons why football in the country is experiencing serious difficulties. He rejects the idea that national governing bodies lack the ability to enact real change. Instead Bairner (2004) asserts that organisations such as the IFA (i.e. governing bodies in small countries) "do have the capacity to initiate their own practical responses to developments within the game, although they are necessarily constrained in their activities by local as well as global circumstances" (p. 27). However, in adopting this stance an assumption is made that governing bodies possess full knowledge of and some control over the activities of individual clubs. In practice this may not always be the case. Nevertheless, when examining the situation in Northern Ireland it could be argued that there is so much overlapping membership between clubs and the game's governing body that claims about a lack of appreciation within the latter are somewhat questionable. Indeed one of the main recommendations arising out a report entitled

'Creating a Soccer Strategy for Northern Ireland' published in 2001 was the formation of better structures for the governance of the game. In practice this proposal was designed to create a clear distinction between the administration of the sport by the IFA and the interests of individual clubs (Department of Culture, Arts and Leisure [NI], 2001; Bairner, 2004). To what extent this becomes reality will be examined with interest as a number of clubs in the Irish League, Northern Ireland's senior domestic league, continue to retain a level of autonomy from the IFA and operate accordingly. Consequently it is neither accurate nor appropriate to apportion complete accountability concerning the state of the game in the country to the IFA.

Initially, this chapter examines the structural context in which senior football operates in Northern Ireland. Historically, the administration of the game there has been complex. The IFA is recognised by *Fédération Internationale de Football Associations* (FIFA) and *Union des Associations Européennes de Football* (UEFA) as the official governing body for football in the country. The Irish Football League (IFL) is the organisation that governs domestic club football in Northern Ireland, including the Irish League Premier, First and Second Divisions. Like most sports confederations, neither the IFA nor the IFL are overly keen on weakening their perceived power bases and thus both have guarded their independence with some resolve (Hassan, 2002). In light of recommendations arising out of the report 'Creating a Soccer Strategy for Northern Ireland' the IFA published an amended development plan in January 2003 (IFA Development Plan, 2003). In it the association proposed a newly constituted executive committee to manage the restructuring of the IFA/IFL and form a newly merged body. One aspect of this process would see a significant downsizing in the administrative structures governing the local game. As a result the focus has been on ensuring the proper administration of the game on the part of the IFA/ IFL with consequently less attention being afforded to the plight of the individual clubs themselves. Whilst the IFA may argue that it is beyond its remit to ensure the proper management and financial solvency of constituent clubs, some of them limited companies, recent developments may serve to sharpen its focus. The introduction of the UEFA Club Licensing System at the beginning of the 2003/4 season placed the spotlight back on the proper regulation of the game in Northern Ireland (UEFA, 2000).

Thus the principal analytical framework underpinning this research examines the findings of an IFA committee formed in August 2003 to oversee the implementation of UEFA's Club Licensing system, which came into force at the beginning of the 2004/5 season. In its simplest form the system requires any club seeking admission to any of the UEFA club competitions to guarantee minimum standards in a range of areas (UEFA, 2000). These include sporting issues, infrastructure, personnel and administration and legal and financial matters. The extent to which these criteria are met by each club is assessed using a scale from A to D (IFA Club Licensing Manual, 2003). All criteria listed under category A are mandatory and must be met as outlined in the UEFA club licensing manual. Under category B clubs are still required to address all criteria but the scheme does allow possible alternatives to be developed in order to achieve the required standard. Failure to address issues outlined under category C will be met with a caution or a fine but will not result in exclusion from UEFA club competitions. Finally category D is not a compulsory aspect of the club licensing system but does contain examples and recommendations relating to good practice in football club management and should be interpreted as such. A consequence of this and similar attempts at imposing greater regulation upon the domestic game in Northern Ireland has been closer scrutiny of the affairs of individual clubs. Leaving aside the obvious difficulties that are present elsewhere, it appears that if a crisis exists within Northern Irish football it is the failings of a number of senior teams throughout the country that are of paramount concern.

This work also affords some consideration to the aforementioned report 'Creating a Soccer Strategy for Northern Ireland', a product of almost two years of deliberations on behalf of a select panel of experts brought together by the then Minster for Culture, Arts and Leisure for Northern Ireland, Mr. Michael McGimpsey. That said Bairner (2004), himself a member of the advisory panel, offers a much more detailed appraisal of its remit than space allows here. Nevertheless some examination of the degree to which the ministerial advisory committee's proposals indicated a need for change within the governance of the game in Northern Ireland, in part because of the mismanagement at club level, will be undertaken. Finally, an underlying theme of this chapter concerns the (mis)use of public funds by sports clubs in Northern Ireland. Whilst investment in sporting infrastructure, raised both directly and indirectly from public monies, is to be welcomed, the proper management and administration of such finance is critical in securing the long term goodwill of the wider community in Northern Ireland. Whilst all of these issues will be dealt with in due course the discussion begins with a brief history of the Irish League, before giving way to a wider examination of a series of policy/position documents concerning the state of domestic football in Northern Ireland.

The Irish League: A Brief History

The IFL was founded in 1890, a decade after the formation of the IFA. From its inception the administration of the game in Northern Ireland became closely associated with a working-class, Protestant culture. This was certainly evident in the make-up of both organisations, which reflected the extent of unionist hegemony prevalent throughout the north-east of the country at this time (Shirlow, 1997). The IFL now controlled all senior club activity, with the exception of the Irish Cup, which remained under the auspices of the IFA. Many of the founding members of the IFL were clubs that had evolved out of large industrial sites in and around the city of Belfast. For example, Linfield Football Club (FC) was founded in March 1886 by employees of the Ulster Spinning Mill and was originally known as the Linfield Athletic Club. The club played its early matches on ground at the back of the mill known as 'The Meadow' (Brodie, 1985; Official Linfield FC Website, accessed 30 July 2004). Similarly, in 1889, when Glentoran FC became a limited liability company, it was the investment of Viscount Pirrie and G W Wolff that allowed the club to prosper. In fact the involvement of Wolff, then Member of Parliament for East Belfast, was viewed as offering an opportunity for workers employed at Harland and Wolff shipbuilders to invest in their local club (Official Glentoran FC Website, accessed 30 July 2004). Over time, interest in these and other clubs competing in the Irish League continued to grow, so that from the 1930s onwards the domestic game began to attract considerable interest amongst the local population.

However from the late 1970s onwards the local game entered a period of marked decline. It continued to experience the negative effects of the internal conflict that had engulfed Northern Ireland during this period (Sugden and Bairner, 1993; Hassan, 2002). Consequently many potential spectators chose to stay away from Irish League matches, as certain games continued to attract only those elements that were intent on expressing sectarian hatred. Of course, in recognising this it is also worth pointing out that some clubs, notably Cliftonville FC, began to receive a larger following precisely because of this opportunity to express opposition to the wider unionist/loyalist culture that had begun to dominate local football. Whilst this remains less of a concern in the current climate, a number of reasons continue to exist that help explain the apparent lack of engagement local people have with the game in Northern Ireland. Two independent pieces of research, designed to reflect the views and experiences of the country's football fans, were carried out during the 2003/4 season. The Department of Culture, Arts and Leisure (DCAL) commissioned both investigations in the context of an £8 million investment it had promised the IFA to improve the overall image of the local game.

The first report, in providing a general overview of the state of football in Northern Ireland, focused primarily upon the experiences of so-called 'armchair fans'. These were individuals who did not physically attend matches but nevertheless had an interest in the game of football. This cohort represented the overwhelming majority (35 out of 38%) of those who took part in the survey and had confirmed an interest in the sport. One of the most interesting findings in this report was the fact that almost half (49%) of 'armchair fans' attended matches in the Scottish league. Only 38% of these fans were from the Catholic community, the remainder almost certainly members of the majority Protestant population. In contrast 46% of 'armchair fans' had never attended a match in the Irish League. Whilst the overall standard of play was cited as the main reason for their non-attendance (59%), forty-seven per cent of those surveyed felt that 'better promotion of IFL soccer' would encourage them to attend local matches and forty-five per cent wished to see the sport become 'more family friendly'. Interestingly, according to the survey findings, seven out of every ten individuals who regularly attend matches in the Irish League have done so for more than ten years. This would suggest that there are very few 'new' fans attending local club games in Northern Ireland. Finally, over twice as many females (17%) are 'armchair fans' than regularly attend

Irish League games (7%). When comparing the percentage of females who attend matches in England and Scotland, the Irish League fails to attract sufficient levels of female support to its games (The Fans Perspective: Summary Findings of Independent Research on the views and experiences of soccer fans in Northern Ireland, 2004).

The second report commissioned by DCAL was entitled 'Research into Attendance at Northern Ireland Soccer Matches' and was published in October 2004. It focused on the experiences of football fans who regularly attended both international and club matches in Northern Ireland. According to the findings of this survey, one in every three of those who attend Irish League matches can be characterised as being male, aged between 30 and 59 years, Protestant and married. Of these, three out of every four have been following their team for more than 15 years and were more likely to have experienced hooliganism when compared to the whole sample. Asked to identify what they considered important in improving the image of the game the three top-ranked responses were 'Better promotion of Irish League football' (97%), 'Improved toilet facilities' (89%) and 'Better management of Irish League football' (85%). These views were echoed by the second key group contained within the survey, women. Indeed the replies offered by this cohort were remarkably similar to those of the first group and, for that matter, those of the final sub-sample 'Catholic, male' (Research into Attendance at Northern Ireland Soccer Matches, 2004). It is possible to conclude therefore that between so-called 'armchair fans' and those who attend football matches in Northern Ireland on a regular basis a level of agreement exists about what must be done to improve the image of the game and encourage more people to attend. Whilst some responsibility rests with the IFA to ensure the proper governance of the sport and to allocate capital funding in an appropriate manner, the onus must also be with the constituent clubs themselves to play their part. During an era when the domestic game in Britain and the Republic of Ireland has experienced an exponential growth in the numbers attending matches, attendances throughout the Irish League have continued to decline. It is argued here that this state of affairs is to a large degree the result of failings on the part of the clubs themselves (The Fans Perspective: Summary Findings of Independent Research on the views and experiences of soccer fans in Northern Ireland, 2004).

Nevertheless one of the most interesting developments within Irish soccer in recent years has been the instigation of an all-Ireland club competition, The Setanta Cup (Ireland On-line, accessed 11 August 2004). The competition is a joint project between the Football Association of Ireland (FAI) and the IFA involving three teams from each jurisdiction. Setanta Sports, the new Irish dedicated sports television channel, signed a four-year deal to be the host broadcasters and sponsors of the tournament. The participating teams in the competition, which began in April 2005, were the winners and runners-up of the premier league competitions in both countries, together with the winners of the annual premier cup competitions in each case. Both the FAI and the IFA have broadly welcomed the move, as have the leading club sides throughout Ireland who view it as an excellent source of additional revenue. Whilst the FAI has always been a governing body that appears comfortable with its own identity and, in latter times, has become increasingly progressive in its outlook, the decision of the IFA to enter into an all-Ireland agreement of this nature is a significant development. It has been claimed that the IFA, as a unionist dominated council, has always been reticent about engaging in any arrangement that suggests movement towards Irish unification (Bairner, 2004). Thus whilst it is keen to demonstrate support for The Setanta Cup it is also eager to reassure football followers in Northern Ireland that such a move should not be seen as a precursor to an all-Ireland league. Nevertheless given the current difficulties within Irish League football a development of this kind might well be necessary — not to mention economically vital — in ensuring the survival and long term prosperity of domestic football. Indeed it has been the absence of this form of progressive administration, particularly in Northern Ireland, that has been a central theme in the game's stagnation and steady decline.

The Way Forward

In October 1998 the IFA issued a consultation document entitled 'The Way Forward' (IFA, 1998). In proposing the instigation of new structures for the local game, including the introduction of a twelve team Irish Premier League, the IFA cited the poor financial status of a large number of local teams. The prospective Premier League 'Mission Statement' aimed at "providing an entirely new cultural environment in which Northern Ireland's foremost football clubs can improve their quality and image, maximise the commercial value of the game and thus ensure football's long-term future and prosperity, both domestically and financially" (p. 1). The report contained a number of reasons explaining the need for change. These included the fact that there were too many senior clubs in Northern Ireland, particularly in the Greater Belfast region, the existence of a negative media image regarding the sport, poor infrastructures to support the game (especially training facilities for young players) and, of course, dwindling crowds attending league fixtures. Central to 'The Way Forward' document was a recognition by the IFA that if the sport locally was to develop and thrive it would have to be self-sustaining. In other words, the clubs would be obliged to place greater emphasis on developing young players and to ensure proper structures and coaching personnel were in place to sustain this move. As far back as 1996, an IFA Development plan concluded that "there is no evidence of any serious attempt at long-term planning or clubs 'managing their future' — as would be evident in their European counterparts" (p. 4). It was apparent that clubs were committing what limited financial resources they had to the pursuit of immediate success and were prepared to offer inflated salaries to arguably very limited players to achieve this end. It was a business model, which certainly from a financial perspective, was short-sighted and lacked sustainability. The report also focused on the public apathy that appeared to exist towards Irish League football. Highlighting the ever increasing demands on leisure spend in Northern Ireland, the report concluded that: "The local football 'product' lacks any form of appeal through a shabby and unwelcoming environment — especially for families and women supporters. Until these matters are seriously addressed, public disinterest will continue"(p. 5).

In spite of the dire warnings contained within the report, club representatives throughout Northern Ireland refused to countenance the level of change suggested in the document and effectively 'sat on their hands' when offered the opportunity to embrace a new way forward. Consequently domestic soccer continued to deteriorate still further until, in October 2000, Michael McGimpsey Member of the Legislative Assembly (MLA), then Minister of Culture, Arts and Leisure in the Northern Ireland Assembly, established an advisory panel to consider how the local game could move forward. Drawing upon his personal involvement with the advisory panel, Bairner (2004) outlines in some detail its remit, including some of the issues it attempted to address. In his foreword to the report the chairman of the panel, Billy Hamilton, was confident that "providing all elements of the report are accepted and acted upon, the game of football will thrive and flourish throughout our community" (p. 5). In view of the abject failure of most local clubs to positively respond to key aspects of 'The Way Forward' document, it was a brave prediction on the part of the former Northern Ireland international. Central to the deliberations of the panel was the issue of governance for soccer in Northern Ireland. From a range of perspectives and as a result of a number of concerns raised, the panel recommended that a closer working relationship be forged between the IFL and the IFA. Whilst it was important that this arrangement was not perceived by the IFL as a take-over, a single governing body was the committee's preferred option (Bairner, 2004). Of concern generally was the sense that under the existing arrangements there was no obvious mechanism in place to guarantee the proper running of the domestic game. There appeared to be some concern that the failure to establish a clear and transparent decision-making body for the sport in Northern Ireland would only perpetuate the very difficulties that had necessitated the advisory panel's formation in the first place. The panel's final report also included a range of other recommendations relating to league structures and measures designed to address the religious imbalance within the sport (including the possibility of inviting Derry City to re-join the Irish League following its decision to resign in 1972). Further suggestions to embellish what is already very commendable work being undertaken in the areas of cross-community reconciliation and anti-sectarianism were also included in the final publication.

The IFA and the IFL took some time to consider the report's implications and initially appeared reluctant to accept them in full. Bairner (2004) presents an accurate and concise overview of some of the issues that help to explain the reticence of the IFA membership on this matter. Furthermore, it is generally accepted that the considerable personal influence of IFA President Jimmy Boyce was required to convince sceptical elements within the organisation of the need to look forward (*Belfast Telegraph*, 31 May 2003). This unwillingness to accede to the advisory panel's recommendations continued up to and including the deadline for a decision set by Angela Smith, who was by then minister with responsibility for sport under direct rule from Westminster. In a context in which change has often been met with the most virulent opposition, resistance to any move designed to lessen unionist control over Northern Ireland football was not entirely unexpected. As if to complicate matters still further, these debates took place against attempts by the governing body of association football in Europe, UEFA, to create a more structured regulatory context for club football within its jurisdiction.

UEFA: A quest for greater regulation of association football in Europe

In January 2004 Lars-Christer Olsson assumed the post of chief executive of UEFA. By replacing Gerhard Aigner, who had held the position for almost fifteen years, Olsson joined his fellow countryman and current President of UEFA, Lennart Johansson, in becoming one of the most powerful men in the world game. Amongst the most pressing concerns for Olsson remains the growing disparity between certain nations and clubs, which have become extremely powerful in financial terms and those, that have stagnated and begun to regress. His belief "that the top end of the game have a responsibility for solidarity and distribution of wealth to the others" (Warshaw, 2004: p. 35) may be somewhat idealistic but reflects a concern that European football has become less the people's game and more that of big business. In order to address concerns that the game may be beginning to over-inflate, Olsson has continued to implement measures designed to ensure clubs adopt a prudent approach to the management of their affairs. Of these, UEFA's club licensing system is the most significant attempt to date to demonstrate the extent of its control over the sport and has forced European clubs to re-evaluate how they conduct their business (UEFA, 2000). It is the financial imperative contained within the licensing scheme that is the cause of most concern for clubs. In future, those wishing to take part in European club competitions will be required to prepare an annual statement for the previous financial year, which must be verified by independent and qualified auditors. Perhaps more significantly, clubs must also prove that they do not have either overdue debt to other clubs, e.g. on transfer activities, or any outstanding payments owed to their employees. All senior clubs playing under the auspices of UEFA have been invited to apply for a club license. No club is obliged to make an application but in its absence teams are prevented from participating in all European competitions, a measure introduced from the beginning of the 2004/5 season.

Individual national governing bodies allocate places in European competitions in a relatively standardised manner. These tend to be awarded to the winners and runners-up in the domestic league championships, whilst the winners of the main cup competitions are also permitted entry to the UEFA Cup, which is widely regarded as a secondary competition to the UEFA Champions League. However, under the new club licensing system, clubs in possession of a license may be able to subvert this arrangement. In practice, clubs finishing in positions that previously would have guaranteed them automatic entry into European competitions will now be prevented from accepting such an offer if they do not hold a valid UEFA club license. Furthermore, such is the importance UEFA attach to this scheme that admission to European competitions may be awarded to clubs that finish some considerable way behind the eventual league winners simply because they are in possession of a license (UEFA, 2000). For example, Ballymena United FC finished sixth at the close of the 2003/4 Irish League Premier League season but were offered a place in the Inter-Toto Cup as those clubs that finished ahead of them did not hold a license. All participants in this competition automatically receive a subsidy of £25,000 from UEFA, despite the fact that they may only play one tie before being eliminated. Indeed it is not beyond the realms of possibility that a club may be relegated from its current division and still secure entry to one of the three main European competitions. Of course its worth recognising that there have always been anomalies associated with Inter-Toto participation by clubs even prior to the introduction of the club-licensing scheme. Nevertheless the scheme remains the most significant development in the European club game since the Bosman ruling, affecting the transfer of out of contract players, in 1996.

The Irish League produced a Club Licensing Manual for its member clubs, which was accredited by UEFA on August 26 2003 (IFA Development Plan, 2003). The manual sets out the criteria that must be met by clubs wishing to represent the league in future European competitions. In effect the publication benchmarks the minimum standards clubs must achieve in order to receive UEFA accreditation. There are a number of key objectives contained within the document, each designed to improve the overall standard of club administration and management. The most significant of these, in the context of a discussion about the relative merits of a number of Irish League clubs, are the first two. The principle objective of the scheme, that of "Improving the economic and financial capabilities of Clubs, increasing their transparency and credibility, and placing the necessary importance on the protection of creditors", requires clubs to closely examine their financial practices in an industry where such activities often lack clarity (IFA Development Plan, 2003: p. 4). As it happens it was on this issue that a number of Irish League clubs encountered problems in meeting the basic requirements of the scheme. The second main objective contained within the document was the "Further promotion of, and continuing priority given to, the training and care of young players in each club" (IFA Development Plan, 2003). Again, this was significant in the minds of Irish League clubs as many have traditionally lacked a discernible youth development programme and have relied instead on a myriad of feeder clubs to both identify and develop talented young players. It was clear therefore that the implementation of the club licensing scheme was designed to pose serious questions about the long-term strategy employed by a number of clubs operating in the Irish League.

The Irish League and the Club Licensing System

All twenty-eight Irish League (Premier and First Division) clubs were invited by the IFA to apply for the award of a UEFA Club Licence for the season 2004/5. Each was issued with a copy of the IFA Club Licensing Manual and a full consultation process was entered into with interested parties. Following this initial dialogue only eight clubs decided to proceed with an application. These were Ballymena United FC, Coleraine FC, Glenavon FC, Glentoran FC, Limavady United FC, Linfield FC, Lisburn Distillery FC and Portadown FC. There is no evidence as to why the remaining twenty clubs decided not to make an application to the scheme (IFA: Report to Club Licensing Committee, 2004). However, it is conceivable that certain issues were central to any deliberations that may have taken place surrounding the application process. Initially, some clubs may have thought it unlikely that they would qualify for European competitions and therefore would have considered the administrative burden associated with the scheme unnecessary. It is also possible that clubs lacked the capacity to make a viable submission, either in terms of personnel, infrastructure or time. Many Irish League clubs continue to be managed by a small, committed group of volunteers, yet a great number of these individuals lack any specific knowledge regarding the management of senior football clubs. Ultimately, anecdotal evidence suggests it may have been reluctance on the part of several clubs to expose their financial practices to external scrutiny that could account for the majority deciding not to proceed with an application.

Of those clubs that did apply only two, Portadown FC and Ballymena United FC, met all the criteria outlined within the club licensing system. A further two, Linfield FC and Glentoran FC, were also awarded a licence despite failing elements of category C, which are considered of relatively minor importance. The remaining four clubs were refused a licence on account of serious concerns being expressed by the committee over the standard of their submissions (IFA: Report to Club Licensing Committee, 2004). In the case of Glenavon FC and Limavady United FC interim financial statements for the year ending 2002/03 were absent. Not only was this also the case with Coleraine FC and Lisburn Distillery FC but both clubs failed to present properly audited financial statements pertaining to the running of the club dating back several seasons. Despite being considered, on the face of it, one of the best appointed club grounds in the Irish League, upon closer inspection the committee found serious shortcomings in the electrical installations at Mourneview Park, home of Glenavon F.C. Such was its concern at the potential fire hazard the defects presented it recommended immediate attention be given to improving this aspect of the ground. Limavady United FC failed to present any evidence of a structured youth development programme within the club, whilst it nominated the Coleraine Showgrounds, home of Coleraine FC, as its preferred ground for any possible home European tie (IFA: Report to Club Licensing Committee, 2004). When the committee sought clarification from Coleraine FC concerning the nature of any such agreement it learned that Coleraine had no such knowledge of any request having been made by Limavady United relating to this matter. Finally, some of the most serious shortcomings were found at Lisburn Distillery FC. Indeed, with reference to almost every aspect of the club licensing scheme the committee identified a series of failings, including financial, structural and personnel deficiencies (IFA: Report to Club Licensing Committee: Club: Lisburn Distillery Football Club, 2004).

Wider concerns regarding the management practices employed at Irish League clubs

It is clear that the concerns raised by the IFA Club Licensing committee about the standard of club management and administration within the Irish League were symptomatic of wider expressions of unease concerning the organisation of senior football in Northern Ireland as a whole. Such issues came to a head following the hosting of three major friendly fixtures featuring Omagh Town FC and Manchester United FC, Liverpool FC and Glasgow Celtic FC. The games, which took place between September 1998 and March 1999, were intended to raise funds for the relatives of those who were killed and injured in the Real IRA bombing of the town in August 1998 (Oliver, 2000, accessed 02 August 2004). Initially it was proposed that the three matches would be played at Healy Park in Omagh, the headquarters of the Tyrone Gaelic Athletic Association (GAA) county board, as its capacity of 25,000 spectators was considerably greater than that of St. Julian's Road, the home ground of Omagh Town FC. However, the presence of Rule 42 in the GAA's constitution, which precludes the playing of non-indigenous games at GAA grounds, prevented this from taking place. It is worth noting that the GAA authorities received widespread criticism for its apparent intransigence on the matter, including from within the ranks of its own membership (Hassan, 2002). Nevertheless, Omagh Town FC was keen to host the games at its own ground and therefore a sub-committee was formed to oversee the successful staging of the charity matches. Not surprisingly each of the three sides proved to be major attractions for football fans throughout Ireland, with applications for tickets far outstripping the number available.

There is no suggestion that Omagh Town FC sought to organise the three fixtures for any reason other than to legitimately raise funds for the

Omagh Bomb memorial fund. However, subsequent investigations into the precise handling of such funds have been the subject of much controversy. A BBC investigation into the hosting of the three matches found that there were major cash discrepancies in accounts relating to the fund raising effort. The Spotlight documentary claimed that thousands of pounds raised for the Omagh Memorial Fund from the games were used to pay off debts incurred by Omagh Town FC (BBC Spotlight, 'A Good Sport': Broadcast 02 May 2000). It cited submissions from an independent accountant, Brian Mellon, who discovered that £14,000 raised as a result of the three matches was used to settle an outstanding Value Added Tax (VAT) bill in the name of the local team (Oliver, 2000, accessed 02 August 2004). Similarly, further sponsorship deals involving *The Mirror* and *The Sun* newspapers, as well as the brewing company Bass, were not declared by the club. Mr Mellon, who was appointed by Omagh District Council to examine the club's accounts following concern over the money, told the programme: "If there was other money received, and it's not in the accounts, you can draw your own conclusions" (BBC Spotlight, 'A Good Sport': Broadcast 02 May 2000). According to figures published in the *Irish Examiner*, "Only £30,000 of the £185,000 raised went to benefit the families of bomb victims and more than a quarter of the cash was used to prepare Omagh's small ground for the glamour games" (Oliver, 2000, accessed 02 August 2004). When Mr Mellon informed Omagh Town FC that it was not permitted to use the Memorial Fund to settle the VAT debt it did refund the money in full. Nevertheless, the club suffered substantial adverse publicity in the period following the investigation.

The alleged misappropriation of funds is central to a further dispute, which arose in May 2004, involving Coleraine FC and the Sports Council for Northern Ireland (SCNI), resulting in a joint Police Service of Northern Ireland (PSNI)/SCNI investigation. Many clubs in the Irish League have experienced acute financial difficulties arising from a combination of excessive wage demands from their playing staff, declining revenue and alleged cases of financial mismanagement (House of Commons Hansard Debates for 17 March 1999 (pt 12)). One such club is Coleraine FC, which from the beginning of the 2000/01 season has been embroiled in an annual battle to secure the Irish League Premier division title and, in so doing, wrest control from the traditional powers of Glentoran FC and Linfield

FC. However, in doing so Coleraine has been forced to sign a number of the League's leading players and thus to divert funds away from the ongoing costs of running the club. The implications for Coleraine FC have been catastrophic. At the time of writing the club continues to owe £18,000 of an unpaid VAT demand and a further £26,000 in back rent to the owners of its home ground The Showgrounds, the North Derry Agricultural Society (*Sunday Life*, 09 January 2005: p. 32). Many sports clubs throughout Northern Ireland rely on revenue raised from the sale of alcohol on their premises to meet spiralling costs surrounding the running of their operations. In particular it is the profit generated from the use of gaming machines that represent a prime source of income for clubs. However, any profit raised from the use of such gaming machines must be declared to the Inland Revenue. It appears that this has not been the case either with Coleraine FC or a number of other Irish League clubs, amongst them Ards FC and Larne FC (Lowry, 2004). During the 2003/4 League season the club also had problems paying its players because of falling gate receipts and the high level of public liability insurance. A number of players refused to play for the team unless their contracts were honoured in full and several subsequently left at the close of the 2003/4 league programme (Lowry, 2004).

However, it is the ongoing PSNI fraud enquiry that is of greatest concern for the club. The investigation concerns the alleged misuse of funds administered by the SCNI, on behalf of the British government, under the Safe Sports Ground Scheme. This programme of funding allowed clubs to apply for up to 80% of capital costs required for urgent stadium repairs, with the rest coming out of their own finances. The head of the PSNI's Fraud squad, Detective Chief Inspector Larry Cheshire, had given Coleraine FC an ultimatum to answer charges of irregularities in SCNI funding amounting to £151,294 (*The Guardian*, 12 June 2003: p. 48). To date Coleraine FC has been unable to provide the SCNI with satisfactory documentation detailing what the money awarded was used for and where it went on no less than five separate occasions (*The Guardian*, 12 June 2003: p. 48).

A number of other Irish League clubs were also investigated by the PSNI Fraud unit concerning awards made to them under the Safe Sports Ground Scheme. In each case the action was initiated at the behest of the SCNI. A total of seven clubs — one quarter of all Irish League Premier and First Division sides — were subject to scrutiny. In addition to Coleraine FC, these were Carrick Rangers FC, Institute FC, Dungannon Swifts FC, Bangor FC, Limavady United FC and Tobermore FC. In March 2004, Carrick Rangers, Institute and Dungannon Swifts each received letters from the PSNI Fraud Squad informing them that no formal criminal investigation would be pursued in respect of its investigations, whilst enquiries were ongoing at the other clubs (McCambridge, 2004). Both Carrick Rangers and Institute Football Clubs demanded a public apology from the SCNI for wrongly referring their cases to the PSNI. Both claimed that irreparable damage had been caused to their image and, in the case of Carrick Rangers FC, sponsors had withdrawn their investment in the club fearing the affects of negative publicity (McCambridge, 2004). Furthermore, whilst investigations into the application made by Institute FC for support under the Safe Sports Ground Scheme were being carried out, the SCNI withheld funds earmarked for the club from a separate grant scheme. It claimed that this decision resulted in considerable financial hardship for the club during this period, spanning twelve months from March 2002 to March 2003 (Official Institute FC Website, 25 March 2004, accessed 27 July 2004). Incidentally, it should be pointed out that irregularities were found in almost half of the 59 football, rugby and GAA clubs involved in the project, which allocated over £3.3 million between 2000 and 2002. At its height the fraud investigation was estimated to be in excess of £250,000 across all clubs that were subject to inspection (*Belfast Telegraph*, 20 June 2003: p. 1). All of which raises serious questions concerning the use/misuse of public monies by sports clubs in Northern Ireland. If, as these figures appear to suggest, the matter is of widespread concern it seems apparent that a much more robust system for applying for, awarding and auditing the use of public money by sports clubs in Northern Ireland should be immediately introduced.

Conclusion

Three important and at times complementary themes have been highlighted and discussed throughout this paper. Firstly, the issue of how effective governing bodies of football in small countries like Northern Ireland are in controlling the game within their boundaries was examined.

A key argument of this chapter has been that rather than laying blame for the crisis within football in Northern Ireland at the door of the IFA, it is more appropriate to examine the activities of individual clubs who have contributed to the difficulties the game has encountered over the years. Due to the overlap of memberships between clubs and the IFA it has not always been easy to distinguish the activities of one grouping from another. Indeed a call for the establishment of proper, transparent and accountable structures for football in Northern Ireland is one of the key recommend-ations contained within the report 'Creating a Soccer Strategy for Northern Ireland' published in 2001. Nevertheless this chapter has outlined a number of examples of clubs failing to administer their activities in a proper and accountable manner. As such it is they, not the IFA, that must accept responsibility for their actions and the impact these have upon the image of the sport throughout Northern Ireland.

The second issue discussed in this chapter examines the extent to which the ministerial advisory committee's proposals, contained within the aforementioned report, indicated a need for change within the governance of the sport in the country. It is quite clear that the way the game was being administered in Northern Ireland gave rise to a series of problems, many of which have been outlined in this work. Fearful of what any such change may have meant for the game it was not surprising that there was a fair degree of resistance within the ranks of the IFA when it was asked to rule on the matter. Nevertheless on May 28 2003 the IFA took the decision to reduce its management committee to a total of seventeen people, thus accepting the advisory panel's report in full. In return it received almost £8 million in direct funding from the government. However Angela Smith, Parliamentary Under Secretary at the Northern Ireland Office, was forced to issue football's governing body with an ulti-matum concerning its apparent reluctance to agree to the recommend-ations of the ministerial advisory panel. She made it clear that the IFA was very close to losing its allocation as a result of its apparent intransi-gence. It was obvious that there remained elements, both working for the IFA and representing the constituent clubs, that were reluctant to accede to outside demands. The investment is designed to address the needs of the sport at all levels, including 'grassroots', women's football, league clubs etc. However when the money is divided between all such groups the impact it is likely to have at Irish League level may prove to be minimal.

The final theme examined in this chapter concerned the use/misuse of public money by sports (specifically football) clubs in Northern Ireland. On account of the way in which football clubs go about their business — in a largely unregulated manner exempt from any threat of investigation from the IFA or independent inspection of their internal affairs — the system has always been open to varying forms of abuse. As businesses that attract considerable amounts of public money, private investments in the form of sponsorships etc., not to mention gate receipts from paying customers, the degree of freedom afforded Irish League clubs is remarkable. It appears obvious to even the most casual observer that the financial management demonstrated by certain Irish League clubs is in urgent need of attention. The fact that a number of clubs are unable to produce properly audited accounts charting their financial transactions, whilst others are incapable of publishing any accounts whatsoever, should be of concern to those with the future of Irish League soccer at heart. It reflects a general substandard level of club administration in Northern Ireland and has resulted in one leading manager, Roy McCreadie of Irish League Premier Division side Newry City FC, threatening "to expose the corruption in Irish League football" (quoted in *The Irish News*, 24 January 2005: p. 41). When one of the game's longest serving managers feels compelled to publicly denounce what he considers to be the unscrupulous nature of the game in Northern Ireland it is surely time for clubs to more closely examine how they conduct their business.

References

Bairner, A. (2004) 'Creating a soccer strategy for Northern Ireland: Reflections on football governance in small european countries', *Soccer and Society* Vol. 5, No. 1: pp. 27–42.

BBC Spotlight — 'A good sport'. Broadcast 02 May 2000. (Belfast: BBC Northern Ireland).

Belfast Telegraph (2003) 'Boyce hails £8 m 'Yes' for change', 31 May: p. 1.

———— (2003) 'Football: Sports club grounds fraud tops £250, 000', 20 June: p. 1.

Drodic, M. (1985) *Linfield 100 years — A book on the history of Linfield F.C.* Belfast: Linfield Football and Athletic Club.

Dempsey, P. and Reilly, K. (1998) *Big money, beautiful game: Saving football from itself*. London: Nicholas Brealey.

Department of Culture Arts and Leisure (NI) (2001) *Creating a soccer strategy for Northern Ireland*. Belfast: HMSO.

Hassan, D. (2002) 'A people apart: Soccer, identity and Irish Nationalists in Northern Ireland', *Soccer and Society* Vol. 3, No. 3: pp. 65–83.

House of Commons Hansard Debates (17 March 1999, pt 12) *Soccer grounds (Northern Ireland)* Column 1079–1082. London: HMSO.

Ireland On-Line. www.irelandon-line/news/story.asp. Accessed 11 August 2004.

Irish Football Association (1996) *Development Plan*. IFA: Belfast.

Irish Football Association (1998) *IFA Premier League: 'The Way Forward'*. IFA: Unpublished.

Irish Football Association (2003) *Club Licensing Manual*. Belfast: IFA.

Irish Football Association (2003) *Development Plan*. Belfast: IFA.

Irish Football Association — National Club Licensing (2004) *Report to Club Licensing Committee — First Instance Committee*. IFA: Unpublished.

Irish Football Association — National ClubLicensing (2004) *Report to Club Licensing Committee — First Instance Committee: Lisburn Distillery Football Club*. IFA: Unpublished.

King, A. (1998) *The end of the terraces: The transformation of English Football in the 1990s*. Leicester: Leicester University Press.

Lowry, B. (2004) 'Turnstiles key to clubs' cash crises', in *Belfast Telegraph*, 09 January: p. 1.

McCambridge, J. (2004) 'Soccer Clubs cleared in fraud probe', *Belfast Telegraph*, 25 March: p. 1.

Official Website of Glentoran Football Club, Belfast. www.members.lycos.co.uk/rafters/1historyclub-Chap1.htm. Accessed 30 July 2004.

Official Website of Institute Football Club, Drumahoe. www.institutefc.com/nw3/publish/. Accessed 27 July 2004.

Official Website of Linfield Football Club, Belfast. www.linfield-fc.com/history.asp. Accessed 30 July 2004.

Oliver, J. (2000) 'Relatives of Omagh dead wonder what became of charity match money', in *Irish Examiner*, www.examiner.ie/archives/2000/may/3. Accessed 02 August 2004.

Report from the Advisory Panel to the Minister for Culture, Arts and Leisure (2001) *Creating a soccer strategy for Northern Ireland*. Belfast: HMSO.

Research into Attendance at NI Soccer Matches (2004). Belfast: Department of Culture, Arts and Leisure.

Shirlow, P. (1997) 'Who are the 'people'? Unionism, protestantism and loyalism in Northern Ireland', in Shirlow, P. and McGovern, M. (1997) *Who are the 'people'? Unionism, Protestantism and Loyalism in Northern Ireland*. London: Pluto Press, pp. 1–15.

Sugden, J. and Bairner, A. (1993) *Sport, sectarianism and society in a divided Ireland*. Leicester: Leicester University Press.

Sugden, J. and Tomlinson, A. (1998) *FIFA and the contest for world football*. Cambridge: Polity Press.

Sunday Life (2005) 'Football: Money is too tight to mention', 09 January: p. 32.

The Fans Perspective: Summary findings of independent research on the views and experiences of soccer fans in Northern Ireland (2004). Belfast: Department of Culture, Arts and Leisure.

The Guardian (2003) 'Cold feet star steps in to rescue Coleraine FC', 12 June: p. 45.

The Irish News (2005) 'Roy insists Newry are in the clear', 24 January: p. 41.

UEFA (2000) *Club Licensing Scheme*. Switzerland: UEFA.

Warshaw, A. (2004) 'Keeping football together', *The Times*, 12 March: p. 35.

FOOTBALL PLAYERS' MIGRATION IN EUROPE: A GEO-ECONOMIC APPROACH TO AFRICANS' MOBILITY

Raffaele Poli, International Centre for Sports Studies (CIES), Geography Institute (IGG), University of Neuchâtel (Switzerland); Centre of Study and Research on Sport and Olympism (CERSO), University of Franche-Comté (France)

Introduction

The goal of this chapter is to understand the reasons for the strong mobility that characterises the careers of professional football players, especially Africans, in the European labour market. In order to do this, an approach called "circulatory" has been formulated. The theoretical framework proposed is based on three concepts that have emerged in the context of the renewal of migration studies in the social sciences: globalisation, transnationalism and circulation. The exacerbation of professional football players' mobility is analysed, taking into account these processes which exist both in human society and in contemporary sport.

The use of the term 'circulatory', introduced in the social sciences field by French sociologist Alain Tarrius (1989), is explained by the desire to emphasise the necessity for footballers to be mobile. Indeed, players are interlocked in specific networks, composed of clubs' officials and players' agents, that regulate their transfers. Such networks are integrated in an economic system in which players' mobility permits the different actors involved to make profits. Instead of staying in the same club for the whole of their professional career, football players are often transferred. Their ability to change club, which is closely linked with their integration in the networks mentioned above, is a "new capital" (Kaufmann, Bergman and Joye, 2004) to take advantage of, and indeed a necessary condition to joining top European clubs.

The theoretical perspective developed starts from the concept of global-isation, defined by Saskia Sassen (1991) as a phenomenon characterised by a double process: the dispersion of productive activities throughout the world and the concentration of the management and control activities in a close number of centres of command. This double tendency can be also observed in the functioning of European professional football. The concentration of power is reflected by the ever-increasing financial gap separating top clubs from the others. The dispersion of productive activities is exemplified by the growing recruitment of players from less well-off continents, such Africa or South America.

In order to train and recruit young players from countries outside Europe, European clubs and players' agents groups follow a policy based on the construction of transnational socio-economic networks. These are not created only by top clubs, but also by middle-range clubs, which, in the context of the dualism present in European football, cannot afford to pay high salaries. Often, players recruited in Third World countries are transferred to Europe as part of an ongoing pursuance of policies aiming at saving money through salary dumping.

Moreover, footballers recruited from southern countries, whose "purchase" or "production" costs are relatively lower than those of their counterparts "nurtured" in the industrialised World, are engaged by middle-range European clubs with the aim of being subsequently transferred to a bigger club in order to make a profit. Integrated from the beginning of their career in a speculative strategy based on transfer accumulation, players in Europe who come from less well-off countries are very mobile. In this manner, circulation in football can be defined as a sequence of short stays in different clubs in order to take advantage of geo-economical discrepancies existing between country leagues, in the context of a labour market in which the ability to move is a capital to be exploited (Poli, 2004).

The chapter introduces, through some examples, the way in which the concepts of globalisation, transnationalism and circulation may be applied to the description of the functioning of the European football industry, in particular with regard to understanding the flux of African players.

Globalisation in European football

Since the end of the Eighties, the concept of globalisation has been increasingly used in the academic world to highlight the compression of time and space and "the intensification of the consciousness of the world as a whole" (Robertson, 1992: p. 8). In the migratory studies field, this notion is useful to describe the acceleration and the diversification of flows (Papastergiadis, 2000) resulting from the technological developments in communication and transport. In this chapter, the growing diversification of the geographical origins of footballers integrated in the European labour market is theoretically linked up to the changes in the professional environment occurring in the context of globalisation.

As Saskia Sassen (1991) pointed out in the case of three "global cities" (New York, Tokyo, London), in European professional football, we observe a concentration of economical and political power in the hands of top clubs taking part in the major leagues (English Premiership, Italian Serie A, Spanish Liga, German Bundesliga, French Ligue). This phenomenon is closely linked to the growing commercialisation of the game, which has coincided with the exponential increase of the rights paid for the retransmissions of matches, notably from Pay-TV, since the beginning of the 1990s.

From the 1995/96 season to 2001/2002, for example, in England, the amount paid by television companies to clubs has grown from 150 to 734 million euros (+489%). In Italy, this amount increased from 199 to 595 million (+299%), in France from 95 to 333 million (+350%) and in Germany from 111 to 414 million (+373%). The average percentage for TV rights of the five major European championships in clubs' budgets is close to 50%. In 1996, this proportion was globally less than 25% (Deloitte & Touche, 2003).

On the other hand, in the less attractive countries' leagues, the money earned by clubs by the sale of television rights increased in a much-reduced fashion. This has further increased the financial divide. In Switzerland, for example, in the season 2001/02, the sale of the rights for retransmission of the games has brought a total of 5.5 million euros to the clubs (*Match Mag*, 12 July, 2000). This amount is equivalent to 0.7% of that received by the Premiership English teams. Because of this and more so than in the past, Swiss clubs, like teams from other countries whose football leagues are unable to generate important funds through the sale of television rights, cannot compete for good results at an international level.

Generally, even within the richest leagues, the money paid in retransmission rights benefited more the powerful clubs which have a vast fan base. This radically changed the European football landscape, especially in the countries where the clubs are the holders of the retransmission rights and can thus individually negotiate their sale, as in the case of Italy, Spain, Greece and Portugal. In Italy, the inequalities in the redistribution to the clubs of the money paid by television led to the start of the 2002/2003 top league season being postponed. In Greece, lots of teams are heavily indebted and in December 2003 the Government gave 600,000 euro to the clubs in order to ensure their short-term financial survival.

In the Italian case, the inequalities are manifest. For the 2004/2005 season, the five most powerful clubs (Juventus Turin, AC Milan, Inter Milan, AS Rome, Lazio Rome) have received 61.2% of the money spent by television for the retransmission rights. On average, they earned 47.2 million euros each, almost five times more than the 15 remaining clubs of the Serie A League. The best-paid club, Juventus Turin, received from the Sky TV network 34 times more money than the worst paid one, Brescia Calcio (*La Gazzetta dello Sport*, 12 October, 2004). Since the 2004/2005 season, Rupert Murdoch's channel Sky TV holds the rights for every club after the bankruptcy of the rival network Gioco Calcio, created in 2002 by the less competitive clubs and by the Italian Lega Calcio. This also reflects the concentration of economic power in the context of the globalisation.

The concentration of power in European football can be observed on a political level too, with the emergence of an organisation such as the "G-14". This lobby groups together 18 clubs from seven countries: England, Italy, Spain, Germany, France, Portugal and the Netherlands. The more or less hidden agenda of the "G-14" lobby is to organise a European Super League, which could widen the existing gap in the European football economy. The "G-14" lobby tries to impose its influence also on FIFA, by demanding financial compensation when players are selected to represent national teams.

The second process highlighted by Saskia Sassen (1991) in the context of globalisation, the dispersion of productive activities, is closely related to the first. Indeed, the deepening of the gulf separating the top clubs from the less well-off ones is directly linked to a change in the geographical origin of players transferred from clubs abroad. The modification of recruitment sources of foreign players has a tendency towards a relative increase in footballers coming from non-European countries, where players can be transferred without a big economic effort.

In Switzerland, for example, according to a statistical analysis carried out through national sport journals — *La Semaine sportive* (1977–1987), *Foot Hebdo* (1987–1994), *Match Mag* (1994–2002) — in the 2002/03 season, African and Latin-American players constituted 67.2% of the total number of players recruited abroad by professional and semi-professional clubs. This percentage, on average, from season 1977/78 to 1981/82, was only 12.8%. Unable to follow the explosion of salaries paid to the players in the main European leagues, Swiss clubs began to look for talent in less well-off countries. In this way, players recruited outside Europe steadily replaced footballers coming from the bordering States (Germany, Italy, France, Austria), Scandinavia (Sweden, Denmark, Norway) and Eastern Europe (Hungary, Czech Republic, former Yugoslavia).

At the level of the UEFA countries, for the 2002/2003 season, according to a statistical analysis carried out through Internet sites (www.soccerassociation.com, www.eufo.de) and football annual reviews (A–Z del Futbol Europeo), footballers from Oceanic, America, Asia and Africa represented 39.5% of the total number of players recruited abroad. Footballers from 135 different countries were integrated into the 1,358 squads of professional and semi-professional European clubs analysed in the study. Even if the historical and cultural links between the countries involved continue to play an important role in the direction of the flows, the recruitment of players by European clubs tends towards a diversification in terms of the geographical origin of footballers.

If we analyse the competition level towards which footballers playing abroad evolve according to their continental origin, it appears that Western Europeans are relatively more recruited by top clubs. On the contrary, African players are concentrated at the lower levels of competition. To demonstrate this, we have elaborated a five level hierarchy of European leagues based on the UEFA ranking. The first level of the hierarchy includes top divisions of England, Spain, Italy, Germany and France. In the second level, we find top leagues of the Netherlands, Portugal, Russia, Turkey and Greece. Inferior leagues of the countries mentioned above are ranked from the third to fifth level, as well as top divisions of the countries that have not been included in the first two levels. From this hierarchy, it results that the recruited players in Africa are comparatively more numerous in the last four levels of competition than in the first one. In fact, they represent 14.1% of the players recruited abroad by first level clubs, 20.8% of the players recruited abroad by second level clubs and 25.7% of the players recruited abroad by third level clubs.

The relative over-representation of players recruited in Africa at the lower levels of competition indicates, on the one hand, the position of a low cost labour force held by footballers of this origin in the European labour market. On the other hand, it illustrates the existence of an extensive number of networks linking European clubs and players' agents based in Europe with existing structures in African football, which is discussed in the next chapter.

Transnational policies of European clubs and players' agents

The concept of globalisation defined in Sassen's terms reveals the existence of a strategy based on the "delocalisation" of player "production" towards less well-off countries, in order to save money. The concept of transnationalism allows us to understand the way in which European clubs and players' agents follow this policy and form social morphologies organised in networks (Vertovec, 1999). The example of Manchester United's organisation for players' transfers illustrates exactly what we want to underline. The richest club of the world is active all over the globe with a close network of recruiters, as shown by this article found on the Internet site of the city of Manchester:

> Despite an extensive scouting network in Britain, the Reds are looking abroad, as well as continuing their efforts on finding the best young talents in the north. That's why they are steadily building a carefully selected network of links with clubs across the globe. They already have alliances with clubs in Norway, Belgium,

France, Australia, Sweden, Ireland, Wales and Scotland, and are looking at a relationship with an Academy in South Africa. For the first time in their history, United are looking at the beaches and barrios of Brazil for talent. Passport laws have made it traditionally difficult for English clubs to sign young South American talent and only established internationals could make the Trans-Atlantic trip. But a new tie-up with Portuguese club Sporting Lisbon will open a doorway to Brazil, due to the historic links between those two countries. Brazilians will be able to pick up European Union passports by joining Sporting and from there they can sign for United. It is just another step towards establishing a world-wide scouting network aimed at trawling the best teenage talents on the planet and bringing them to United. (www.manchesteronline.co.uk)

Like Manchester United, more and more European clubs follow a policy of world-wide recruitment of young players through the setting up of global networks. The Dutch club of Feyenoord Rotterdam, for example, owns football academies both in Africa and Latin America. An official of the club asserted that "the days when Feyenoord could afford to just scout in Ommoord and Croswijk are over. The club goes all over the world looking for young talents. Just like all the other international top clubs, Feyenoord now has a network of tipsters that stretches to all continents: from Ghana to Brazil and from Sweden to Japan" (www.feyenoord.com).

Feyenoord's main rival, Ajax Amsterdam, follows the same strategy and collaborates with clubs from Mexico to South Africa. On 17 July 1999, the most successful club of the Netherlands became the first European team to purchase a club situated outside Europe. In fact, the merger between the teams of Seven Stars and of Cape Town Spurs gave birth to Ajax Cape Town, a club owned 51% by Ajax Amsterdam. Since then, several players "nurtured" in South Africa, such as Steven Pienaar, crossed the Mediterranean Sea to reach the main team of the "Ajax transnational company".

Arsenal is also a good example that illustrates the setting up of global networks for the recruitment of young players. The London club has a partnership agreement with Beveren, a Belgian club. Beveren in turn is linked with a football academy on the Ivory Coast, owned by the French manager Jean-Marc Guillou. With Arsenal's help, Guillou took control of the Flemish club in 2001. The agreement between Arsenal and Beveren, in place until 2006, stipulates that the English club has first preference regarding Beveren players. Moreover, Arsenal loans young players to Beveren for them to become more seasoned. This was the case, among others, with Ireland's Graham Stack, the English player John Halls and the Latvian Igor Stepanovs.

An agreement with a Belgian club is particularly interesting for an English club because in Belgium no limits for non-communitarian players exist and an uninterrupted stay of three years is sufficient to apply for Belgian citizenship. This allows the bypassing of the rules regarding the recruitment of players from countries outside the European Union, which are still in force in England. Manchester United has an agreement with Royal Antwerp and Chelsea collaborates with Westerlo. In this manner, players recruited in Africa by English teams find that Belgium is a good place to develop their skills. It was notably the case of the Gambian player Arthur Gomez, recruited by Manchester United and loaned to Royal Antwerp, likewise with the South African footballers Jeffrey Pule, Mosia Boy-Boy and Michael Modubi who were transferred by Chelsea and loaned to Westerlo.

The globalisation of the recruitment of players through the setting up of transnational networks is not limited to European clubs. Players' agents' groups also follow the same policy. For example, the Pro Active Sports Group, an English corporation created in 1987, owns offices in ten different countries. In September 2002, the Group purchased the Norwegian corporation International Sports Management (ISM). In 2003, a partnership agreement was reached with the Portuguese Group Geste Futi. This agreement allowed the transfer, among others, of Cristiano Ronaldo from Sporting Lisbon to Manchester United for 17 million euros. In the future, the group "believes that the focused development of Central and Southern Europe is key to the Player Representation Division's long term objectives and remains committed to expanding its presence in France, Germany and Spain" (www.proactivesports.co.uk).

Regarding Africa, the main players' agents' companies active on this continent have also developed a close network of relations in the most important "exporting" countries. For example, the French corporation

InterContact Marketing, has several collaborators in different African countries. The owner of the company, Lucidio Ribeiro, explained that, most of the time, his corporation works with "former players, coaches and clubs officials. In the field, they perform discreetly a deep detection work and they also give advice on some players. The first approaches are generally made by them" (Afrique Football, May/June 2003). Once a player is considered good enough to be recruited by a European team, Ribeiro manages to obtain a visa for him. In this way, the player has the possibility of making a trip to Europe to be tested by clubs with which InterContact Marketing works.

The circulation of players in European countries

For a long time, the European football federations curbed the international circulation of players by quotas limiting the presence of non-national footballers in clubs. With the emergence of the European Union, since the season 1996/97, all quotas were abolished for players with a community passport. Hence, according to the statistics elaborated by Paolo Piani (2003), from season 1995/1996 to 2001/2002, the average percentage of non-national footballers playing in the first divisions of thirty UEFA country championships almost doubled, rising from 13.3% to 25.9%.

The "Bosman" judgement of the European Court of Justice, pronounced on December 15th 1995, brought profound changes regarding the transfer of footballers. This decree has in fact put an end to the practice according to which a club could prevent the departure without compensation of a player, even if the contract signed by him had expired. Henceforth, when a contract binding a football player to a club expires, the officials of the latter cannot prevent the player from signing a new contract with another club, nor can they demand a compensation fee.

As well as free movement for players of the European Union, the abolition of the rule allowing the clubs to keep footballers beyond the stated period in signed contracts has provoked a strong increase in players' mobility. In fact, the clubs began to sign long contracts with players, not to keep them, but to sell them before their work contract expired, which lead to a major increase in players' circulation. In the new legal context of footballers' transfers, more so than in the past, players' mobility, as underlined by French economist Jean-François Bourg (1989: p. 156), is "necessary to the good functioning of the system, which is based on the selection and movement of players".

Moreover, in the context of the dualisation of the European football economy, as mentioned before, more and more clubs depend on the "discovery" of young players, whose "purchase" is inscribed in a logic which consists of reselling them to a richer club in order to make a profit. Clubs that follow this kind of strategy recruit in areas where players can be transferred at a low cost, such as in Sub-Saharan Africa. Historically, Belgium was a starting point for African players in Europe. Even nowadays, this country continues to play an important role in this capacity.

In 2001, for example, Belgian club La Gantoise transferred from SC Zamalek the Egyptian Hossam Mido for 361,000 euros. One year later, La Gantoise resold Mido to Ajax Amsterdam for 4.5 million euros. In 2003, the player was transferred for 6 million euros to Olympique of Marseille. La Gantoise earned 500,000 euros according to the agreement made with Ajax. This stipulated that 30% of the profit of a new transfer had to be paid to the Belgian club (*Sport/Foot Magazine*, 14 May, 2003; 16 July, 2003; 11 February, 2004). One year after his arrival in France, Mido was resold to AS Rome. Considering that during the season 2002/2003 Ajax loaned him out to Celta Vigo, Mido moved between five clubs in five different countries within a period of three years.

Like professional Belgian leagues, the Swiss championship is sometimes a stepping-stone for players coming directly from Africa. For example, the Congolese player Shabani Nonda played three seasons for FC Zurich before being transferred to the Stade Rennais. In 2000, the French club resold Nonda to AS Monaco for almost 23 million euros (France Football, 1 April, 2003). The Senegalese players Henri Camara and Papa Bouba Diop also began their European career in Switzerland, from where they were transferred to French clubs. Finally, after a few years, they joined the "eldorado" of British teams.

As in the Belgian case, top European clubs use Swiss clubs as a "holding bay" for young talents to develop. It has been notably the case of Mohammed Kallon, a player born in Sierra Leone, recruited in Gambia by Inter Milan when he was fifteen and loaned, among others, to the Swiss club FC Lugano. The strategy pursued by top clubs of purchasing players and lending them to less competitive clubs leads to an increase in the mobility of footballers. Kallon, for example, changed clubs six times in five years before coming back to Inter Milan.

One of the eight Cameroonian players interviewed, Thimothée Atouba, has also experienced a spectacular rise. Transferred from Union Douala to Neuchâtel in 1999 for 27,000 euros, one and a half years later he was resold to FC Basle for 270,000 euros. In the summer of 2004, Tottenham London bought the player for 3.5 million euros. This example shows that the situation of African players, as a "low cost" labour force and with a very low "purchase" price at the outset of their career, lends them perfectly to the pursuit of a profit-oriented strategy based on their movement.

One other player interviewed, Hervé Tum, stressed that for African players, the stay in Swiss clubs is considered as a possible stepping stone to being recruited by more prestigious European clubs. According to this, integration in the host society is not considered as essential. On the contrary, Tum asserted that "to me, Switzerland, France or Europe is the same thing. I've not any particular link. I'm here and I do a job. I can have relationships with people, but I'm not linked to a place. If I link myself, it's like if I'll finish my life here, but for me the future is situated elsewhere". In the typologies elaborated by Joseph Maguire (1999) for professional sportsmen and by Ralph Grillo (2000) and Nina Glick-Schiller (in Potot, 2003) for migrants in general, Hervé Tum and six other Cameroonian players interviewed may be portrayed as "mercenary crossborders" living abroad in a situation of "enclavement in the permanent transmigration".

Only one player interviewed, Augustine Simo, asserted that for his personal well-being, it was important to become integrated in Switzerland. Indeed, at the beginning of his European career, he crossed four countries in three years (Italy, Switzerland, France and Spain) and ended up finding himself without a contract. Forced to return to Cameroon, after a few months, he reintegrated the European professional football circuit with a different outlook. Consequently, despite his good performance during the rest of his career, he preferred to stay in Switzerland rather than go abroad and earn more money. In 2004, Simo got married to a Swiss girl with whom he plans a future, between Switzerland and Cameroon.

Like Stig-Inge Bjornebyë, Shaun Goater and Gerard Weikens in the interview-based analysis on foreign professional players in England performed by Jonathan Magee and John Sugden (2002), Augustine Simo can be considered as a settler. In 2001, he became the first African player chosen to be captain of a Swiss team, Neuchâtel Xamax.

Downward mobility and precariousness of African players

If some African players have an upward mobility which allows them to reach the top European clubs, we should not neglect the examples of downward mobility of a great number of players, who are very often victims of the speculation system based on players' transfers. In Switzerland, for example, from 1990 to 2002, only 31 African footballers have been transferred to more important clubs after their training time in a Confederate club. In 127 other cases (76.6%), they have been recruited by less competitive clubs or they have simply disappeared from the professional circuit.

One footballer interviewed, Frédéric Ayangma, also went through a very tough period in France at the age of fifteen, one year after his transfer from Cameroon. At the age of 14, through former player Roger Milla, Ayangma joined the football academy of Montpellier. His performances did not satisfy the French club, which resulted in Ayangma being left on the street. Luckily, Ayangma's brother lived in Paris and was able to help him. After two years, Ayangma reintegrated himself into the football professional circuit, but since February 2004 he is again without a contract.

Ayangma explains the mechanism by which lots of African players coming to Europe end up going underground:

> There are a lot of problems linked to players' agents. Some come to Cameroon to see local matches. They imagine that you are highly skilled and they send you where they think you can get a contract. If it doesn't go as they hoped, they abandon you on your own and disappear. I know of a lot of such cases in France. You get a tourist visa, you go around searching for a club; sometimes they don't even know the officials. They hope that a club will be convinced anyway. If they see that they pay for you but nothing works, they abandon you. Once your visa is expired, you can't do anything. It's like a spiral. You don't have a residence permit; clubs don't want you anymore, even for a test. If my brother had not been in Paris, after Montpellier, I think that I would have got caught up in the same system.

As suggested by Frederic Ayangma, a Belgian report (2001) asserted: "most of the players arrive in Belgium after the issuing of a tourist visa of three months for a simple trial, which allows the players to transit from one club to another until their agents find satisfaction". According to the authors of the report, in a general way, it was noted that there are a very few contracts proposed in comparison with the amount of circulation. Consequently, an important number of players hesitate to return to their country of origin and attempt by any the means to remain in Europe.

Because of this, many African players who migrated "with the ball" (Lanfranchi and Taylor, 2000), and who are not able to practise the profession that had brought them to Europe, end up by finding themselves in very precarious situations. In a recent work, Evariste Tshimanga Bakadiababu (2001) furnished several examples of players who had been exploited and then dropped out from the professional European football industry, in particular Cameroonian, Nigerian and Guinean nationals. As well, John Bale (2001) presented a case of Cameroonian player Bodo Njiki, who was a victim of trafficking both in France and in Belgium. The geographer analyses this case as an instance of "neo-colonial exploitation".

Moreover, even players who sign contracts as professionals in European clubs do not earn as much money as is generally thought. On the contrary, the interviews with Cameroonian players revealed the existence of discrimination in terms of salary. Thimothée Atouba, for example, received from the first European club for which he played, Neuchâtel Xamax, only a third of the sum stipulated in the contract that he signed. Only after one year did he manage to obtain two thirds of the sum, almost 3,300 euros per month. During this first year, the club officials and his agent reacted to his complaints by threatening to send him back to Cameroon.

Similarly, Augustine Simo stressed that some players' agents work only with African footballers "because they know that they can take away from us up to 70% of our salary. When we come to Europe, we look at the positive side of the things. We are already happy if we can earn a small amount and help our family". Thus, African players, at the beginning of their career lend themselves perfectly to the role of a flexible and easily exploitable labour force, of which European clubs and players' agents do not hesitate to take advantage.

Conclusion

To understand professional football players' migrations we need a theoretical framework, which allows us to lean from a macro sociological to a micro sociological perspective. The "circulatory" approach proposed permits us to take into account these different aspects of migrations. The concept of globalisation is useful to analyse the context of European professional football in geo-economic terms. Transnationalism is a concept that allows the analysis of the general geo-economic context to be bound to strategies pursued by clubs in order to take advantage of the latter. This notion, with the social network, is the link to the micro sociological approach based on the reconstruction of players' career paths through a longitudinal approach based on life history interviews.

Taking into account different scales and perspectives, our analysis integrates social and economic criteria and differentiates itself from a pure market approach. Indeed, we share Patrick McGovern's (2002: p. 26) point of view of considering that the "pattern of international migrations within the football industry are socially embedded". This means that to fully appreciate professional football players' flows, it is necessary to go beyond the analysis of the labour market economic structure in which these migrations take place.

Applied to African players' migrations, the theoretical approach proposed illustrates the situation of extreme socio-economic dependency in which the continent finds itself. Firstly, in the context of globalisation, we observe a concentration of power in the hands of top European clubs. This concentration is responsible for a growing internal and external economic gap. Because of this, African clubs cannot retain their players and are even forced to sell them if they want to ensure their financial survival. In some ways, an agreement with a European club or with players' agents with good connections with European clubs is a necessity in order to have monetary resources which then allow clubs to be competitive even at a local scale.

This explains the reason which makes African football structures look for partnerships beyond the Mediterranean Sea, whatever the price. In reality, the terms of the exchange for African players' transfers are characterised by a strong inequality. The monetary value of a footballer in the African market is clearly inferior to his value once a European club has recruited him. Equally, his financial value varies considerably according to the State and the club in Europe to which he has been transferred. These strong geo-economic discrepancies stimulate the development of a speculative profit-oriented strategy which provokes significant movements of players.

In this context, players' mobility takes a unilateral direction from Africa toward Europe and transnational networks set up in order to provide European clubs with young footballers are controlled from above, by the latter or by players' agents based in Europe. Because of this, most of the income coming from players' transfers ends up in European bank accounts. Under these conditions, as John Bale (1996, 2001) and Paul Darby (2001) pointed out, African "muscle exodus" inhibits the development of African football or, at the very least, creates dependent development.

Finally, in the multi-stranded approach proposed, the reconstruction of African players' career paths indicates that dependency is also evident at an individual level. Once they reach Europe, African footballers are victims of speculation, discrimination and abuses in terms of salary, labour stability and work access. Very often, they are obliged to accept dreadful conditions in order to obtain a work permit, allowing them to stay in Europe. This will continue until the moment when, in the global labour market of footballers, players recruited in Third World countries fill the role of a low cost labour force through whom European clubs pursue a policy based on salary dumping.

Bibliography

Bale, J., (2001) 'African footballers and Europe: Migration, exploitation and postcolonialism', Paper presented at the Annual Conference of British International Studies Association, Bradford.

Bale, J. and Sang, J. (1996) *Kenyan running: Movement culture, geography and global change*. London: Frank Cass.

Bourg, J.-F. (1989) 'Le marché du travail sportif', in W. Andreff (ed) *Economie politique du sport*. Paris: Dalloz, pp.145–169.

Centre pour l'égalité des chances et la lutte contre le racisme belge (2001) 'Mécanisme des filières et des trafics de recrutement de joueurs', http://www.antiracisme.be/fr/rapports/traite/2001/06b-traite01.pdf

Darby, P. (2001) 'The new scramble for Africa: African Football Labour Migration to Europe', in: J.A. Mangan (ed) *Europe, sport, world: Shaping global societies*. London: Frank Cass, pp. 217–244.

Deloitte&Touche (2003) *Annual review of football finance. Appendices*, Manchester: Deloitte&Touche.

Grillo, R. (2000) 'Transmigration and cultural diversity in the construction of europe', Paper presented at the symposium "Cultural Diversity and the Construction of Europe", Barcelona. http://www.uoc.edu/ webcat/promocio/simposium/english/Grilling.rtf

Jimenez Macias, J. (2003) *A–Z del futbol europeo. Premium*, Caceres: Ediciones-JJM.

Kaufmann, V., Bergman, M. and, Joye, D. (2004) 'Motility: mobility as a capital', Paper presented at the International Sociological Association Research Committee on social stratification and mobility (RC 28), Neuchâtel.

Lanfranchi, P. and Taylor, M. (2001) *Moving with the ball: The migration of professional footballers*. New York, Oxford: Berg.

Magee, J. and Sugden, J. (2002) 'The world at their feet. Professional football and international labor migration', *Journal of Sport & Social Issues* Vol. 26, No. 4: pp. 421–437.

Maguire, J. (1999) *Global sport. Identities, societies and civilizations*. Cambridge: Polity Press.

Mc Govern, P. (2002) 'Globalization or internationalization? Foreign footballers in the English League, 1946–95', *Sociology* Vol. 36, No. 1: pp. 23–42.

Papastergiadis, N. (2000) *The turbulence of migration: Globalization, deterritorialization and hybridity*. Cambridge: Polity Press.

Piani, P. (2003) 'Globalizzazione e flussi migratori nel calcio', Coverciano: Federazione Italiana Giuoco Calcio, Paper presented at the Conference "Aspetti politici, giuridici e sociali della circolazione dei calciatori, Florence.

Poli, R. (2004) *Les migrations internationales des footballeurs. Trajectoires de joueurs camerounais en Suisse*. Neuchâtel: CIES.

Potot, S. (2003) *Circulation et réseaux de migrants roumains: une contribution à l'étude des nouvelles mobilités en Europe*. Nice: Université Sophia Antipolis, http://tel.ccsd.cnrs.fr/documents/archives0/00/00 /34/80/tel-000 03480-00/tel-00003480.pdf.

Robertson, R. (1992) *Globalization. Social theory and global culture*. London: Sage.

Sassen, S. (1991) *The global city: New York, London, Tokyo*. Chichester: Princeton University Press.

Tarrius, A. (1989) *Anthropologie du mouvement*. Caen: Paradigme.

Tshimanga Bakadiababu, E. (2001) *Le commerce et la traite des footballeurs africains et sud-américains en Europe*. Paris: L'Harmattan.

Vertovec, S. (1999) 'Conceiving and Researching Transnationalism', *Ethnic and Racial Studies* Vol. 22, No. 2: pp. 447–462.

LAW, REGULATION AND THE 'EUROPEANIZATION' OF A GLOBAL GAME

Simon Boyes
Nottingham Trent University

Introduction

This chapter discusses the role of regulation, in particular legal regulation, in the development of association football. It seeks to argue that law and regulation in Europe have had a significant impact upon the form and operation of the game at a global level.

This argument is broken down into two distinct elements. The first emphasises the importance of law and regulation in Europe, most significantly in Britain, in initial moves toward codification and formalisation of association football in respect of the way in which the game is played. This first strand recognises the role of law as being facilitative of this process and as providing parallels in terms of broader societal trends at the time of codification.

The second strand of the discussion is itself partitioned into two separate elements. The first emphasises the important role European law has played in shaping football on a global scale in the modern era, noting in particular that this has occurred at the administrative level rather than impacting directly upon the physical nature of the game. The second element of this discussion considers the extent to which players have become 'Europeanized' as a result of these legal and regulatory interactions.

Phase 1: Law, regulation and the creation of a global game

The European nations, Britain foremost amongst them, were key actors in the initial development of the system of global sport and its regulation. The development of the football codes beyond largely localised, un-codified practices is often described as coinciding with the industrial revolution period in Britain (Elias, 1978; Elias and Dunning 1986). Though it could never be claimed that Britain was responsible for the invention of 'football', there being evidence of similar games and rituals over thousands of years across the globe (Hutchinson, 1996: p. 60), it was during this period that the British took the game and produced a coherent and structured package.

The industrial revolution fuelled the drive towards regulation and codification. Interaction between increasingly disparate locations across Britain required that there be some commonality of understanding between participants in sporting activity. For interdependence to occur successfully there is a requirement for a degree of stability, organisation and direction. Sport as a spectacle or participatory event becomes unintelligible and largely unplayable where the participants are not playing to at least substantially similar sets of rules. This is fertile ground for regulation. Where prevailing social conditions do not provide the necessary conditions for such activities, intervention is required in order to facilitate this. Rule-making, monitoring and enforcement, the *sine qua non* of regulation (Black, 2001: p. 129), were utilised to alter the underlying conditions. Thus common rules in sport, and the football codes in particular, were developed as a result of increasing interdependence and the subsequent need for facilitative frameworks (Cashmore, 1996: p. 79).

The modern game of association football has its roots in the early nineteenth century, when clubs and teams were formed in order to engage in competition. Despite this, football remained largely un-codified, with the rules of each particular contest being largely localised and transmitted orally rather than being a centralised written code (Dunning, 1993: p. 51). Aspects foreign to the modern game, such as the handling of the ball and tackling by making use of the shoulder and arms, were variously in use during this period:

Football, at this stage, was not so much a single game as an array
of roughly similar tribal codes preferred by different public schools.
(Birley, 1993: p. 257)

Regulation, then, had a clear facilitative function in respect of permitting
football to be played, but the nature and substance of that regulation has
also had a significant impact upon the manner in which the game is played.
The development of the regulation of football and other sports was
paralleled and, perhaps, promoted by a significant growth in the state
regulation of personal conduct, primarily concerned with reducing violence
and disorder. At the heart of this was the Offences Against the Person Act
1861. And so, while the regulation of football may well have been brought
about by the need for a common understanding of the game for the
purposes of facilitation, much of its substance was derived from a broader
drive towards the control of violent and disorderly behaviour and reckless
conduct likely to result in injury.

The role of law in shaping football's regulation is exemplified by the
case of *R v Bradshaw* [1878] 14 Cox CC 83. While regulatory impulse
moved toward the outlawing of violent and disorderly behaviour, the law
appeared to look favourably on the facilitation and control of sport, in
particular football, exercised by the creation and maintenance of rules. In
Bradshaw, a criminal case, the defendant was tried for charging another
player after the ball had been played. The victim was seriously injured
and later died. In his judgment Lord Justice Bramwell stated that while
the rules of football could not make any unlawful act lawful, they could
act as a key indicator as to the mental state of the participant in a game
such as football. If a player, playing according to the rules of the game,
caused injury or death then, according to Lord Justice Bramwell, it would
be reasonable to infer from his adherence to the rules that the qualities of
intent or recklessness required in order to be guilty of an offence were
unlikely to be present. The rules of the game were validated by the courts
and consequently the game itself gained status as being considered 'lawful'
(Opie, 1987: p. 27).

The position adopted by the court in *Bradshaw* can be usefully
contrasted with that in a case involving sporting practice, closely associated

with the prevailing social impulses of the day. *R v Coney* [1882] 8 QBD 534 involved a case brought against the participants in a bare-knuckle prize-fight. The fight drew a large and noisy crowd, many of whom were involved in gambling on the outcome of the contest. The court found the two combatants to be causing a breach of the peace and considered that the members of the crowd were aiding and abetting them in this, contrary to the Justices of the Peace Act 1361. While violent and rowdy sports were still considered unlawful, the 'civilized' game of association football was considered to be an appropriate pastime.

Previous legal responses to the coarse, un-codified football-style games of the past, practiced by the lower-classes, were clearly disapproving. Such games were often outlawed on the basis that participation was at the expense of militaristic activities, such as archery, undermined public order, or was directly disapproved of by the Church. Football and other such sports were,

> ... widely viewed as valueless diversionary spectacle closely connected to idleness, gambling, drink, and violence — at best crude folk culture, at worst a manifestation of cultural decline and barbarism. (Gruneau, 1993: p. 86)

In 1314 the Lord Mayor of London outlawed football within the city on pain of imprisonment. King Edward III enacted measures in 1331 to outlaw football and from 1338–1453, during the 100 years' war between England and France, Edward III, Richard II, Henry IV and Henry V outlawed football on the basis that it distracted the masses from practising useful military disciplines, most notably archery (Gerhardt, 1994). The Oxbridge football matches of the 16th Century were also considered to be on a par with prize-fighting (Opie, 1987: p. 22).

However, the new 'civilized' game won the approval of the state as being,

> ... a disciplined, codified, responsible game: a game which Victorian schoolmasters could not only enjoy, but could also introduce to their flocks with a clear conscience, happy in the knowledge that by playing football the boys were learning teamwork, restraint, fairness and the meaning of rules. (Hutchinson, 1996: p. 17)

The first 'hands-free' code is widely considered to have been adopted at Cambridge University (Curry, 2004) and was followed by the inception of the Football Association in 1863, as an overarching regulator for the new sport of association football. The code adopted in 1863, whilst predominantly concerned with providing a facilitative framework of rules, also included rules outlawing tripping, hacking and pushing. The protection of players from physical harm was also enhanced through the outlawing the wearing of "projecting nails, iron plates, or gutta percha on the soles or heels of … boots". The broader societal drive towards orderly and responsible conduct was manifested through the adoption of playing rules specifically aimed at this, rather than the facilitation of the playing of the game itself.

So the game of association now had 'in game' regulation, it had a regulator to oversee the operation of the rules, and this regulatory package had the support of the law, through a willingness to allow the rules of the game to preclude legal regulation, a willingness which continues today (Gunn, 1998; p. 221 *et seq.*), though the game has evolved under the influence of broader societal trends (Opie, 1987: p. 34). The beauty of such a package was that it was easily exportable.

The game shaped by Victorian Britain's impulses towards codification and regulation, coupled with the permissive approach of the law, spread across its borders into Europe and beyond. The spread of association football appears to have occurred in two separate ways. First, there are specific examples of the game being spread by foreign workers taking it with them from Britain home to Germany, the Netherlands, Czecho-slovakia, Austria, Italy, Brazil and Hungary. Second, the inverse process occurred, with British workers and students taking the game abroad with them. Direct examples of this means of transmission can be seen in respect of France, Denmark, Belgium, Russia, Uruguay, Spain, Uganda and Mexico (Guttmann, 1993: pp. 129–130). Once this diffusion began from Britain, it is clear that it continued apace. The self-same methods of propagation which had taken the game to Europe also took it further abroad. Clubs were founded by Britons in Europe and further afield. Other European nationals did likewise, carrying the British/European sport of association football worldwide (Lanfranchi, 1994: pp. 27–28; Giulianotti, 1999: p. 7). A British game, honed in Europe, spread very quickly throughout the world, where the associated administrative and regulatory structures were adopted almost without question (Guttmann, 1993: p. 144). Once happily in place around the globe, the rules and regulations exported from Britain facilitated further integration on an international level; where peoples from disparate geographical locations have a common understanding of a game it is easy to play even where linguistic or cultural barriers might otherwise exist (Giulianotti, 1999: p. 1)

Once operating across the globe, it took little time before international competition was commenced. As with the initial development of football as an organised and structured activity, where interaction exists there comes the need for a regulator to maintain the commonality of under-standing that had fostered the growth in the first instance (Boyes, 2000: p. 69). So the Fédération Internationale de Football Association (FIFA) was created; a global regulator for a global game. Despite the well documented reticence of the British associations in FIFA's early years, the global regulator remained solidly European both in terms of leadership and location (Sugden, Tomlinson and Darby, 1998: p. 13). The European hand would remain on the regulatory tiller well into the twentieth century, so by the time that control was wrested from the Europeans with the election of João Havelange as president in 1974 the global game had a European stamp deeply embedded within it.

Phase 2: Law, regulation and the 're-Europeanization' of football

With the creation of FIFA and the massive expansion of football across the globe, the power base shifted. Now individual nation states did not have the influence they might have had in the initial stages of the game's development:

> ... the game was bigger than any one nation. If national associations, governments or legal systems objected to the manner in which FIFA regulated the sport then that was largely inconsequential. Because of its global reach FIFA had an almost unchallengeable control over the way in which the game was run, however much anyone might object.

Before Bosman: Bogotá, retention and the Irish problem

There were occasional skirmishes. In 1948 a dispute arose between the Colombian football authorities and FIFA over the creation of a new professional league in the country. This lead to Colombia's membership of FIFA being suspended, with the consequence that the 'Dimayor', Colombia's newly conceived professional league, was able to operate outside of the constricture of FIFA's regulations. Most notable in this regard were the regulations pertaining to the transfer of players: Colombian teams were no longer required to pay transfer fees and could therefore contract players with the only expense being wages. Colombian teams attracted large numbers of Argentines and Uruguayans during this period, football in both nations being afflicted by strike action at the time (Taylor, 1998: p. 167). However, the financial rewards available also attracted players from Britain. Foremost amongst these was the Manchester United winger Charlie Mitten who left Europe to join Millionarios of Bogotá. Millionarios were able to increase Mitten's basic wage tenfold, as well as offering a generous win bonus. Such riches, and the ability to move without the need for a transfer fee, were unprecedented in British football at a time when the maximum wage still applied and the case of *Eastham v Newcastle United* [1963] 1 Ch 413, had yet to make inroads into the system of 'retain and transfer' (Grayson, 2000: p. 402). However, of all those British footballers who subverted FIFA regulation by moving to Colombian clubs, only Mitten lasted a year and on their return the footballers were harshly treated by the football establishment, being fined and suspended for their audacity in daring to move outside of the football mainstream and subvert the regulatory hegemony. Colombia's return to the fold was negotiated in 1950, with the proviso that the 'illicitly' acquired players could be retained until 1954 (Taylor, 1998: p. 170). The brief flirtation with free-agency was over and football settled back into regulatory uniformity.

Legal challenges which did arise during this period were confined within national boundaries. George Eastham's challenge to football's retain–and–transfer system represented a limited victory, both geographically in terms of the court's jurisdiction and in the fact that many regard it as being somewhat pyrrhic (Grayson, 2000: p. 402). A decade after *Eastham* the futility of any regulatory or legal challenge to the dominance of FIFA was emphasised by a related case which came before an English court. In 1972 a dispute arose between the Football Association (FA) and a player over the compatibility of FIFA regulations with English law. *Cooke v Football Association* [1972] came about through a situation involving a player wishing to transfer between Irish and English clubs (reported in *The Times*, 24 March, 1972). FIFA regulations required that any player transferring between two clubs coming under the authority of different national associations would be required to obtain a transfer certificate from his former association before he could be registered as a player with his new club. In the instant case Cooke was unable to obtain such documentation from the Football Association of Ireland, and thus the FA refused to allow him to register with his English club. In finding for the player, the judge commented that if FIFA's regulation were contrary to English law, then the FA would simply have to withdraw from the organisation. Cooke obtained his transfer, but there was no withdrawal and FIFA's regulations remained intact and unrevised.

The European Union: The re-regulation of football

But a change came and a potential rival to FIFA as a regulator of aspects of football emerged, with the initiation, growth and development of the European Union (EU). It is indisputable that one name has become synonymous with intervention of EU law in football. A swift glance over the details of transfer activity conducted between football clubs in the recent past serves as clear evidence of this. Of most note is that there is a significant number of players after whose names, where the transfer fee would normally be listed, one will simply find the word 'Bosman'; not 'free transfer' or 'out of contract', as would be more legally correct, but the surname of a Belgian journeyman footballer. That this name has penetrated the consciousness of the football world to such a degree is testament to the shift which has taken place.

This chapter is not an appropriate forum for the minute dissection of the case in question; nevertheless, it is useful to briefly recite the facts of the case. In *Union Royale Belge des Sociétés de Football Association ASBL v Bosman* Case C-415/93 [1995] ECR I-4921 (*Bosman*) the European Court of Justice (ECJ) found that rules preventing the transfer of players after the conclusion of a playing contract, and those including EU nationals amongst those restricted by limitations imposed on the number of 'foreign' players that could be fielded by any one team, were contrary to EU laws which prohibit nationality-based discrimination and restrictions on the freedom of movement of economically active persons. Why then did the case have such an impact? Why did it not simply disappear in the same way as *Cooke v FA*? Here the football authorities were not simply dealing with one dissenter: the application of EU law spanned what remained the world's most politically powerful geographic region, encompassing the world's biggest (and richest) clubs and leagues, a vast majority of the world's best international sides and huge swathes of the world's top players attracted from all over the globe to the opportunities available in Europe (Maguire and Bale, 1994: p. 2). FIFA could not simply sweep this challenge aside.

The problem for the football authorities was further exacerbated as the decision appeared to re-invigorate the European Commission, whose forays into the football sphere had previously been limited to problems pertaining to the ticketing arrangements for the Italian World Cup of 1990 and a 'soft law' agreement with the Union of European Football Associations (UEFA): the infinitely complicated '3+2 rule', which regulated the inclusion of a limited number of 'foreign' players in club sides. The European Commission went for the jugular, suggesting that the whole of football's transfer system — not just the aspects condemned by the European Court of Justice in *Bosman* — was contrary to EU law. The result was negotiation rather than litigation and resulted in further amendments being made to the transfer system, though the reorganised transfer structure still bears strong resemblance to its forerunner.

Although there is no case-law or legislation here to declare the transfer system as being unlawful, the influence of the EU is clear. The implicit threat of regulation through litigation from the EU was sufficient to force a change in the rules of the game in line with the norms and principles embodied by EU law. Most notably, from the perspective of this chapter at least, the new transfer system has not just taken effect within the EU, but because of the need to operate on a 'level playing field' in these matter, the European approach has been enacted worldwide. With a shift in the power dynamic, a global game has become 'Europeanized' once more. The 'old' position, in which FIFA's political dominance allowed it to impose its regulations on member nations, these rules being effectively 'internalized', was reversed. Now a political power-bloc overlapping FIFA's jurisdiction both geographically and subjectively was able to effectively 'externalize' its own rules and norms by forcing a change to global regulation. Where, in the past, legal and regulatory interventions had largely impacted on the manner in which the game was played, through its playing rules, or had been sufficiently weak to enable them to be delimited within one, or a small number of nations, the geographic reach and political weight of the EU essentially provided FIFA with a *fait accompli* — regulate or be regulated. When faced with such situations self-regulators generally respond in a defensive manner and amend their regimes in order to reduce the likelihood of legal or legislative intervention (Kaye, 2003: p. 7).

Transforming footballers' nationalities

The 'Europeanization' of the game through the impact of EU law and regulation has not been limited to the externalization of norms and principles; it has also resulted in the internalization or 'Europeanization' of growing numbers of footballers.

The measure, designed to liberalise the movement of professional footballers within the European Union, has had some unexpected side effects. The *Bosman* judgment has not impacted upon the ability of the sport's ruling bodies to impose restrictions upon the number of non-EU nationals featuring in club sides. Both the Italian Serie A and the English Premier League, for example, restrict their teams to playing three non-EU nationals in competitive games. In addition to these restrictions, obtaining a work permit to play professionally can be extremely difficult. For would-be Premier League players originating outside of the EU the task is an onerous one (Gardiner and Welch, 2000: pp. 116–117): generally, in order to qualify, the player will be required to have represented their nation in at least seventy-five percent of competitive internationals for which they were available for selection over the preceding two-years. In addition only those players who have represented a team in ranked by FIFA in the top 70 nations can qualify in this way. Work permit applications for players not meeting these criteria are considered by an Independent Football Review Panel, which considers the application on the basis of whether the player is an international player of the highest calibre and thus likely to make a significant contribution at the highest level of the game in the United Kingdom (Home Office, 2004).

Thus the opportunity to play in the Premier League and the other leading leagues throughout Europe is potentially limited to the cream of players possessing non-EU nationalities. However, players and their agents have identified and seized upon flaws in the system. Once recognised as an EU national, the law requires that a player be allowed to ply his trade anywhere within the Union, thus negating the rigorous work permit requirements and circumventing nationality quotas imposed in domestic and European club competitions.

Divergent trends: Legal controls on 'Europeanized' players

Consequently non-EU players have become increasingly keen to become recognised as EU nationals. They have sought to achieve their aim in a number of different ways, not all of them legitimate. The trend appears to have been most prevalent amongst players of South American origin. In both of Europe's leading leagues in Italy and Spain, it has become commonplace for non-EU players to make applications to become naturalised and thus obtain citizenship, bringing with it the obvious benefits of obtaining free movement across the EU.

Such players appear to have been remarkably successful in tracing distant European relatives. Juan Sebastian Veron, who once plied his extremely lucrative trade as a midfield playmaker for Italian champions Lazio, faced a judicial inquiry and criminal charges in relation to the manner in which he had obtained Italian citizenship. Argentine Veron claimed that a maternal great-great grandmother gave him the right to Italian citizenship; later investigations suggested that he had not provided adequate documentary evidence to support his claim. Other players and agents have been thoroughly unscrupulous; three players (two Brazilians and a Paraguayan national) of Italian club Udinese faced prosecution after the Portuguese passports they held were deemed to be forgeries. The players were subsequently registered as 'non-EU nationals' for the purposes of the Serie A nationality quota. French side St Etienne were deducted six points in their domestic league championship for fielding players holding false documentation. Monaco and Metz also faced disciplinary procedures.

The impact of the affair was not really felt within the United Kingdom; however, the National Crime Intelligence Service (NCIS) launched inquiries into the validity of the documents of 80 players playing in England. Derby County encountered difficulties when their Argentine striker Esteban Fuertes was deported from the UK for travelling on forged Italian documentation. Because of the Fuertes affair the Premier League issued clubs with guidelines regarding their dealings with non-EU nationals. Arsenal suffered similarly, with two Brazilian would-be signings, Edu and Edmilson, unable to provide the appropriate documentation to gain entry to the United Kingdom. Edu was, however, subsequently signed by Arsenal.

Endgame? The globalization of a European game?

The ability of non-EU nationals to ply their trade freely within the EU has been further expanded by the decisions of domestic courts in Italy and Spain. These landmark decisions concerned two east-European footballers, Ukrainian Andrei Shevchenko and Estonia-born Valeri Karpin. Both had complained that nationality restrictions concerning the number of non-EU nationals allowed in teams offended against their employment rights as nationals of states with trade agreements with the EU. These mirror the earlier decision in the *Malaja* case (CE 30 December 2002), which determined that a Polish basketball player could not be discriminated against under the terms of nationality quota restrictions. A similar case was brought before the European Court of Justice by a Hungarian footballer, Tibor Balog (Case C-246/98 *Tibor Balog v Royal Charleroi Sporting Club*). In Balog's case, the imminence of legal action was a prime driver behind the amendment by FIFA of the transfer regulations to the effect that the *Bosman* approach to transfers was extended beyond the EU and across the globe (Lowrey, Neatror and Williams, 2002). This view was finally recognised by the ECJ in the case of *Deutscher Handballbund v Maros Kolpak* C-438/00. The case involved a Slovakian handball player who was employed as a professional by a German second division team. As a national of a non-European Economic Area (EEA) State, Kolpak was not considered by the German regulator to qualify for the benefits emergent from the decision in *Bosman*. Thus the regulator limited the number of non-EEA nationals which a team could field at any given time. Kolpak argued that an association agreement between Slovakia and the European Union entitled him to be treated in the same manner as an European Economic Area (EEA) national as regards access to employment. The key element in the judgment of the ECJ was that the relevant part of the association agreement was capable of 'direct effect', that is being applied by a EEA Member State court, and thus that sporting bodies were, in effect, unable to discriminate against nationals of association agreement countries once they were legally employed within an EEA Member State (Boyes, 2003: pp. 72 *et seq.*; van den Bogaert 2004: pp. 267 *et seq.*). Ostensibly, this is a relatively limited expansion of the *Bosman* ruling, as the EU has a small number of association agreements with European states. However, the ruling has the potential to have a significantly greater impact because of the existence of the Cotonou Agreement. This is an international agreement signed between the EU and nations from forming the ACP (Africa, Caribbean, Pacific), now numbering over 70. Article 13(3) of the Cotonou Agreement contains provisions substantially similar to those applied in *Kolpak*, meaning that this is likely to spread the impact of the judgment to nearly 100 nations (Branco Martins, 2004: p. 26).

However, it is important to note that this ruling applies only to the treatment of affected players once lawfully employed in an EU Member State, and does not provide a right of entry or access to employment for association agreement State nationals or a right of movement between EU Member States (Branco Martins, 2004: p. 27; *cf* Gardiner, 2000: p. 1). Nevertheless, the judgment has some serious implications for football as it shifts regulatory responsibility from the football authorities onto the State, as the rules applied in the granting of work permits is now key if football is to avoid "a flood of imported cheap foreign players" (Gardiner, 2000: p. 1).

Conclusions: The end or just the beginning?

The role of law and regulation in the development of association football is clear. Although this work focuses on the sculpting function played in the development, there is an ongoing role. Footballers today are still subject to legal sanction, criminal and civil, for wrongdoings which fall outside of the rules and spirit of the game (James, 2002). Similarly, though the

European Commission has now closed its file pertaining to football, not all in the game are satisfied and the players' international representative body FIFPro continues to support action by players seeking to challenge FIFA's new regulations on the basis of European Union law (Parrish, 2004: p. 149). As this new wave of legal challenges reaches the European Court of Justice, there is significant potential for further liberalisation within Europe and for the extension of that across the globe.

Bibliography

Birley, D. (1993) *Sport and the making of Britain*. Manchester: Manchester University Press.

Black, J. (2001) 'Decentring regulation: Understanding the role of regulation and self-regulation in a 'post-regulatory' world', *Current Legal Problems* Vol. 54, p. 103.

Boyes, S. (2000) 'Globalization, law and the re-regulation of sport', in Gardiner, S. and Caiger, A. (eds) *Professional sport in the EU: Regulation and re-regulation*. The Hague: TMC Asser Press.

———— (2003) 'In the shadow of Bosman: The regulatory penumbra of sport in the EU', *Nottingham Law Journal* Vol. 12(2), p. 72.

Branco Martins, R. (2004) 'The Kolpak case: Bosman times 10?', *International Sports Law Journal* Iss. 1–2: p. 26

Cashmore, E. (1996) *Making sense of sports*, 2 ed. Oxford: Blackwell.

Curry, G. (2004) 'Eton-Rugby status rivalry and the bifurcation of football', Paper presented at the International Football Institute Conference, 2 September.

Dunning, E. (1993) 'Sport in the civilising process: aspects of development of modern sport', in Maguire, J. and Pearton, R. (eds) *The sports process: A comparative and developmental approach*. Champaign, IL: Human Kinetics.

Elias, N. (1978) *The civilizing process*. Oxford: Blackwell.

Elias, N. and Dunning, E. (1986) *Quest for excitement: Sport and leisure in the civilizing process*. Oxford: Blackwell.

Gardiner, S. (2000) 'Support for quotas in EU professional sport', *Sports Law Bulletin* Vol. 3(2), p. 1.

Gardiner, S. and Welch, R. (2000) 'Show me the money: Regulation of the migration of professional sportsmen in post-Bosman Europe', in Gardiner, S. and Caiger, A. (eds) *Professional sport in the EU: Regulation and re-regulation*. The Hague: TMC Asser Press.

Gerhardt, W. (1994) 'The colourful history of a fascinating game', Available from: *http://www.fifa.com/en/history/history/0,1283,1,00.html*

Giulianotti, R. (1999) *Football: A sociology of the global game*. Cambridge: Polity Press.

Grayson, E. (2000) *Sport and the law*, 3rd edn. London: Butterworth.

Gruneau, R. (1993) 'The critique of sport in modernity: Theorising power, culture and the politics of the body', in Maguire, J. and Pearton, R. (eds) *The sports process: A comparative and developmental approach.* Champaign, IL: Human Kinetics.

Gunn, M. (1998) 'The impact of the law on sport with specific reference to the way sport is played', *Contemporary Issues in Law* p. 221

Home Office, (2004) 'Work permit arrangements for footballers — 2004/2005 season', Available from: *http://www.workingintheuk.gov.uk/working_in_the_uk/en/homepage/work_permits/applying_for_a_work/sports_and_ents/criteria/football.html*

Hutchinson, R. (1996) *Empire games: The British invention of Twentieth Century sport.* Edinburgh: Mainstream.

James, M. (2002) 'The trouble with Roy Keane', *Entertainment Law* Vol. 1(3) p. 72.

Kaye, R. (2003) 'Professionals, politicians and the strange death of self-regulation', *Risk & Regulation* Vol. 6, p. 7.

Lanfranchi, P. (1994) 'Exporting football: Notes on the development of football in Europe', in Giulianotti and Williams (eds) *Game without frontiers: Football, identity and modernity.* Aldershot: Arena Publishing.

Lowrey, J. Neatrour, S. and Williams, J. (2002) *The Bosman ruling, football transfers and foreign footballers.* Leicester: Leicester University of Leicester, Sir Norman Chester Centre for Football Research.

Maguire, J. and Bale, J. (1994) 'Sports labour migration in the global arena', in Bale, J. and Maguire, J. (eds) *The global sports arena: Athletic talent migration in an interdependent world.* London: Frank Cass.

Opie, H. (1987) 'Changing concerns in the legal control of participant violence in sport', in Vamplew, W. (ed) *Games, rules and the law.* ASSH Studies in Sports History, No. 4.

Parrish, R. (2004) *Sports law and policy in the European Union.* Manchester: University of Manchester Press.

Sugden, J., Tomlinson, A. and Darby, P. (1998) 'FIFA versus UEFA in the struggle for the control of world football', in Brown, A. (ed) *Fanatics! Power, identity and fandom in football.* London: Routledge.

Taylor, C. (1998) *The beautiful game.* London: Phoenix.

Van den Bogaert, S. (2004) 'And another uppercut from the European Court of Justice to nationality requirements in sports regulations', *European Law Review* Vol. 29(2), p. 267.

SENSIBLE SOCCER: SPORT FANDOM
AND THE RISE OF DIGITAL GAMING

Garry Crawford
Sheffield Hallam University, UK

Introduction

This chapter provides an introduction to the study of sport-related digital games[1], and a basis for further research. Digital gaming has a long and cemented relationship with sport, where almost every sport and competition now has its digital version, while many sport teams and athletes have often profited (both economically and in terms of increased exposure) from this relationship. Moreover, sport-related games constitute one the most popular forms of digital games. However, to date there exists little empirical research on this relationship.

Specifically in this chapter, I focus upon the consumption of sport-related digital games by their players, and argue for a consideration of the players as an 'active audience', who not only frequently 'interact' with these texts, but also draw on them in the construction of their identities and social interactions. This work draws on 392 respondents to a questionnaire-based survey[2] of undergraduate students at two Sheffield (UK) universities studying on Sociology, Social Work or Cultural Studies degrees. The questionnaire specifically focused on the students' digital gaming and sport participation patterns. Additionally, this data is supported by forty follow-up interviews.

The sample group consisted of sixteen (eight male, seven female) undergraduate students who were selected for interview on the basis of their availability and willingness to participate in a follow-up interview.

Additionally, a copy of the original questionnaire had been posted on my own university's website, and this was completed by an additional 124 respondents who had been directed to this page via a number of notices posted on various sport and/or digital gaming related websites and mailing lists[3]. From this, eighteen (fifteen male, three female) individuals indicated that they would be willing to participate in further research, and were subsequently interviewed via email correspondence. Finally, an additional six interviewees (five male and three female) were contacted via digital game related web-based discussion boards; three of these were subsequently interviewed via email, and the remainder were interviewed over the telephone.

Hence, the skewed nature of this sample (consisting solely of undergraduate students and users of the Internet) provides a sample which is unlikely to be representative of the general adult population. However, to date there exists very little empirical research on adult gamers (Crawford, 2005), and hence this research provides an important foundation for further research into this area.

Gaming and game studies

Digital gaming is over forty years old. *Spacewar!*, which is generally viewed as the first ever computer game, was developed in 1962 by Harvard University researchers (game research, 2003), though ten years prior to this Cambridge University student A. S. Doulgas had developed a computer based version of noughts and crosses (digiplay, *n.d.*). However, it was not until the late 1970s and 1980s that digital gaming began to develop as a major leisure industry, with the rapid rise in popularity of arcade-based games such as *Space Invaders* and the introduction of home based video games consoles and home computing, such as the release of Nintendo's *Famicom* and the *Commodore 64* both in 1983 (digiplay, *n.d.*). Today, video and computer games are a major global leisure industry. The largest digital game market is still undoubtedly in the US, where a recent poll by the Entertainment Software Association (ESA) suggested that 41 percent of all Americans, and 63 percent of parents, planned on purchasing at least one digital game in the following year (ESA, 2004). In the US alone, digital games software sales in 2003 were worth in excess of $7billion, and this figure continues to rise year on year (ESA, 2004). Following the US and Japan, Britain constitutes the world's third largest games market, with digital game sales now exceeding those of both cinema box office takings and VHS/DVD rentals (ELSPA, 2003). Moreover, today more digital games are sold in the US and UK than books (Bryce and Rutter, 2001).

However, the academic study of digital games as a cultural and social phenomenon is still relatively young. A large proportion of the literature published on digital gaming, particularly in its earliest days, has been firmly located within the media effects debate, and specifically, has looked for causal relationships between digital gaming and aggressive behaviour (see Bryce and Rutter, 2003b). It is certainly evident that violence is a key component of many digital games, and this is also true for some sport-related games. For instance, in 2002 Dutch game publishers *Darxabre* realised a 'football hooligan' inspired computer game, *Hooligans: Storm Over* Europe, where the object of the game is to 'kill, maim and destroy the opposing hooligan teams' (hooligans-thegame, 2002). Furthermore, one of the key selling points of the soccer game *Red Card (Midway*, 2002) is that it allows the gamer to carry out numerous illegal tackles and fouls.

The relationship between violent games (as with violence on television) is far from conclusive (Colwell and Payne, 2000). Much of this theory is based in psychology — specifically 'social learning theory' (Bandura, 1973) — and suggests that digital gaming can either reinforce or help generate aggressive and violent behaviour in its players (see Dill and Dill, 1998). However, such research has been heavily criticised for its often varied methodology and skewed sample groups, and "has also been criticized theoretically for overestimating the ability of game content to influence the development of specific attitudes and behaviour in different demographic groups, and for conceptualising gamers as passive and vulnerable to representations of violence within games" (Bryce and Rutter, 2003a: p. 4).

A further criticism often levelled at digital gaming is that this is frequently an anti-social and isolating activity, producing a generation of passive 'couch potatoes'. However, again, this negative attitude towards digital gaming has been questioned by many. For instance, Cowell and Payne (2000), in their study of over two hundred London school children, found no evidence to suggest that those who regularly played digital games had fewer friends. Moreover, Bryce and Rutter (2001) convincingly argue that digital gaming can involve *virtual, psychological* and *physical* presence for gamers. They argue that the gamer is not 'absent', but rather constitutes an active participant within the games they play. Digital gaming is an expression of human performance (Wright *et al.*, 2002) and gamers can frequently become deeply engaged with these and enter into a state of 'flow' (Csikszentmihalyi, 1990). However, most importantly they suggest that digital gaming can be a very sociable activity, with gamers playing each other online, meeting up at conventions and 'LAN parties[4]', but more commonly simply playing with friends or family members. For instance, Mitchell (1985: p. 134) suggests that digital gaming enhances family interactions and is "reminiscent of days of Monopoly, checkers, card games, and jigsaw puzzles" (cited in Squire, 2002). And a survey by the ESA recently suggested that 60 percent of parents would play 'interactive' (*i.e.* digital) games with their children at least once a month, while 44 percent say they play games with their children daily or weekly (cited in Guzman, 2004).

However, much of the growing literature on digital gaming has in recent years attempted to move beyond the over-deterministic approach of media effects theory, and in particular has sought to understand the inter-action between gamers and the games that they play. As with most dis-ciplines, the fissures within this field have also become more apparent as this literature has developed. In particular, there appears to be a growing divide between theorists who have sought to understand digital games from the perspective of 'narrative' structure (developing out of Media Studies debates) and those who adopt a more psychologically influenced focus upon patterns of play (or ludology) (Wolf and Perron, 2003; Frasca, 2003). Rather than being understood as an 'audience', digital gamers are still frequently situated as 'individual' players, and hence the location and importance of gaming within social and cultural networks is often overlooked (Yates and Littleton, 2001). However, as with wider changes in Cultural Studies, there is an increasing awareness within the literature on digital gaming that academic focus needs to be shifted towards considering the location of digital gaming within the social context, and understanding how gaming is located within people's everyday lives and social networks (see Squire 2002). Although digital games are often attributed with the label of 'virtual',

Jakobsson and Taylor (2003: p. 89) suggest that "there is nothing unreal about the people participating, their interactions with each other or the emotions ... [this] experience evokes in them".

Hence, this chapter seeks to understand the contemporary relationship between sport and digital gaming, but more specifically, to locate this within the social and cultural patterns of its gamers. In particular, I argue that gamers can be understood as an 'active audience', interacting and adapting with gaming technology, and moreover, drawing on these as a 'resource' in the construction and maintenance of their social identities and networks (Abercrombie and Longhurst, 1998).

Sport and digital gaming

There exists a lengthy, and to some extent reciprocal, relationship between sport and digital gaming. In particular, sport has proved an extremely popular subject for digital game developers. For instance, one of the earliest arcade games (and the first to make it into our homes as a games console), *Pong*, was more than loosely based on the sport of table-tennis (or ping-pong), and there now exist digital versions of almost every existing sport and major sporting competition.

Digital gaming has also proved (at times very) profitable for the sport industry. Digital games manufactures and publishers, particularly those wishing to promote sport related games, will frequently advertise their products via billboard or hording at sport venues, or sponsor teams and competitions, such as *Sega's* endorsement of the 1997 UEFA Champions League and their 1999/2000 shirt sponsorship of Arsenal, Sampdoria and St Etienne football clubs (Poole, 2000). Individual sport stars and teams can also make sizable profits by endorsing sport-related games, and athletes such as 'Tiger' Woods and David Beckham, and clubs such as Manchester United, have several games bearing their names and likenesses. In particular, in the US, digital games are now only second to replica shirts in generating merchandising income for the NFL (O'Connor, 2002).

It is also possible to view new media technologies as potentially beneficial for the followers of sport. For instance, new media, such as digital television and the Internet, provide sport fans with greater levels of 'interaction[5]', allowing audiences to view sport events from different angles or discuss and comment on the sports that they follow, such as in Internet chat rooms or discussion boards. This is extended further by digital gaming, which allows the gamer to take control of 'virtual' sport teams or athletes either as participants or coaches, controlling their direction and destiny. Digital games are also becoming increasingly 'realistic' in their portrayal of sports, with characters, movement and characteristics of athletes painstakingly replicated within many games — as the slogan of *EA Sports* declares, increasingly "if it's in the game, it's in the game".

The digital games industry has also been known to move beyond these parameters and dream up new sports and competitions (or adapt old ones) in creating new entertaining formats — for example the *Bitmap Brothers'* game *Speedball*, a futuristic variation of soccer (heavily influenced by the film *Rollerball*), which proved an extremely popular game in the early 1990s; or *Electronic Arts'* placement real NFL and NBA stars in competitions in urban locations, such as *NFL Street*. Digital gaming also allows gamers to go beyond what would be possible with conventional sports, such as pitting contemporary sport stars and athletes against sporting legends of yesteryear or allowing gamers to place electronic representations of themselves in the games.

Digital games allow gamers at least the fantasy that they too can play sport at its highest level, and for some who may have been excluded from sport participation due to their perceived (or actual) lack of ability, digital gaming provides a chance to participate in this culture. Tim Willits, a leading games developer for "*id*" argued, "There are large groups of kids who would love to play on a hockey team or a football team, but they aren't the right kind of kids … it's all virtual, but it's still a team" (cited in King and Borland, 2003: pp. 141–2). It is this element of 'fantasy' that proves popular for many gamers, particularly in relation to sport management games such as the highly popular soccer management simulation series *Championship Manager*. 'Dean' (male, aged 29, PR consultant, telephone interview, UK) commented:

> I don't really play any other games … just *Champ Man* … I don't know why, I suppose you can really get into it. I've got a pretty good grasp of reality, normally [but] you do get very emotionally involved in the game, and feel like you are managing a real team, and you

want to interact with your players more. Like tell them to pull their socks up, or that their performance was rubbish or praise them.

This recent rise in popularity of sport-related digital games has led some academics and journalists alike to suggest that there is probably more sport being played on video and computer game screens than in parks and fields. Giulianotti (1999: p. 85) suggested in relation to soccer related digital games, that "[football] has indeed come home[6]". As O'Connor (2002: p. 2) wrote in *The Times* in respect of football (soccer) related digital games:

> The rate at which these games are flying off the shelves would suggest more football is being played on home computers than local fields. Which raises the question, could it be possible that virtual football is even bigger than the real thing?

For some, this has led to a 'moral panic' over a new generation of 'mouse potatoes' (Kline *et al.*, 2003) whose only contact with sport will be via video screens and their only exercise the rapid thumb movement of the avid gamer (Bryce and Rutter, 2001). However, these fears have not been borne by recent research. For instance, Fromme's (2001) study of over one thousand German school children suggested a positive relationship between 'daily use' of digital games with levels of sport participation (though this was not statistically significant). This assertion is supported by my own survey of the sporting and gaming participation habits of undergraduate students (see Crawford, 2005), which suggests no discernable relationship (either positive or negative) exists between the tendency for these respondents to play digital games and 'real' sport.

However, empirical data gathered from this survey and the follow-up interviews does suggest a strong relationship between sporting interests (both as participants and followers of sport) and digital gaming. In particular, it is evident that the kinds of sport people participate in and their sporting interests as fans can play an important role in influencing the nature of digital games they play. For instance, 43 percent of respondents (N=161) suggested that their participation in sport, while 47 percent suggested that 'following' a particular sport, had encouraged them to play a digital version of this. These finding were reinforced by the follow-up interviews, such as the comments made by 'Stephen' (male, aged 21, student, UK):

> Yeah I play *FIFA* [digital soccer game] mostly [and] I love American
> sports, I love watching them and playing them. In fact, well I used
> to a lot more than I do now. *NBA Jam* [television show] I used to
> love ... I used to be well into it. That was when I was big into the
> NBA, when I was about 12–13 yrs old. I wish I had played a bit
> more NFL [digital game]. I play a little bit of golf [on the computer],
> but usually it's what I am interested in.

It is also evident that digital gamers will frequently demonstrate (often quite
high) levels of loyalty and emotional connection between the teams and
sports they follow and those they play in digital games. Of the twenty-six
(twenty-four men, and two women) interviewees who suggested that they
regularly played sport-related digital games, all but one indicated that they
would (if possible) usually 'play' the team they supported; such as indicated
by 'Brian' (male, aged 25, graduate student, Internet respondent, UK):

> I tend to play my beloved Newcastle Utd, though they're never the
> best team in the game and it's not easy when I'm to play against the
> likes of Man Utd, Real Madrid ... that my friend plays. On the other
> hand I'm quite good when playing England.

As 'Brian' indicates, sporting allegiances and interests can often be a much
greater influencing factor in determining the way many gamers play
digital games, than are more calculated or instrumental factors, such as
simply selecting the best team or character. This is particularly noted in
relation to sport management games, where several interviewees indicated
that they would often select or reject certain players on the basis of how
much they liked them as inividuals, rather than on the basis of their
ability in the game:

> Oh God, yeah. Well, yeah, yeah. I mean you can't [let emotions
> influence you]... it's just crazy I mean there are certain players you
> have to play. Straight away pick my favourite players [and] with
> some players you don't like you just get rid of you know ... It gets
> very emotional but ... very frustrating game as well, it's crazy. I
> remember I won...first time I won the FA Cup round my mates at
> midnight. Don't know, I wouldn't usually do, I mean his parents

were asleep, I woke his dad up I got so excited and you know, crazy. It's weird like that... it has this hold over you. ('Mark', male, aged 23, graduate student, UK)

However, this relationship between sporting interests and digital gaming appears less notable for the majority of female participants in this research. For instance, of the female survey respondents who indicated that they regularly played digital games (N=69), only 18 percent suggested that their participation in a sport, and 12 percent indicated their following of a sport, had encouraged them to play a digital version of this [compared with 52 percent and 57 percent for men respectively (N=92)]. It is evident that the themes and goals of majority of digital games do not reflect the interests of many women, and rarely feature female characters (Bryce and Rutter, 2003a, 2003b). This is particularly true for the vast majority of sport-related games, which tend to focus around male team participation sports such as American football, baseball, ice hockey and soccer (see Crawford and Gosling, 2005). However, it has been suggested that women's increased participation in many traditionally male sports (such as soccer) may constitute a fresh and new market for sport-related games developers in the future (Cassell and Jenkins, 2000).

Digital gaming has often been viewed as a traditionally male preserve (Cassell and Jenkins, 2000). However, a sizable amount of research has developed since the early 1990s (such as Funk, 1993; Kafai, 1996; Roe and Muijs, 1998; Littleton et al., 1998; Colwell and Payne, 2000), which suggests that women are participating in digital gaming in increasing numbers. However, such studies tend to be based largely (if not solely) upon sample groups of school children. Elsewhere (Crawford and Gosling, 2005) I argue that these patterns of female participation are not replicated for adult gamers, and that women continue to be marginalised within adult gaming patterns. This, I suggest, can be explained by the propensity for many girls to have their access to digital games granted (and restricted) by male family members. Control of leisure technologies usually remains within the hands of men, and is seen as not 'symbolically' belonging to women (McNamee, 1998). Hence women are less likely to continue playing digital games as they progress into adulthood and move away from their family home (see Crawford and Gosling, 2005).

Gamers as 'active audience'

In Media Studies there is an increasing move away from viewing audiences as 'passive dopes' (Garfinkel, 1967), particularly since the publication of Stuart Hall's now classic paper 'Encoding and Decoding in the Television Discourse' (1980 [1973]) — though the origins of this argument can be traced back to the work of Benjamin (1931), if not before. I would suggest, that likewise, it is important that we consider how digital games are utilised by gamers, and more specifically, how these are socially and culturally located. As Poole (2000: p. 101) suggests, digital gaming is "every bit as revolutionary, in its form, as cinema was for Benjamin...". Not only do digital games allow gamers to 'interact' more fully than other (traditional) forms of media, they often provide the gamer with multiple opportunities to change (to some degree) and adopt the text (the game) to fit their personal tastes and interests — either via options built into the game, or via more 'illegitimate' methods, such as 'hacking' or modifying games. Hence, it is not only important that we understand gamers as an 'audience' (*i.e.* located within a wider group of consumers), but also see this as an 'active' audience. For instance, 'Stephen' (male, aged 21, student, UK) recounted adapting soccer related games to include his favourite team and even friends:

> ... [what] I would do sometimes is put my home team in there, put the Luton team in there so I would have the Luton eleven so they were the best. I would have me and all my friends in the same team. You defiantly have to name your own cup, you have to work out how it's going to work out, whether it's going to be one leg or knock out. We customise our figures, shapes and hair colours, everything has got to be perfect.

Other interviewees indicated that they would adapt games more conspicuously, by creating game add-ons (or 'mods') such as new game levels or scenarios; as related by 'Pete' (male, age and occupation unknown, Internet respondent, USA):

> I made some pretty killer *StarCraft* [science-fiction strategy war game] levels in high school for the sake of perfecting my craft in level design. I should note that my interest in game creation is not usual.

However, beyond these examples of gamer 'creativity', gamers are also 'active' in the way games are drawn on and used as a basis for their social interactions within everyday life. As cited earlier, authors such as Bryce and Rutter (2001) and Squire (2002), suggest that for many digital gaming can be a quite 'sociable' activity, often played by groups of friends, family members or with others via Internet or LAN links. However, it is not just the playing of these games that involves social interaction, but rather conversations, social networks and identities can be built around the use of digital games. As King and Borland (2003: pp. 7–8) write:

> Much of what we do in our lives — from organizing our music and movie collections so that visitors can see what we like, to joining recreational sports teams — is about finding other people who like what we like, and making the connections that make us feel less alone in a hurried world ... For millions of people, computer games have provided an opportunity to find people who share similar backgrounds, stories, hopes and dreams. It may seem strange to think of computer game communities in the same light as sports teams, writing groups, or ordinary offline friends ... but for gamers, those virtual worlds are just an extension of the real world.

Digital gamers can be seen as a 'knowledge community' (Levy, 1997), where individuals will exchange information about games via websites, Internet discussion boards and face-to-face conversations. Rutter (2004) has suggested that digital gamers may follow a social career path (Goffman, 1968), where they are inducted and schooled into this particular 'community'. Elsewhere (Crawford, 2003) I have applied the idea of career development to the induction and social progression of sport fans, and it may be seen how digital gamers follow a similar form of path, particularly for players of sport related games, where their 'status passage' (Glaser and Strauss, 1971) as a gamer and sport fans may complement and fuel each other. Certainly, all of the interviews were able to name individuals who had influenced them in the types of games they played, and most indicated that over their life course they had become more knowledgeable and skilled in the games they play. Again, this was in some part due to 'schooling' from friends and/or relatives, as indicated by 'Julie' (female, aged 20, student, UK):

> Yeah, my brother influenced me loads in the games I play. I'd play
> the games he bought, and he'd suggest games that I might like and
> wanna buy...and like he'd help teach me how to play 'em and I'd
> pick other stuff up from his magazine...and we'd talk about what to
> do in the games, and like how to get past levels, and stuff, loads.

However, knowledge and information gained from digital gaming is not
simply used to fuel conversations and interactions based around gaming,
but can also be drawn on as a resource in other areas. In particular,
interviewees who indicated that they frequently played sport-related games
suggested that discussions of these would frequently combine and
interchange with wider conversations about sport. Again, this was most
notable with players of sport management simulations (such as
Championship Manager), who would frequently discuss tactics and
exchange game knowledge with friends; as 'Mark' (male, aged 23, graduate
student, UK) recounted:

> Oh, God, yeah yeah. Like *Championship Manager* is probably the
> most talked about one [game] we do ... it'll be referenced somewhere
> in my day and me and my mate Tony always talk about it ... and
> we'll talk about real football as well, 'cause they're pretty much the
> same thing aren't they? You're still talking about tactics and players
> and stuff, but with *Champ Man*, you're in control ain't you?

Erickson's (1996) study of conversations in Canadian workplaces suggested
that 'sports talk' was a useful source of conversation for men of all social
classes as a means of social interaction and inclusion. Similarly in the
present study, the majority of male interviewees suggested that digital
gaming was something that they would discuss with friends and family
members, and it is evident that knowledge and information gained from
digital games was drawn on to inform general conversations about sport.
Moreover, 33 percent of respondents (*N*=160) indicated that digital gaming
had increased their interest in following sport, while 63 percent (*N*=161)
stated that digital games had increased their knowledge of certain sports.
In particular, this was most notable for many North American sports (such
as ice hockey and baseball), which have less of a media presence and
following in the UK. Such as the comments made by 'Mark' (aged 21,

student, UK): "Yeah, it [digital gaming] has increased my knowledge of basketball and American sports loads".

Abercrombie and Longhurst (1998), drawing on the work of Appadurai (1990), suggest that the mass media surround and envelop our everyday lives in a 'mediascape', and — as with the landscape beneath our feet — this often goes unnoticed, but is fundamental in shaping the nature of the world around us. This mediascape provides a knowledge base and resource that individuals draw upon in their conversations, social interactions, and in the construction of identities. Likewise, new media technologies, such as the Internet and digital gaming, contribute to contemporary mediascapes, blurring with other forms of mass media and entertainment, such as film, music and sport, to provide the resources individuals draw on in their everyday lives.

It is not only men who discuss sport-related games. One interviewee 'Elaine' (female, journalist, aged 25, Internet respondent, UK) indicated that she was an avid player of *Championship Manger* and would frequently discuss this with friends, both in-person and online. As she indicated:

> My interests are closer to those of the average bloke than average girl. I am interested in sport and military history. Most girls are not obsessed with footy or keen gamers ...

'Elaine' readily acknowledged that she is in a minority, and even sometimes hides her identity as a female gamer when using web-based discussion boards and Internet sites, as she feels "people would view me differently [as a woman]".

Conclusion

The evidence collected in this research suggests that interest in sport can influence the type and nature of digital games that individuals play, and likewise, these games in turn can inform some individuals' interest and knowledge in sport. I have argued that research and theory on digital gaming needs to move away from a consideration of the relationship between the individual gamer and the games they play, and rather locate these within a wider social and cultural setting. Doing so allows for an under-standing of the 'active' nature of the games audience; gamers will frequently interact with and adapt games, and also draw on knowledge obtained from these as a resource in conversations, identity formations and social interactions, and often beyond those that focus specifically on gaming.

However, the relationship between sporting and gaming interests is more noted for men, as the vast majority of sport-related digital games focus upon male participation sports. Moreover, women's interests have frequently been marginalised within digital gaming (Bryce and Rutter, 2003a, 2003b). However, there is evidence to suggest that some women do play sport-related games, and that these may also constitute a source of conversation and social interaction for them. Moreover, Bryce and Rutter (2003a) draw on the literature on 'oppositional reading' (such as that of Fiske, 1989a, 1989b; and Jenkins, 1992, which suggests that readers of cultural 'texts' (such as digital games) can often reinterpret and even subvert these), to argue that some female gamers may draw pleasure from games that are not necessarily aimed or marketed towards them. However, I would suggest that the potential for audiences to 'reinterpret' the messages embodied within cultural texts is often overstated within the 'oppositional reading' argument, and moreover, this should not be taken as justification for the continued marginalisation of women's interests within digital gaming; as it is important that game developers and publishers produce games that have an appeal beyond the current core market of male gamers.

By suggesting that gamers should be considered as an 'active' audience, I am not advocating that they are necessarily (or in anyway) 'resistant'. For as Abercrombie and Longhurst (1998: 30) argue, "activism does not of itself give power or even the capacity to resist". They suggest that it is important that we move away from restrictive arguments that see audiences as either resistant and/or incorporative of dominant ideological messages, and towards an understanding of how power relations are played out through social interactions and located within people's everyday lives, and it is this argument that I wish to advocate here. Hence, it is important that further research considers the location that media texts (such as digital gaming) occupy within patterns of everyday life and social interactions.

Notes

1. Though terms are used interchangeably, the term 'video games' is often used to refer to games played on home-based game consoles or on arcade machines, while 'computer games' are generally defined as those played on PC or Apple Macintosh systems (see Poole, 2000: p. 35). However, to help avoid confusion, the term 'digital gaming' appears to be the preferred term growing in acceptance within the literature on gaming to refer to all forms of electronic gaming, including video, computer and mobile gaming (see DiGRA, *n.d.*).

2. For further consideration of the methodology of this questionnaire see Crawford (2005).

3. However, due to the skewed demographic nature of users of the Internet, and particularly for many fan (Clerc, 2000) and sport sites (Redhead, 1997) that continue to be (in the majority of cases) excessively male dominated, respondents who completed this survey online were excluded from the questionnaire analysis used in this chapter.

4. A 'LAN' is a 'local area network', which consists a series of computers networked (linked) together (such as in an office). LAN parties however, have developed in recent years, where groups of gamers come together (often at one of their homes or local halls) with their computers and link these together to play against each other (see King and Borland, 2003).

5. In this chapter I use the term 'interactivity' quite loosely, for as Gansing (2003) suggests, this is an often overused term, which is frequently overstates the potential power of gamers to influence the games they play.

6. This quotation draws on the lyrics of the song 'Three Lions', which was an anthem for the English soccer team in the Euro '96 competition, which features the line 'Football's Coming Home' (see Carrington, 1998).

References

Abercrombie, N. and Longhurst, B. (1998) *Audiences*. London: Sage.

Appadurai, A. (1990) 'Disjuncture and difference in the global economy', *Theory, Culture and Society* No. 7: pp. 295–310.

Bandura, A. (1973) *Aggression: A social learning analysis*. Englewood Cliffs: Prentice Hall.

Benjamin, W. (1931) 'A small history of photography', in W. Benjamin (1979) *One way street and other writings*. London: Verso.

Bryce, J. and Rutter, J. (2001) 'In the game — in the flow: Presence in public computer gaming', poster presented at *Computer Games and Digital Textualities*, IT University of Copenhagen, March <http://www.digiplay.org.uk>.

—— (2003a) 'The gendering of computer gaming: Experiences and space', in S. Fleming and I. Jones (eds) *Leisure cultures: Investigations in sport, media and technology* (LSA Publication No. 79). Eastbourne: Leisure Studies Association.

———— (2003b) 'Gender dynamics and the social and spatial organization of computer gaming', *Leisure Studies*, No. 22: pp. 1–15.

Carrington, B. (1998) 'Football's coming home but whose home? And do we want it? Nation, football and the politics of exclusion' in A. Brown (ed) *Fanatics! Power, Identity and Fandom in Football*. London: Routledge.

Cassell, J. and Jenkins, H. (2000) 'Chess of girls? Feminism and computer games', in J. Cassell and H. Jenkins (eds), *From Barbie to Mortal Combat: Gender and computer games*. London: MIT Press.

Colwell, J. and Payne, J. (2000) 'Negative correlates of computer game play in adolescents', *British Journal of Psychology*, No. 91: pp. 295–310.

Crawford, G. (2003) 'The career of the sport supporter: The case of the Manchester storm', *Sociology* Vol. 37, No. 2: pp. 219–237.

———— (2005) 'Digital gaming, sport and gender', *Leisure Studies (forthcoming)*.

Crawford, G. and Gosling, V.K. (2005) 'Toys of boy? The continued marginalization and participation of women as digital gamers', *Sociological Research Online*, March.

Csikszentmihalyi, M. (1990) *Flow: The psychology of optimal experience*. New York: Harper Perennial.

Digiplay (no date) *Digiplay Interactive* <http://www.digiplay.org.uk>.

DiGRA (no date) *Digital Games Research Association* <http://www.digra.org>.

Dill, K.E. and Dill, J.C. (1998) 'Video game violence: A review of the empirical literature', *Aggression and Violent Behaviour*, No. 3: pp. 407–428.

ELSPA (2003) *The cultural life of computer and video games: A cross industry study*, Entertainment and Leisure Software Publishers Association <http://www.elspa.com>.

Erickson, B. (1996) 'Culture, class and connections', *American Journal of Sociology*, No. 102: pp. 217–251.

ESA (2004) Entertainment Software Association <http://www.theesa.com/>.

Fiske, J. (1989a) *Understanding popular culture*. London: Unwin Hyman.

———— (1989b) *Reading the popular*. London: Unwin Hyman.

Frasca, G. (2003) 'Simulation versus narrative: Introduction to ludology', in M.J.P Wolf and B. Perron (eds) *The video game theory reader*. London: Routledge.

Fromme, J. (2003) 'Computer games as a part of children's culture', *Game Studies* Vol. 3, No. 1 <http://www.gamestudies.org/0301/fromme/>.

Funk, J.B. (1993) 'Reevaluating the impact of computer games', *Clinical Paediatrics*, No. 32: pp. 86–90.

Gansing, K. (2003) 'The myth of interactivity? Interactive films as an imaginary genre' paper presented at *MelbourneDAC2003* conference, <http://hypertext.rmit.edu.au/dac/papers/Gansing.pdf>.

Garfinkel, H. (1967) *Studies in ethnomethodology*. Englewood Cliffs, Prentice-Hall.

Glaser, B. G. and Strauss A. L. (1971) *Status passage*. London: Routledge.

Goffman, E. (1968) *Asylums*. London: Penguin.

Giulianotti, R. (1999) *Football: A sociology of the global game*. Cambridge, Polity Press.

Guzman, R.A. (2004) 'Video games can be bonding tool for families', *San Antonio Express*, 27 February 2004.

Hall, S. (1980) 'Encoding and Decoding' in S. Hall, D. Hobson, A. Lowe and P. Willis (eds) *Culture, media, language: Working papers in cultural studies, 1972–79*. London: Hutchinson.

Jakobsson, M. and Taylor, T. L. (2003: 89) 'The Sopranos meets EverQuest: Social networking in massively multiplayer online games', paper presented at *MelbourneDAC2003* conference < http://hypertext.rmit.edu.au/dac/papers/Jakobsson.pdf>.

Jenkins, H. (1992) *Textual poachers*. Routledge: London

Kafai, Y.B. (1996) 'Electronic play worlds: Gender differences in children's construction of video games', in Y.B. Kafai and M.Resnick (eds) *Constructionism in practice: Designing, thinking and learning in a digital world*. Ablex: Mahwah NJ.

King, B. and Borland, J. (2003) *Dungeons and dreamers: The rise of computer game culture, from geek to chic*. New York: McGraw-Hill.

Kline, S., Dyver-Witherford, N. and De Peuter, G. (2003) *Digital play: The interaction of technology, culture, and marketing*. McGill-Queen's University Press: London.

Levy, P. (1997) *Collective intelligence: Mankind's emerging world in cyberspace*. Cambridge: Perseus.

Littleton, K., Light, P., Joiner, R., Messer, D. and Barnes, P. (1998) 'Gender, task scenarios and children's computer-based problem solving', *Educational Psychology* Vol. 18, No. 3: pp. 327–340.

McNamee, S. (1998) 'Youth, gender and video games: Power and control in the home' in T. Skelton and G. Valentine (eds) *Cool places: Geographies of youth cultures*. Routledge: London.

Mitchell, E. (1985) 'The dynamics of family interaction around home video games', Special Issue: Personal Computers and the Family, *Marriage and Family Review* Vol. 8, No. 1–2: pp. 121–135.

O'Connor, A. (2002) 'Even better than the real thing?', *The Times, The Game* supplement, 9 December 2002, 2–3.

Poole, S. (2000) *Trigger happy: The inner life of videogames*. London: Fourth Estate.

Roe, K. and Muijs, D. (1998) 'Children and computer games', *European Journal of Communication* Vol. 13, No. 2: pp. 181–200.

Rutter, J. (2004) 'Gamers as consumers as producers', paper presented to *Digiplay: Experiences and Consequences of Technologies in Leisure* conference, Manchester 14–15 January 2004.

Squire, K. (2002) 'Cultural Framing of Computer/Video Games, *Game Studies*, 2 (1), <http://www.gamestudies.org/0201/squire/>.

Wolf, M.J.P. and Perron, B. (2003) 'Introduction', in M.J.P Wolf and B. Perron (eds) *The video game theory reader*. London, Routledge.

Wright, T., Boria E. and Breidenbach, P. (2002) 'Creative player actions in FPS Online Video Games: Playing counter strike', *Game Studies* Vol. 2, No. 2 <http:// www.gamestudies.org/0202/wright/>.

Yates, S. J. and Littleton, K. L. (2001) 'Understanding computer game culture: A situated approach' in E. Green and A. Adams (eds) *Virtual gender: Technology, consumption and identity*. London: Routledge.

REPORTING THE MEDIA: THE OCCUPATIONAL SUBCULTURE OF THE SPORT JOURNALIST

John Doyle
University of Brighton

Sport and the media

There has been little academic attention paid to the occupational culture of sports journalists and to how they contribute to the production of the meanings, ideologies and cultures of sport. Lowes (1999) and Palmer (2001) are exceptions, and their ethnographic work examines aspects of the creation of sports texts. Rowe (1999: pp. 36–63) and his collaborators interviewed more than 40 sports journalists in the mid-1990s. These included television and radio specialists, but most were print journalists, and they were from three English-speaking countries. He identified different types of journalist: 'anorak' journalism akin to sports fandom; "traditional sports reporting and recording" (p. 48); and a more engaged, 'crusading' approach to the journalistic task. This chapter is a preliminary study of a specialist area of the second of these categories.

    The chapter explores the nature of the relationships that characterise the occupational culture, and points to connections between sport journalism and other media; and, overall, places the occupation in its wider social context. The chapter discusses how recent changes in the European football industry contribute to the formation of a subculture of football writing. These changes have seen football clubs and governing bodies adapt to the intensity of the media gaze and attempt to accommodate the twin demands of the new commercial reality and the mass media.

The subculture of sports journalism

Sports journalism is a specialist type of journalism, "with professional practices, 'news values' and readerships that are similar to but distinctive from those of journalism in general" (Brookes, 2002: p. 33). Sports journalists both conform to the norms of the wider culture of journalism, and also negotiate many structures that are distinctive to the sports media world.

A distinctive aspect of sports journalism is the paradox of its profile in relation to its prestige. The sports departments of newspapers have a high profile: an expensive department and its sports journalists are expected to deliver a large readership. Their labour is crucial to the economic success of papers: "sport sells newspapers" (Creedon, 1998: p. 89). The outcome of economic success for the newspaper is that its sports journalists are well rewarded financially. Yet, sports journalists are seen within the wider culture of journalism as having low prestige. In addition, sports journalists are under pressure of tight deadlines, so their production is "rationally arranged to achieve this quota through an institutionalisation of routines" (Brookes, 2002: p. 36). In order to operate within these routines sports journalists are expected to conform to occupational norms. They may be assigned to particular 'rounds' or 'beats', which will provide their source of daily copy, or they will be expected to be specialists in a particular sport or region. As with news journalists, this system has implications for the kind of sports news generated, which is often reported,

> ... from press conferences arranged by key organisations on the beat, or from personal relationships with important sources, both on and off the record. (Brookes, 2002: p. 37)

In addition, the economic demands on sports journalists on 'beats' mean that they are expected to produce copy whether there is any news or not. This ensures an intense relationship between sports organisations and journalists that Brookes (2002) has characterised as "mutually beneficial interdependency" (Brookes, 2002: p. 38).

In his occupational ethnography of North American sports journalists, Mark Lowes (1999) argues that this interdependency occurs because the sports section is a "high performance promotional vehicle for the North

American (and increasingly global) sports entertainment industry" (Lowes, 1999: p. 100). His research is concerned with the manufacture of sports news for the daily press, the professional ideologies and "institutionalised work routines" of sports journalists. Lowes finds that "media relations people must understand media logic and media formats to facilitate sports news-work" (Lowes, 1999: p. 49).

Given the interdependency of sports organisations, journalists and media relations staff, any study of the occupational culture of sports journalists should also comprise an examination of the power dynamics of these relationships within the "media sports cultural complex" (Rowe, 1999: p. 34).

Europe, UEFA and the press

Recent research into European football and the media has been based on a textual analysis of media content. Blain *et al.* (1993) outline the particular representations of national identity in the European media, concentrating on a textual analysis of selected European media. They have noted the homogeneity of the European press in its articulation of regional or national identities, and the high profile that 'nationalism' has for sports journalists. They see the sports media as 'agents' in the perpetuation of the dominance of the state and the ideologically driven perpetuation of fixed images of national traits.

Crolley and Hand's (2002) study is a textual analysis of the football press in France, Spain and England which aims to uncover what the "language of football writing says about perceptions of identity in Europe" (Crolley and Hand, 2002: p. 15). They conclude that European print media discourses on football contain stereotypical portrayals of national, gender and ethnic identities that,

> ... reinforce if not inculcate myths of national character which are rooted in wider politico-diplomatic and socio-economic objective realities. (Crowley and Hand, 2002: p. 161)

Both these studies provide valuable data on the role of the sporting press in the sustaining of national identities and dominant ideologies. However, neither examines the producers of the content to uncover

how the occupational routines of sports journalists and their professional interactions with clubs, players and governing bodies contribute to
the creation of football texts. This chapter is offered as a pre-liminary
analysis of the mores and the *modus operandi* of that occupational group.

A snapshot of a subculture

The context, and methods of studying the culture

The research reported in this chapter focused upon the everyday realities
of football's media sports cultural complex, and centred on the European
Football Confederation's (UEFA) Champions League. This competition was
transformed by UEFA in response to pressure from the group G-14, which
represents 18 of Europe's elite clubs. G-14's negotiations with the group
Media Partners, and their threat in the early 1990s to break away from
UEFA and form their own competition, pressured UEFA to create a
competition that favoured clubs from the most powerful football nations,
ensured that they qualified regularly, played more games, and kept the
most revenues. In addition, the huge financial investment of broadcast
corporations now sustains European football but has also led these
broadcasters to justify the cost of their investment by providing constant
coverage. This has led to an increasing synergy in the messages the
broadcasters and football elites emit. The football press has been relegated down the 'food chain' and is now required to hunt for sustenance
that the 'rights holders' cannot use or access in order to justify their
usefulness and distinguish themselves from the broadcast media.

The central section of this chapter outlines how journalists have
adapted and interact with employees of elite clubs and UEFA in the creation
of sports news texts. It examines whether football texts are a co-production,
and whether they are homogenised collaborative projects, produced within
the subculture in association with football clubs and the governing body
in order to 'promote' the brand of UEFA and the football industry. Finally
it seeks to develop some understanding of the occupational routines and
professional ideologies that impact on the creation of football texts.

The data for the study were collected through observation at Champions League press conferences and interviews with national newspaper

journalists working on the Champions League. The fieldwork was conducted during the 2003–4 English/European football season, much of it around the training *environs* and match-day schedules of Chelsea Football Club in its Champions League campaign. I attended press conferences at Chelsea, and at Arsenal Football Club and Monaco. To gain access to these, I either simply walked into the conference room or location, or displayed my NUJ (National Union of Journalists) student press pass. The empirical data that are reported in the chapter derive from three in-depth interviews with experienced journalists familiar with this particular sports beat. To preserve anonymity of these respondents, no indication is given of their personal profile or characteristics.

The occupational routines of football journalists

Consideration of the routine of the football journalist is helpful in understanding how the journalists, the clubs and UEFA combine to create sports news. To understand this routine it is useful to outline the newspaper's commitments in terms of content, the resources that go into covering the Champions League matches and how the structure of the Champions League press conferences impacts on the deadlines of journalists.

With games every two weeks during the group stage, clubs play up to 12 games en route to the final. Thus with four of the highest profile English clubs taking part and most of the world's top players, coverage of the Champions League takes up a considerable amount of a newspaper's midweek football content. The journalist must therefore structure his routine around the events that are set up by UEFA and the clubs to manage the media's requirements. The organisation of this routine is facilitated by the beat system whereby journalists cover a particular area, competition or club. This system allows journalists to become familiar with the routines and the day to day happenings on the beat.

The routines of other media workers also impact on the print journalist: the growth in importance of the Champions League is reflected in increased demands from TV and radio. This translates as competition for access to the 'gatekeepers' who act as guardians of the information that journalists require in order to produce football texts.

The timing of press conferences allows broadcasters to preview the games, thus impacting on the ability of the journalist to produce a 'scoop' from the conference. Some newspapers negotiate this by using the standard copy syndicated by the wire services. However the press occasionally work around the structural constraints of the conference and adapt their routines for their own occupational purposes. As one interviewee related:

> The print journalists don't want to ask the clever question in front of the television because that goes out straight away, you want to keep something for yourself, inevitably you get print journalists in huddles in corners keeping things off-mike and away from the action and because they won't be out until the next day.

The routine of the journalist therefore involves not only attending these events and getting the standard quotes but also extracting something extra from them. The standard quotes can be sourced from TV, radio or the wire services. The press attend these events to keep their relationships, sources and networks alive. In essence, journalists have to use their initiative and skills to cultivate sources and circumvent the structural barriers and gatekeepers of the sport media business.

The sports news event

The Champions League press conference is an event linked to commercialisation of European football and ensures that the Champions League brand is dispersed by the media. One journalist explained that a UEFA press conference "ensure[s] that a Champions League match is given a status". This 'status' in his view ensured that clubs adhered to a standard template and enabled the UEFA and Champions League brands to be promoted. Another added that the clubs,

> ... apply basic standards and they are not being altruistic. They are not trying to please journalists but they are doing it because they want a page and if Capello sits there for 10 minutes and talks to journalists then it's a page in the *Gazetta del la Sport*, it's a page in the *Sun*, it's a page in *El Pais*, it's a page in the *Telegraph*. You know we're talking about an audience of 300 million people, everyone will be reading Champions League.

The sports news event is divided into four distinct phases. The first phase consists of the training photo opportunities that take place an hour before the conference begins. Here the focus is on providing the images that will fill the TV screens and newspapers around Europe. This phase is essentially the public staging of a training session — the public represented by the media, with the images of players training offered up for media consumption. During this phase the press are less evident, with TV and photographers taking up most of the space alongside the touchline.

It is in the pressroom when many journalists are hanging around waiting for the conference to begin that much of the unseen work is done. Journalists talk about rumours, the upcoming games and share personal and professional opinions — both out of necessity and due to the boredom of long periods of time waiting around. The structure of the managed sports news event forces journalists to fit their working practices into a rigid structure, and this in turn forces them to share information.

After the training session is over there is usually a delay before the next phase, the press conference. At this point the press are usually working on their copy. When the conference begins the broadcasters initiate the questions. As the conference progresses the press become more vocal. As everything is recorded for the broadcasters it usually provokes a highly managed response from players and managers. One journalist described the UEFA press conferences as "very stage-managed". The journalist explained that this was a distinctive feature of UEFA conferences, as was the desire of those employed in the football industry to conform to expectations of UEFA and a pan-European media. He remarked:

> It's quite interesting because at those conferences the manager of the English club you're following talks in a different way, in a more diplomatic way; really what they want to say is how pleased they are to be in this country, how much they admire the team they are going to play, and give a bit of team news. It's all very polite, it's not like a normal one.

This stage-managing disappears with the cameras when the third phase of the conference begins, the press briefing. This takes place immediately after the conference and is characterised by a less formal structure than the recorded conference. The manager, offering a more focused and personal view, is surrounded by the journalists in a huddle and is asked more intimate questions about the opponents, players' injuries and personal opinions. This phase shows the competitive edge — some journalists jostle for a good position in the circle while others stay on the periphery capturing the quotes. It is here that much of the content for the papers is produced, where the best quotes from the manager are given. At Chelsea, the manager used this opportunity to put his side of the Chelsea saga across: this was where he began to change his relationship with the press. The duel-like nature of the press briefing is demonstrated by the following exchange:

> The manager responds to a question about support outside the club and how he feels about this: 'I am aware of support outside of Chelsea. Thank you, you do a great job'. A lone voice shouts from the press pack, 'After we killed you, everyone liked you!'. There's lots of laughter from the manager and everyone in the huddle. Another journalist shouts, 'Then we brought you back to life' and everyone laughs again. (Fieldnotes)

This exchange reveals the way in which the press briefing can be used by individuals, clubs and the press for their own ends. The deal means that the manager gets his views into the press and the press gets what it wants, a good supply of quotes and a running story.

The fourth stage of the conference is the post-conference discussion period when many of the TV people have departed. It is a forum where journalists return to mixing the personal and professional, where quotes and facts are checked and validated.

News sources — UEFA

UEFA also offer other formal news sources for journalists covering the Champions League. One source prepared for journalists is the press pack. Bound in a UEFA branded folder it contains all the facts about the forthcoming game, a summary of the club's recent form, some basic quotes, squad details and Champions League statistics. One journalist described the press pack as "second to none" and thought that it was particularly useful to help "spark an idea". Many journalists also flick through a new addition to the press pack — the Champions League magazine. This new commercial publication adds to UEFA's portfolio of Champions League information. It is a glossy high quality magazine with contributors from across European football. Translated into various European languages it acts a source of UEFA-sanctioned information for the journalist. Significantly the editor-in-chief is UEFA's director of communications.

Another UEFA-sanctioned source is UEFA's web-site. This sophisticated site offers news sources, a vast amount of UEFA-sanctioned information and edited content from the games. Every game is covered in detail with on-line press packs and information about the games. It is here where UEFA also manages the media through an on-line accreditation system. For UEFA Champions League draws and the final, the accreditation process is overseen by UEFA; in order to be UEFA-accredited, journalists must prove to be accredited members of the 'football family', through a registration process. Once registered by UEFA they can then apply for media accreditation at these events and UEFA can oversee which media participate in the making of sports media texts. Some journalists are resistant to UEFA's media relations becoming increasingly based upon on-line systems. One journalist stated in interview that "everything with UEFA has to be done by e-mail and internet; that's slightly annoying".

News sources — the clubs

The system of press accreditation for entry into the clubs' press boxes at Champions League games is handled by clubs' press officers. To gain match accreditation from the clubs, journalists must work for a paper, magazine or a media outlet. Working journalists without a staff job on a paper, a commission or a relationship with the press office will be unable to attend games. Even well-known journalists writing for national papers occasionally have difficulties getting accreditation to some games. One interviewee explained how this impacted on him:

> I mean, I go in there to write a serious article about the games. Often you can't get match accreditations ... if it's a Champions League game, I tried to appeal to UEFA but they just go [shrugs shoulders].

It is here where tensions between UEFA's and clubs' interests and processes emerge, and difficulties in supporting the media and the pan-European football network appear due to a lack of dialogue and consistency.

As well as the match conferences, other less structured news sources are also handled by clubs and their press officers. These form part of the formalities of hosting a Champion's League game. The 'mixed zone' after the game is the area where selected players provide quotes for the media. This area and the atmosphere within it cause difficulties for a number of journalists. One interviewee said:

> I treat mixed zones like mine fields. I hate them. That's only because I can — I don't have to go into them so I don't. You know no one goes into there voluntarily, hanging around like a bloody hooker waiting for players to talk to you. It's not a nice job but sometimes you have to do it.

Gatekeepers — managers and players, press officers and agents

In many ways the manager sets the tone for the relationships between journalists and the club's staff and also acts as the key gatekeeper. At Chelsea the manager's relationship with the press changed markedly over the 2003–4 season, from a normal sparring approach to a sympathetic stance by the press in response to the manager's dignified demeanour in the face of boardroom rumours and his likely impending dismissal. This was evident at the manager's last game in charge, when it was clear to all that he would not be at the club for much longer:

> The manager appears and everyone rushes to the seats. He looks emotional. One journalist, the reporter from *Corriella de la Sport* shouts, 'I saw Kenyon clapping'. The manager laughs and shouts, 'Ah! an Italian Shark' to much laughing, and rhetorically shouts 'What will you do without me?' Then the manager, still emotional, breaks off from discussing football and says, 'You had me a long time and now you give me something more, thankyou'. This recognition of the press support during a difficult period draws a spontaneous standing applause from the press benches. (Fieldnotes)

The other key gatekeepers are the players themselves, although during more recent years access to players has become more problematic for journalists. Players are increasingly asked to answer questions at the formal press conferences or in the mixed zone rather than in one-to-one interviews. Another group journalists use as information sources are the hidden gatekeepers in football clubs, such as club employees and players' agents. Stewards, security and general staff, usually cited as 'club insider' or 'anonymous', are valuable sources of rumour and gossip, easily cultivated during the long waiting periods and the time journalists spend on routine tasks in and around the training ground and stadium. In interview, one journalist explained how his sources extended to,

> ... agents or the club. Some press officers don't have the authority to really guide you, so you need to go to other people — the chief executive or club secretary, directors or members of the coaching staff.

However other journalists recognise that some agents or press officers do not act as reliable sources because it is not in their interests. As one interviewee commented:

> It's almost part of their job description to keep you away from the player — the agent because unless it's a pay job, then he gets nothing out of it, and the press officer has a strategy which is based on what the club wants rather than [what] you might want, so that's generally what I do ... but it's always tempting to go with them, and you always regret it in the end.

Occasionally anonymous sources allow journalists to extract information or stories out of clubs, but away from official or monitored channels. One journalist explained to me that if he had a quote from an anonymous source he could,

> ... go back to the club and say, ' I know you don't want to talk about it but I'm going to print this and so-and-so's agent says this. I do feel the club ought to respond to that'. That might prompt a response. So you need to have a contact on the board, or an agent.

This type of collaboration means that to do his job a journalist needs to ensure that his working relationship with the gatekeepers is effective. One interviewee stated that his relationships with press officers differed from

club to club. When asked whether these were formal relationships, he
answered:

> No, informal — it depends really. It's about building contacts with
> people, some you know well and you use to run stories by. Others
> you just phone to find out what time the press conference is. It
> depends on the quality and the information that they know.

Networks, teams and loops

The media networks that cover the Champions League can be divided into
two subgroups. One journalist stated these are either socially or
professionally determined:

> There's a split between radio, TV and the written press and that's a
> definite split and within that there's just friends. It's just that you're
> better friends with some people than others so you would rather
> spend your time with someone you like.

These occupational networks are vital for sharing information. This same
journalist also explained how the network operates. The sharing of
information is limited to

> ... journalists that you trust, you would work with a friend, you
> might get information back. You would work with little small
> pockets and groups.

As well as being invaluable sources of information and stories, these
networks allow journalists to socialise and learn behaviour. A newer
journalist quickly learns the norms of the press pack. After asking a
manager a question and being ridiculed for his lack of knowledge, senior
journalists berated a younger colleague for his 'school-boy error'. These
occupational networks aid the validation of stories, the sharing of
information, and act as a support network. They are socially constructed,
nurtured through familiarity and routine and firmly embedded in the media
structure.

Networking is a natural part of journalists' professional existence and
provides a way to cope in a competitive industry. The networks allow an

individual to gain status, influence and power by acting as part of a group: this forms the press pack so firmly fixed in the public's mind. The structured nature of the media event in many ways enforces these networks and generates a 'pack mentality' within the subculture.

Sports news networks occasionally become more formalised and are manifested as teamwork. This teamwork differs depending on the type of publication, but for some the experience is akin to genuine collaboration. As one interviewee said:

> You know we all have a our little tasks and then we pool the information, we email it to each other and everyone has got lots of stuff so we do work together as a team and that would certainly be true of tabloid boys. If you get a huge massive exclusive you keep it to yourself, but by and large you do deals. That way everyone gets a lot of material. So, yes it's very much a case of teamwork throughout the football writing profession.

However, teamwork, while aiding the journalist, can also mask more competitive instincts, as one journalist explained:

> Tabloid journalists are like the Borg in Star Trek. They are like a single entity and if you go on a trip with them it can be laughable. They are so terrified that one will get something and not share it, that they all move around in a globule and if one person goes off they all follow that person. He might have just gone to the loo, [but] they all follow him in case he's filing a story.

Operating as a member of the press team is referred to in the subculture as being 'in the loop'. This is integral to the journalist's quest for access to information but can also be used by individual journalists to influence the news agenda. The practice of 'holding back' involves quotes or stories being saved until a quieter news period or to cause maximum impact. This can be determined by the interaction of professional seniority and individual pragmatism, as described by one interviewee:

> You know it would be quite a good sociological study to see how it works; it varies. It might be simply that the chap who went down to get the quotes has total say, he did the work. If he is a junior or

someone quite new and he is dealing with a more senior bunch of guys ... they might manipulate it and say 'well done well done, great quotes but we really think we should use them earlier' or the opposite, 'don't you think we should hold them back, don't you think that's a good idea?' If there's one chap and 5 others all nodding, he's going to succumb, because he needs to keep the relationship going. Next week there will be someone else getting the quotes.

One journalist explained that it was a mixture of occupational norms and power relations that led journalists to hold stories, and that holding was more important for journalists on beats, as they have to produce copy every day. This shows how the subculture colludes to create football texts:

You're only allowed two passes to interview players and the tabloid guys want to go, they are desperate. So I let them go. I'm not going to fight about something I don't care about. We don't quote players that much. They go down the tunnel and they bring the stuff. Well if they have done all the work with the player and want to hold it then I'm not going to say I'm going to use them. That would be horrible of me and if you're involved from a start of story ... and sometimes I've been involved and I've said, 'I think you're mad holding them', because I don't think it will last. But it matters more to them because they have to produce something every day. So if they are in collusion with their mates that a certain news piece will be held over until Wednesday, [and] if all the public only read it on a Wednesday, but in fact it was out on the Monday, then no one knows, do they? The average reader doesn't know, their editors don't know.

It is in situations like these that journalists can utilise the occupational networks and teamwork to their advantage, acquiring vital knowledge of how to negotiate the channels of the sports media world and control aspects of their professional life. Being 'in the loop' is an integral part of the journalist subculture.

The journalists also work with press officers who occasionally take control of situations. Thus teamwork — when it emerges outside the vocational culture — can sometimes resemble control. In one incident a young French journalist was asked to 'go back to the stadium to translate quotes' under the supervision of the press office. The collaboration of press officers and journalists to produce sport texts is important because it illustrates how the journalist can be incorporated into a wider project. If a journalist's independence from managed sources is compromised, his relationship with his editor or the gatekeepers can be affected. Journalists therefore have to balance the desire for a good relationship with the club with their desire for professional integrity. This explains why journalists occasionally resist information from press officers. For the press officers, the ability to mediate coverage of the clubs in the press is an important aspect of this control.

Thus networks, teamwork and loops are integral in the creation of football texts, and involve a collaboration of press, press officers, players and managers to produce the discourse of European football. Those journalists who either by choice or inexperience refuse to collaborate can work only within the prescribed parameters set by the clubs and governing bodies and will struggle to go beyond these managed sources.

The subculture's relationship with governing bodies is more difficult to decipher. As these relationships are not essential in order for the journalist to operate it is more difficult to observe how they are managed. However, just as it is important for journalists to stay 'in the loop', it is important for them to cultivate relationships with officials within governing bodies. These relationships have to be both managed and supported. Some journalists forge these relationships to facilitate news work but also to smooth potential accreditation difficulties.

Discussion and conclusions

The observation and interview data acquired in this investigation reveal that football texts are forged in a three-sided partnership between a rela tively closed journalist subculture, various news sources and gatekeepers with economic or political interests in the game, and the media managers of governing bodies and the clubs. The football journalist working on the Champions League has to negotiate a period of assimilation into the working practices and norms of a subculture, work in a homogenised environment, negotiate structural barriers and consistently cultivate a myriad of relationships in order to successfully work in the profession. A journalist working alone, without accreditation, sources or networks will be unable to work on the Champions League.

The journalist's success is governed by relationships with the clubs and governing bodies who combine to collude in the creation of consensual stories that promote UEFA and the most powerful clubs. Palmer (2001) has argued that these interactions create an occupational category of the "cultural broker", who works to "produce (and profit from) the ideologies, images and resources of popular culture" (Palmer, 2001: p. 366). The resulting consensus of cultural brokers creates formulaic football texts reliant on information generated by the press conferences and briefings. However, the quest by journalists for 'exclusives' and for different viewpoints can challenge the consensus-building of UEFA and the clubs.

The clubs' and UEFA's support of accredited media mask the increasing structural limitations that impact on football journalists' ability to perform in their roles. On a number of occasions I heard journalists lament the "good old days" when they could talk freely with the players. As one remarked, "Now they're like the royal family". In attempting to control the news agenda and sources, UEFA and the clubs seek to plug all the gaps through which journalists might obtain unapproved or unauthorised information. While they can efficiently enforce the working of certain aspects of the media through erecting news management strategies, press officers cannot stop stories they would like to suppress being leaked by other sources. Only occasionally, during the press briefings I witnessed, were stories critical of the hierarchy of Chelsea openly discussed.

Any consensus created through these interactions could be, and sometimes is, challenged by a more critical investigative approach, or by the interest of political or economic reporters, who can more realistically pitch a football story for the front page. But the consensus in elite European football is widely accepted: the investigative dimension of football journalism is rarely pursued to full effect because of the difficulties for journalists in retaining news sources and relationships with gatekeepers in the football industry. One journalist explained that an investigative story into the football industry would ensure that the journalist would "never be allowed back to football, you would blow all your contacts straight away and it would seem petty". Another journalist opined that the lack of an investigative imperative was due to journalists' inability to get contacts "to stand things up, and nobody ever will unless they have got a grudge or unless you can pay them".

For some journalists the love of the game was a factor in their incorporation into the 'football family'; the investigative role was viewed by them as being for others outside the football industry to pursue. Another interviewee believed that being investigative would compromise him, but he also conceded that he worked for the general good of the football industry, as he was "not a pure journalist — I am a football lover who gets a living from the game". The lack of a critical imperative in sports journalism is therefore bound up with the increasing synergy between the media and football; and it is evident, futher, that some journalists feel comfortable in these collaborations.

Employees within the clubs also resist the consensus-making mechanism by stepping outside these structures to provide less managed forms of football texts and acting as news sources and gatekeepers. Nevertheless football texts created by the English football press increasingly reflect the homogenisation and concentration of ownership of the sports media and are increasingly dependent on the corporate nature of the bodies that control football. If these groups are manufacturing consensus for the new football family, whose interests do the sports press serve and what broader conclusions can be drawn?

Lowes's (1999), in his study of North American sports journalism argues that it inherently reproduces dominant ideologies and that it,

> ... constitutes a discourse that serves the promotional interests of the major league sports industry's primary stake holders — media commentators, equipment and apparel manufacturers, civic boosters and the like. (Lowes, 1999: p. 99)

He calls sports news the "promotional domain" of the sports industry, and clearly UEFA's Champions League brand has been nurtured as such a domain. Clubs also maintain a tight control of their own press relations, to cement their place at the top tier of European football. Press officers act as promoters of a club's media profile and collude in the production of football texts. When clubs fail to exercise these controls, journalists have to use diverse sources and alternative strategies, and this disrupts the club. Occasionally, even clubs with a strategic media management structure cannot always control the stories that emanate from the club because of the number of stakeholders who provide information to journalists. Paradoxically, an intense news management strategy can also promote a parallel level of interest from journalists who probe the gaps and weak points in the news structures.

Football texts produced by the national sporting press are therefore collaborative projects that reproduce the dominant ideology of prominent institutions within the cultural industries of contemporary capitalism, serving the promotional agenda of UEFA and the elite European clubs. Such texts generally enhance the homogenising features of European football. However this is not always the case. But tensions in the relationships between the subculture and the news structures are also identifiable. Football texts, while produced collaboratively and often collusively, are also the results of negotiation between news sources, gatekeepers and journalists.

Within sports journalism, there are struggles over access and meaning, both within and outside the subculture. Journalists contest access to sources, the rights-holders' power and the formal structures that UEFA and the clubs enforce. The occupational subculture constantly negotiates and renegotiates consent to enter the sports world, to produce football texts and to produce meanings.

This preliminary study and commentary upon the occupational subculture of British football journalists over a season of Champions League football has produced some understanding of the nature of a little-researched occupational subculture. The football journalist may have an increasingly high profile, but must continually balance the editorial with the personal, the corporate with the public, and the need for access to information with the desire to sustain access to sources. It is in the making of these decisions and the exercise of what are often limited choices that the sports journalist will be judged not just by a loyal readership but by peers from other specialist areas within the wider professional subculture.

References

Blain, N., Boyle, R. and O'Donnell, H. (1993) *Sport and national identity in the European media*. Leicester: University of Leicester Press.

Brookes, R. (2002) *Representing sport*. London: Arnold.

Creedon, P.J. (1998) 'Women, sport and media institutions: Issues in sports journalism and marketing', in Wenner, L.A. (ed) *MediaSport*. London: Routledge.

Crolley, L. and Hand, D. (2002) *Football, Europe and the press*. London: Frank Cass.

Lowes, M. (1999) *Inside the sports pages: Work routines, professional ideologies and the manufacture of sports news*. Toronto: University of Toronto Press.

Palmer, C. (2001) 'Spin doctors and sportsbrokers: Researching elites in contemporary sport: A research note on the Tour de France', *International Review for the Sociology of Sport* Vol. 35, No. 33: pp. 364–377.

Rowe, D. (1999) *Sport, culture and the media — the unruly trinity*. Buckingham: Open University Press.

Index

FIFPro *246*
finances, in football
　consumption of digital games
　　250
　crisis, in Scottish football *183–194*
　English Football League *165–180*
　industry and clubs *43–59*
　licensing scheme, and Irish
　　football *204–208*
　migration of players, geo-economics of *217–232*
　rights, broadcasting
　　*165, 167, 168, 169, 170,
　　184, 219*
　television, income/revenue
　　185, 186, 188, 191, 201, 219
　top clubs in Europe *14–15*
　West Ham club turnover *107–108*
Fine, G. A. and Kleinman, S. *79*
Fiske, J. *262*
fitness *84, 87, 91, 138*
'flow' in digital gaming *252*
football academies *223*
football as lingua franca of 'Christmas truce' *39*
football as sign of modernity in
　France and Italy *43*
Football Association (inception) *237*
Football Association of Ireland
　(F.A.I.) *65*
football culture
　31, 122, 123, 125, 138, 139
'football hooligan' computer game
　251
Football League
　*165, 166, 167, 168, 169, 170,
　171, 173, 176, 178, 179*
Fordist *101*
foreign/foreign players
　*45, 46, 48, 55, 56, 125, 136,
　137, 138, 139, 143, 154,
　158, 183, 221, 227, 234,
　237, 241, 245*

Forrest, D. Simmons, R. and
　Feehan, P. *171*
Fort, R. and Quirk, J. *166*
Frasca, G. *252*
fraud *209, 210, 211*
freedom of movement *241*
French Cup 1943 *54*
Fridenson, P. *46*
Frier, G. *187*
Fromme, J. *255*
Fuertes, Esteban *244*
Funk, J. B. *257*

G

G-14 *220, 270*
Gaelic Athletic Association (GAA)
　208, 211
Gale, F. J. *24, 25, 34*
game studies *250*
gaming machines *210*
Garate, M. and Martín, J. *146*
Gardiner, S. *245*
Gardiner, S. and Welch, R. *242*
Garfinkel, H. *258*
Garland, J., Malcolm, D. and Rowe,
　M. *5*
gate receipts *210, 213*
gatekeeper/s
　*271, 272, 276, 281, 282,
　283, 284*
gay *85, 86, 91*
　clubs *86*
　minority *94*
　scene *91*
　women *94*
Gay-Lescot, J. L. *54*
'gentleman elite' *99*
gentrification *101, 114*
George, Ric *137*
Gerhardt, W. *236*
Gerry Morgan *77*
Ghirelli, A. *47, 48*
Gibson, Victor *50*
Giulianotti, R. *99, 128, 237, 238*

Thomas, W. I. *140*
Thornton, S. *86, 92, 93, 96*
Through the Wind and Rain
    131, 132, 133, 136
ticket price/pricing *152, 173, 176*
Tobermore FC *211*
Tomlinson, A. *8*
toponymy *113*
topophilia *113, 114*
Torino AC *51*
'tourist reds' *107*
tradition
    122, 126, 133, 134, 135, 136
traditional
  Basque sports *144*
  class-based culture *4*
  footabll club *99–119*
  forms of media *258*
  knock-out style cup *13*
  male sports *257*
  sources of revenue *169*
  sports reporting *267*
  urban society *147*
  work *5*
trafficking *229*
training
    44, 50, 52, 54, 55, 84, 87,
    89, 90, 132, 135, 202, 206,
    228, 272, 273
  ground *122, 128, 277*
  session *273*
transfer
    217, 221, 224, 225, 226, 228,
    239, 240, 241, 244
  accumulation *218*
  certificate *240*
  fee *14, 239, 240*
  system *5*
  window *187, 190*
transnationalism
    217, 218, 222, 230
Treaty of Rome *125*
trusts *191*

truth *36*
Tshimanga Bakadiababu, E. *229*
Tum, Hervé *227*
Tuohy, M. *61, 63*

U
UEFA
    115, 166, 185, 189, 192,
    196, 197, 204, 205, 206,
    241, 269, 270, 271, 272, 273,
    274, 275, 282, 283, 284
Ugarte, J. *147*
Ulster Unionist Party (UUP) *62*
Unzueta, P. *149*
Updike, John *125*
upper middle class *146*
Upton Park *112*
Usher, D. *132, 133*

V
Vamplew, W. *103, 113*
Van den Bogaert, S. *245*
Venables, Terry *7*
Venglos, Josef *133*
Vertovec, S. *222*
Viareggio charter, 1926 *47*
violence *235–236, 236*
  in digital games *251*
  sectarian (NI) *61–78*
violent
  behaviour *235, 251*
  sports *236*
Vizcaya *145*
Vogts, Berti *183*

W
wage
  capping/setting *166, 193*
  cuts *183*
wage/s
    5, 56, 130, 170, 171, 172, 173,
    176, 177, 178, 185, 186, 188,
    209, 239